NEW STUDENT LITERACIES
AMID COVID-19

INNOVATIONS IN HIGHER EDUCATION TEACHING AND LEARNING

Senior Series Editor: Patrick Blessinger, St John's University and Higher Education Teaching and Learning Association, USA

Associate Series Editor: Enakshi Sengupta, American University of Afghanistan, Afghanistan

Published Volumes:

Volume 25	Integrating Community Service into Curriculum: International Perspectives on Humanizing Education – Edited by Enakshi Sengupta, Patrick Blessinger and Mandla Makhanya
Volume 26	International Perspectives on Improving Student Engagement: Advances in Library Practices in Higher Education – Edited by Enakshi Sengupta, Patrick Blessinger and Milton D. Cox
Volume 27	Improving Classroom Engagement and International Development Programs: International Perspectives on Humanizing Higher Education – Edited by Enakshi Sengupta, Patrick Blessinger and Mandla Makhanya
Volume 28	Cultural Competence in Higher Education – Edited by Tiffany Puckett, and Nancy Lind
Volume 29	Designing Effective Library Learning Spaces in Higher Education – Edited by Enakshi Sengupta, Patrick Blessinger and Mandla S. Makhanya
Volume 30	Developing and Supporting Multiculturalism and Leadership Development – Edited by Enakshi Sengupta, Patrick Blessinger and Mandla S. Makhanya
Volume 31	Faculty and Student Research in Practicing Academic Freedom – Edited by Enakshi Sengupta and Patrick Blessinger
Volume 32	International Perspectives on Policies, Practices & Pedagogies for Promoting Social Responsibility in Higher Education – Edited by Enakshi Sengupta, Patrick Blessinger and Craig Mahoney
Volume 33	International Perspectives on the Role of Technology in Humanizing Higher Education – Edited by Enakshi Sengupta, Patrick Blessinger and Mandla S. Makhanya
Volume 34	Humanizing Higher Education through Innovative Approaches for Teaching and Learning – Edited by Enakshi Sengupta, Patrick Blessinger and Mandla S. Makhanya
Volume 35	Humanizing Higher Education through Innovative Approaches for Teaching and Learning – Edited by Enakshi Sengupta, Patrick Blessinger and Mandla s. Makhanya
Volume 36	Integrating Research-based Learning across the Curriculum – Edited by Enakshi Sengupta and Patrick Blessinger
Volume 37	International Perspectives in Social Justice Programs at the Institutional and Community Level – Edited by Enakshi Sengupta and Patrick Blessinger
Volume 38	The Role of External Examining in Higher Education: Challenges and Best Practices – Edited by Enakshi Sengupta, Patrick Blessinger, Andrew Ssemwanga, and Barbara Cozza
Volume 39	International Perspectives on Supporting and Engaging Online Learners – Edited by Jaimie Hoffman and Patrick Blessinger
Volume 40	International Perspectives in Online Instruction – Edited by Jaimie Hoffman and Patrick Blessinger

INNOVATIONS IN HIGHER EDUCATION TEACHING AND LEARNING   VOLUME 41

NEW STUDENT LITERACIES AMID COVID-19: INTERNATIONAL CASE STUDIES

EDITED BY

ENAKSHI SENGUPTA
American University of Afghanistan, Afghanistan

and

PATRICK BLESSINGER
International Higher Education Teaching and Learning Association, USA

United Kingdom – North America – Japan
India – Malaysia – China

Emerald Publishing Limited
Howard House, Wagon Lane, Bingley BD16 1WA, UK

First edition 2022

Copyright © 2022 Emerald Publishing Limited

Reprints and permissions service
Contact: permissions@emeraldinsight.com

No part of this book may be reproduced, stored in a retrieval system, transmitted in any form or by any means electronic, mechanical, photocopying, recording or otherwise without either the prior written permission of the publisher or a licence permitting restricted copying issued in the UK by The Copyright Licensing Agency and in the USA by The Copyright Clearance Center. Any opinions expressed in the chapters are those of the authors. Whilst Emerald makes every effort to ensure the quality and accuracy of its content, Emerald makes no representation implied or otherwise, as to the chapters' suitability and application and disclaims any warranties, express or implied, to their use.

British Library Cataloguing in Publication Data
A catalogue record for this book is available from the British Library

ISBN: 978-1-80071-467-0 (Print)
ISBN: 978-1-80071-466-3 (Online)
ISBN: 978-1-80071-468-7 (Epub)

ISSN: 2055-3641 (Series)

Printed and bound by CPI Group (UK) Ltd, Croydon, CR0 4YY

ISOQAR certified Management System, awarded to Emerald for adherence to Environmental standard ISO 14001:2004.

Certificate Number 1985
ISO 14001

INVESTOR IN PEOPLE

CONTENTS

Series Editors' Introduction   vii

PART I
SOUTH ASIAN COUNTRIES

Chapter 1   Introduction to New Student Literacies Amid COVID-19 – International Case Studies
Enakshi Sengupta and Patrick Blessinger   *3*

Chapter 2   Online Teaching, Learning, and Assessment During COVID-19: A Case of a Management Faculty in Sri Lanka
A. W. Janitha C. Abeygunasekera   *13*

Chapter 3   Preparedness of Students for Future Teaching and Learning In Higher Education: A Bangladeshi Perspective
*M. Mahruf C. Shohel, Md. Ashrafuzzaman,
Atm Shafiul Alam, Arif Mahmud, Muhammad Shajjad Ahsan
and Md Tariqul Islam*   *29*

Chapter 4   The Impact of Online Education on The Learning Experiences of Tertiary Students During The COVID-19 Pandemic: An Indian Case Study
Nandita Mishra   *57*

Chapter 5   Uncertainty in an Uncertain Land – Battling of COVID-19 In Afghan Educational System
*Enakshi Sengupta, Mohammed Gul Sahibbzada,
Madina Ibrahimi, Nelab Haidari and Elaha Yousufi*   *69*

PART II
MENA REGION, AFRICA AND EUROPE

Chapter 6   University Preparedness for Online Teaching and Learning Amid COVID-19 In Kenya
Stanislaus Agava, Sahaya G. Selvam and Judith Pete   *83*

Chapter 7 Transitioning From Physical Classroom to Distance Education During the COVID-19 Crisis: A Lebanese Case Study in Higher Education *Ahmad Samarji*	*101*
Chapter 8 COVID-19 Chronicles in Education: Overcoming Global Pandemic Challenges in Turkey by Empowering Educators to Become Digitally Literate *Ayşegül Liman Kaban and Sinan Aşçı*	*115*
Chapter 9 Self-Directed Learning Competencies – A Key to Success in Online Learning: A Lithuanian Case Study *Rasa Poceviciene*	*135*
Chapter 10 Which Attitudes Helped the Academics to Overcome the Difficulties of Online Education During COVID-19? *Veronika Végh, Klára Soltész-Várhelyi and Henriette Pusztafalvi*	*153*
About the Authors	*169*
Name Index	*177*
Subject Index	*185*

SERIES EDITORS' INTRODUCTION

INNOVATIONS IN HIGHER EDUCATION TEACHING AND LEARNING

The purpose of this series is to publish current research and scholarship on innovative teaching and learning practices in higher education. The series is developed around the premise that teaching and learning is more effective when instructors and students are actively and meaningfully engaged in the teaching–learning process.

The main objectives of this series are to:

(1) present how innovative teaching and learning practices are being used in higher education institutions around the world across a wide variety of disciplines and countries,
(2) present the latest models, theories, concepts, paradigms, and frameworks that educators should consider when adopting, implementing, assessing, and evaluating innovative teaching and learning practices, and
(3) consider the implications of theory and practice on policy, strategy, and leadership.

This series will appeal to anyone in higher education who is involved in the teaching and learning process from any discipline, institutional type, or nationality. The volumes in this series will focus on a variety of authentic case studies and other empirical research that illustrates how educators from around the world are using innovative approaches to create more effective and meaningful learning environments.

Innovation in teaching and learning is any approach, strategy, method, practice, or means that has been shown to improve, enhance, or transform the teaching–learning environment. Innovation involves doing things differently or in a novel way in order to improve outcomes. In short, innovation is positive change. With respect to teaching and learning, innovation is the implementation of new or improved educational practices that result in improved educational and learning outcomes. This innovation can be any positive change related to teaching, curriculum, assessment, technology, or other tools, programs, policies, or processes that leads to improved educational and learning outcomes. Innovation can occur in institutional development, program development, professional development, or learning development.

The volumes in this series will not only highlight the benefits and theoretical frameworks of such innovations through authentic case studies and other empirical research but also look at the challenges and contexts associated with implementing and assessing innovative teaching and learning practices. The volumes represent all disciplines from a wide range of national, cultural, and organizational contexts. The volumes in this series will explore a wide variety of teaching and learning topics such as active learning, integrative learning, transformative learning, inquiry-based learning, problem-based learning, meaningful learning, blended learning, creative learning, experiential learning, lifelong and lifewide learning, global learning, learning assessment and analytics, student research, faculty and student learning communities, as well as other topics.

This series brings together distinguished scholars and educational practitioners from around the world to disseminate the latest knowledge on innovative teaching and learning scholarship and practices. The authors offer a range of disciplinary perspectives from different cultural contexts. This series provides a unique and valuable resource for instructors, administrators, and anyone interested in improving and transforming teaching and learning.

Patrick Blessinger
Founder, Executive Director, and Chief Research Scientist,
International HETL Association

Enakshi Sengupta
Director – Centre for Teaching Learning & Associate Professor Business –
American University of Afghanistan

PART I

SOUTH ASIAN COUNTRIES

CHAPTER 1

INTRODUCTION TO NEW STUDENT LITERACIES AMID COVID-19 – INTERNATIONAL CASE STUDIES

Enakshi Sengupta and Patrick Blessinger

ABSTRACT

The world has seen a lot of disasters which have affected some part of the globe and healed in due course but rarely has any health disaster affected the entire world like COVID-19. It not only affected the health sector but caused a downward spiral of the world economy. The world was not prepared to face such a magnitude of the disaster. Overnight, schools and universities declared a lockdown affecting 1.57 billion students in 191 countries (UN, 2020). The sudden closure of educational institutions negatively impacted education around the world and much of the education sector shifted to remote learning. This exacerbated the shortcomings of those institutions who were unprepared for the sudden shift to remote learning. The global pandemic triggered the need to reconceptualize how educational institutions provision teaching and learning. Universities resorted to intensive use of different technology platforms and resources to achieve their learning outcomes. This volume explores how educational institutions needed to rethink teaching, learning, research and innovation, and implement innovative approaches to address such complexities. International case studies have been compiled that highlight the issues related to the impact of the COVID-19 pandemic on higher education and how different countries tried to cope with the sudden shift of remote learning and tried to resolve challenges around the issues of digital pedagogy.

Keywords: COVID-19; digital pedagogy; accessibility; higher education; online; teaching and learning; global pandemic; affordability; preparedness

INTRODUCTION

In December 2019, a virus slowly made its way from the Wuhan District of China and quickly spread throughout the world in less than a month until it was declared a global pandemic by the World Health Organization (WHO, 2020) on March 11, 2020. The pandemic was not only creating havoc in the health sector when people were dying every day, but was also shattering the economic system of many countries and was having a devastating impact on human lives (Xiang et al., 2020). Social distancing and masking were the main solution left to flatten the curve of this infection which spread rapidly due to human contact.

Governments around the world declared the closure of educational institutions hoping that physical distancing and reducing interpersonal contact will minimize the transmission of this deadly virus mainly in places like universities where the population tends to be dense (Weeden & Cornwell, 2020). The transition was made almost immediately to the online mode of learning. The institutions were not prepared, and students and parents found the system to be alien. At the same time, it exacerbated other issues such as low connectivity, absence of hand-held devices or computers, lack of electricity, and unpreparedness of faculty to align content with online teaching. It also exposed inequalities, marginalization and the plight of disadvantaged students to pursue education.

The global crisis triggered the realigning of resources and educational provisions at all levels. The rapid, global transition to remote learning has been one of the boldest and most daring "experiment" the educational sector has ever implemented. The current crisis required all universities to become the vanguard of change and become more resilient and agile by building more effective teaching and learning platforms.

Dealing with disaster is not new for mankind. Gaus (1947), in his classic *Reflections on Public Administration*, recognized the role that catastrophe plays in reshaping public administration and policy systems. He argued that to be most effective, the government should be viewed as an integral part of an ecological system, which can exist and thrive only in relationship with their environments. He listed several factors useful to explain "the ebb and flow of the functions of government … people, place, physical technology, social technology, wishes and ideas, catastrophe, and personality" (p. 9).

For Gaus (1947), catastrophe

> not only is destructive, so that relief and repair are required on a scale so large that collective action is necessary, but it also disrupts, jostles or challenges views and attitudes, and affords to the inner self as well as to others a respectable and face-saving reason for changing one's views as to policy. (p. 16–17)

Thus, catastrophic events can be considered as change agents and when introduced into an ecological system, the system will react to achieve a new equilibrium. This note of positive thought as proposed by Gaus (1947) led institutions to seek newfound opportunities even amidst pandemic and chaos.

CHALLENGES AND OPPORTUNITIES

The current educational situation is unique and one cannot find its precedence in history. The transition to the online mode of education comes with challenges of providing quality education, adoption of the right mode and the correct platform for delivery, accessibility for all and the role of educators whose traditional form and work has changed drastically, almost overnight. Universities are conducting training modules to equip the faculty members to adapt to the online mode along with the support of the government who aims to boost digital literacy and digitization of educational services (Rashid & Yadav, 2020).

Some academics are also of the opinion that remote learning offers a myriad of advantages for individuals who are unable to attend a traditional full-time face-to-face university due to personal circumstances. The flexibility of asynchronous remote learning may provide wider access to those individuals and provide a chance to them to complete their education. Traditional higher education institutions are also exploring the concept of hybrid or blended forms of learning that may help improve the quality of face-to-face teaching by moving content delivery online and focusing in-person sessions on active learning, post-pandemic (Bowen, 2012; Riffee, 2003).

Higher educational institutions have faced financial losses with cut down on fees and the drop-in enrollment rates for students. Countries that relied on international students saw a dwindling of student mobility and a negligible population willing to pursue their study abroad program online paying a higher amount of fees. "A decline in international student mobility in these countries risks affecting productivity in advanced sectors related to innovation and research in the coming years" (OECD, 2020 p. 11).

The economic disruption has resulted in budget cuts and retrenchment in educational institutions. Departments that were once thriving with international students and their recruitment has been downsized overnight (DePietro, 2020; Friga, 2020). The local governments have announced a significant reduction in the resources allocated to boost higher education (Ferguson, 2020). Declining of the budget is not a recent phenomenon. The last couple of years has seen a cut in expenses, increasing tuition fees, aggressive marketing strategies to enroll more students and innovative method of teaching–learning and the pandemic will only aggravate such situations and defer the growth of the institutions. One tends to apprehend the serious ramifications that this chaotic situation might cause toward social equity.

Universities are known to be significant contributors to social equity and viewed as institutions that can help provide a conduit for social mobility (Hazelkorn & Gibson, 2019; Hu, 2009; Marginson, 2018). Social mobility can be gained only when one can access higher education and success therein. Budgetary shortfalls may weaken the access to pursuing higher education as a result of increasing costs, diminished scholarships, reduced academic supports, this could have serious ramifications for social equity (Blankenberger & Williams, 2020).

CONCLUSION

Continuing education for students remains a top priority among academics and policy makers in universities. Efforts have been made in every possible way to minimize interruption in studies and there has been an urgent need for faculty who are capable of imparting education through online and other modes of long-distance communication. There are short term goals of finishing the semester and the designated curriculum, evaluating the students and assigning grades. Along with it exists a long-term planning process of being prepared in a futuristic manner for any impending crisis and designing an education system that can manage and set up a contingency plan that is capable of dealing with risks in the future.

Assessing and evaluating students remains a challenge and it is difficult to monitor how the online tests are being taken by the students. Lab-tests, practical exams and hands-on demonstration of knowledge can be more difficult to conduct online. In addition, not all students will have access to a computer, laptop or uninterrupted internet supply at home. Mental health and physical well-being of staff and students and ensuring a safe environment is now a top priority of universities. Universities have to ensure that regular communication channels are fully operational and careful attention is given to ensure that all queries and apprehensions are addressed.

This book volume discusses case studies and interventions that has been implemented by academics to ensure high quality, uninterrupted education for students. Strategic plans are explained with different theoretical models and framework which is being currently utilized and benefits gained. The information provided in this book volume is meant to benefit educators, leaders, policy makers, government organizations, faculty members and students.

CHAPTER OVERVIEWS

"Online Teaching, Learning, and Assessment during COVID-19: A Case of a Management Faculty in Sri Lanka" by A. W. Janitha C. Abeygunasekera is about COVID-19 Pandemic that has affected the smooth functioning of all aspects of life, while the education sector is one of the most influenced fields. This chapter presents a case of a faculty in a state university in Sri Lanka which underwent a transformation toward online teaching, learning, and assessment mode with the COVID-19 pandemic. The unexpected conversion to online mode impacted many parties, and among them, the lecturers and students were mostly affected within universities. The author explored the perception of students and lecturers on this unexpected compulsory transformation and identified how they perceive this new normal in teaching, learning, and assessment. In addition, the benefits and challenges faced, and the pre and post views on online experience were also studied. An online survey with students and a series of interviews with lecturers were exercised for data collection. The views that students have on online learning were different among the various study program levels, and the benefits and challenges faced by the different student groups also varied. Further, the lecturers had different perceptions on teaching the different level programs and subjects. These aspects are discussed in detail throughout the chapter, and at the end, suggestions for making the online mode more effective are presented.

"Preparedness of Students for Future Teaching and Learning in Higher Education: A Bangladeshi Perspective" by M. Mahruf C. Shohel, Md. Ashrafuzzaman, Atm Shafiul Alam, Arif Mahmud, Muhammad Shajjad Ahsan and Md Tariqul Islam is about COVID-19 pandemic that has had a significant impact on higher education across the globe, including in Bangladesh. The Bangladeshi higher education system is going through an abrupt transformation to cope with the crisis time. This chapter is based on data collected from teachers and students of Bangladeshi public and private higher education institutions regarding teaching and learning during the COVID-19 lockdown. In Bangladesh, some universities switched to online distance teaching and learning quickly during this period, and others lagged behind in this regard. Teachers and students from both groups participated in the study, including those who attended online teaching and learning activities and those who did not participate. This chapter highlights both teachers' and students' perspectives regarding students' future preparedness for participating fully in the changing landscape of higher education, especially technology-enhanced teaching and learning. Understanding the perspectives of teachers and students is important to address the digital divide and social justice issues in the policy and practice. Within the higher education sector in Bangladesh, it is especially vital while transforming its education system and adapting emerging technologies to address the challenges of education in future emergencies.

"The Impact of Online Education on the Learning Experiences of Tertiary Students during the COVID-19 Pandemic: An Indian Case Study" by Nandita Mishra talks about COVID-19 that has shown its pandemic powers to the whole world. At times when many countries are forced to go for total lockdown of its economic activities, unusual economic crisis is inevitable. Amid all the crisis, the impact on education sector was also massive. In India also COVID-19 has resulted in a country-wide lockdown, which led to closure of schools and colleges. University Grant Commission, an apex educational body has come up with several guidelines for Higher Education Institution. This study is an attempt to understand the perceptions of Indian tertiary students toward online teaching which has become the no-other-choice method of instruction for educational institutes during the pandemic. An online survey was conducted in October 2020, to collect information from the students through Google form about their perceptions and experiences with online learning. A total of 248 students completed the survey. Factor analysis has been applied on the collected data to understand the factors which most impacted the students. Results showed that "less effectiveness," "stress and boredom" and "connectivity challenges" were among the major challenges faced by these students in their online learning experience. This study urges the need for an educational strategy to be set by policy makers to respond to the challenges encountered during online learning.

"Uncertainty in an Uncertain Land – Battling of COVID-19 in Afghan Educational System" by Enakshi Sengupta, Mohammed Gul Sahibbzada, Madina Ibrahimi, Nelab Haidari and Elaha Yousufi highlights about the battle to fight and resist the COVID-19 virus which continues worldwide and even the vaccination drive is failing to control the new strains of viruses which are resulting in death and disruption of a normal life. The higher education sector, like others, has been affected by billions of students unable to return to their campus life. Universities have been forced to scale up their online learning ability, try out new and effective learning management systems and train their faculty and staff members to teach and operate remotely. This has led to a financial strain on the higher education institution with dwindling enrollment and student mobility. Afghanistan's vulnerable and fragile higher education system, fraught with war and internal strife, has suffered a huge setback. Electricity and access to the internet is a perilous problem and with the additional burden of students studying online, both providers of utility services and educational institutions are finding it increasingly difficult to face the unprecedented demand. This chapter aims to highlight such issues that are plaguing the already uncertain future of this country – even when the presence of the COVID-19 virus was unheard of. Qualitative interview method was used to gather data from the officials from the Ministry of Higher Education, faculty members from different universities and students from various provinces who voiced their opinion and hardships that they are facing in the current pandemic situation. The data were analyzed to suggest possible outcomes and recommendations were based on the data collected.

"University Preparedness for Online Teaching and Learning Amid COVID-19 in Kenya" written by Stanislaus Agava, Sahaya G. Selvam and Judith Pete writes about how globally, the COVID-19 pandemic took institutions of learning and the workplaces by surprise. Offering online learning was an alternative for institutions of higher learning. Were the Kenyan institutions adequately prepared for this? The present study had three specific objectives: (a) to establish the status of policy-preparedness of online teaching and learning in Kenyan universities; (b) to explore the infrastructural-preparedness of the universities; and (c) to find out the level of competency-preparedness of lecturers and students in embracing the facilities for online teaching and learning. The study had an embedded mixed method research design. Data was gathered using an online questionnaire, from 112 lecturers and 372 students, who were conveniently sampled, representing 34 universities and university colleges. Findings suggest that almost all represented institutions have a policy on online teaching and learning, though 50% of participants' report that the policy did not exist prior to the onset of COVID-19. On the level of infrastructural preparedness, the personal ownership of digital devices among participants is very impressive, though 50% of institutions do not provide any device. Thirdly, the level of competency in the use of the three sets of online platforms for teaching and learning is far below the expected average, but this is improving since the onset of COVID-19. Lecturers have statistically more perceived competence than students ($p<0.01$). The implication of these results is discussed. And we conclude that the period of forced online teaching and learning need not be considered as a stop-gap measure during COVID-19, but as a way forward for improved self-learning and lifelong learning.

"Transitioning from Physical Classroom to Distance Education during the COVID-19 Crisis: A Lebanese Case Study in Higher Education" by Ahmad Samarji explains that distance Education (DE) is neither a new concept nor process. Learning through postal correspondence can be traced back to more than 150 years. The avenues of DE have evolved from postal correspondence, videotaped lessons, electronic communications, to distance teaching higher education institutes. Up until the start of 2020, DE was an educational process of choice or preference. However, when WHO declared COVID-19 as a pandemic in March 2020, DE was no longer an option but rather the only choice and educational avenue for the majority of the universities worldwide; Lebanon is no exception. This chapter considered the case study of DE at Phoenicia University, Lebanon, studying instructors' attitudes and perceptions about some of the quality attributes of DE such as interactivity, inclusiveness and immediacy prior to and after their first online semester. A mixed methods approach was adopted, where pre- and post-test surveys were administered with 54 instructors in Spring 2020. Semi-structured interviews were conducted with 12 instructors toward the end of that semester. This study found that the participants held a more positive stance when it came to instructor immediacy following their first online semester. On the contrary, instructors' attitudes and perceptions toward interactivity and inclusiveness did not significantly change between the pre- and post-test results, maintaining a less favorable stance of DE for these particular attributes in comparison to physical classroom education. The study concluded that overall, participants perceived DE as an efficient approach given the unprecedented crisis; nonetheless, the effectiveness of such an approach was challenged by many obstacles and limitations due to internet connection issues and the unreliable power infrastructure.

"COVID-19 Chronicles in Education: Overcoming Global Pandemic Challenges in Turkey by Empowering Educators to Become Digitally Literate" by Ayşegül Liman Kaban and Sinan Aşçı is about applying digital literacy skills in face-to-face or online classrooms that started ringing the changes during the COVID-19 pandemic in recent months. Stating the obvious, well-planned distant learning experiences are different from courses offered online in response to a crisis or disaster. Every institution around the world has worked on preserving instruction throughout the COVID-19 pandemic. The extent to which educators being aware of their own and their students' digital literacy skills perceived how and what kind of information and communication technologies are used under such an emergency remote teaching and learning. The preparedness level of learners in using online information and communication technologies is a naturally regulated phenomenon because they are born to live a life of technology. Yet, educators have applied experience, and practical knowledge in face-to-face classroom settings remains a mere curiosity to remote teaching. This study was conducted to investigate educators' level of preparedness to use online information and communication technologies for their emergency remote teachings and their experiences from the field by focusing on moderating variables – asserted by Means, Bakia, and Murphy (2014) – like modality, instructor role online, online communication synchrony, source of feedback, and role of online assessments. Based on self-report scaled and open-ended questions in the same questionnaire, the participants were recruited online via convenience and accidental sampling, and the data were analyzed by using SPSS 22.0 and thematic analysis.

Within this study, how educators experience remote teaching during the global pandemic and what they prefer to carry out for the same effectiveness of the courses are discussed based on their digital literacy skills and digital readiness.

"Self-directed Learning Competencies – a Key to Success in Online Learning: A Lithuanian Case Study" by Rasa Poceviciene highlights that March 30, 2020 was a day of qualitative changes in the Lithuanian education system. This day in history – at least in the history of education – will record the day when mass distance learning began in the entire Lithuanian education system. All educational activities from kindergarten to higher and adult education were organized at a distance. In fact, the idea of distance learning was not so new in Lithuania. The first steps in developing a distance learning system in Lithuania were taken 25 years ago, but before the pandemic, it was more the exception than the norm and, of course, it had never been global. But in Spring 2020 all educational institutions (in general education during 2 weeks, in higher – even only during 2-3 days) were transformed from contact to distance learning. From a few-month perspective, it can be said that, despite all the circumstances, this transformation has been quite successful. In order to better understand the reasons for this quite sufficiently successful transition, it would be worthwhile to briefly review the organization of distance learning in Lithuania until the 2020 pandemic.

"Which attitudes helped the academics to overcome the difficulties of online education during COVID-19?" by Veronika Végh, Klára Soltész-Várhelyi and Henriette Pusztafalvi is about Hungarian school communities that also faced with the challenging situation posed by COVID-19 in March, 2020. The transition to emergency remote teaching could be affected by many factors. The attitudes of educators are important as their decisions largely determined the methods of digital education. In the present study, 147 high school teachers and 58 academics' data were analyzed. Academics were more likely to maintain interactions during their courses, and they preferred to make their own material for the lessons, while high-school teachers more often borrow material from pre-existing sources. We also found that the effect of self-efficacy on resilience is mediated through the intention to create teaching materials and through the willingness to adopt them as well. It can be concluded that the assistance cannot be one-dimensional, as teachers of different ages, with different IT competencies, teaching at different levels of education, teaching different subjects, have different needs and need to be supported in different ways.

REFERENCES

Blankenberger, B., & Williams, A. M. (2020). COVID and the impact on higher education: The essential role of integrity and accountability. *Administrative Theory & Praxis, 42*(3), 404–423. doi: 10.1080/10841806.2020.1771907

Bowen, J. A. (2012). *Teaching naked: How moving technology out of your college classroom will improve student learning.* San Francisco, CA: Jossey-Bass. ISBN 1118238087, 9781118238080

DePietro, A. (2020). Here's a look at the impact of Coronavirus (COVID-19) on colleges and universities in the U.S. Forbes. Retrieved from https://www.forbes.com/sites/andrewdepietro/2020/04/30/impact-coronavirus-covid-19-colleges-universities/#6d4f9cb061a6

Ferguson, H. T. (2020, April 8). Cuts expected for state higher education funding in the wake of COVID-19. Retrieved from https://www.nasfaa.org/news-item/21469/Cuts_Expected_for_State_Higher_Education_Funding_in_the_Wake_of_COVID-19

Friga, P. N. (2020). Under Covid-19, university budgets like we've never seen before. *The Chronicle of Higher Education*. Retrieved from https://www.chronicle.com/article/Under-Covid-19-University/248574

Gaus, J. M. (1947). *Reflections on public administration*. Tuscaloosa, AL: University of Alabama Press.

Hazelkorn, E., & Gibson, A. (2019). Public goods and public policy: What is public good, and who and what decides?. *Higher Education*, 78(2), 257–271. doi:10.1007/s10734-018-0341-3

Hu, S. (2009). *Walter W. McMahon: Higher learning, greater good: The private and social benefits of higher education*. Baltimore, MD: John Jopkins University Press.

Marginson, S. (2018). Public/private in higher education: A synthesis of economic and political approaches. *Studies in Higher Education*, 43(2), 322–337. doi:10.1080/03075079.2016.1168797

Means, B., Bakia, M., & Murphy, R. (2014). *Learning online: What research tells us about whether, when and how*. New York, NY: Routledge Taylor & Frances.

OECD. (2020). Flattening the COVID-19 peak: Containment and mitigation policies. Retrieved from https://read.oecd-ilibrary.org/view/?ref=124_124999-yt5ggxirhc&title=Flattening_the_COVID-19_peak-containment_and_mitigation_policies

Rashid, S & Yadav, S. (2020). Impact of Covid-19 Pandemic on Higher Education and Research. Indian Journal of Human Development, 14(2), 340–343. DOI: 10.1177/0973703020946700

Riffee, W. R. (2003). Putting a face on distance education programs. *Syllabus*, 16(7), 10–13.

United Nations. (2020). Policy Brief: Education during COVID-19 and beyond. Retrievd from https://www.un.org/development/desa/dspd/wp-content/uploads/sites/22/2020/08/sg_policy_brief_covid-19_and_education_august_2020.pdf

Weeden, K. A., & Cornwell, B., (2020). The small-world network of college classes: Implications for epidemic spread on a university campus. *Sociological Science*, 7, 222–241.

WHO. (2020, March 11). *WHO Director-General's opening remarks at the media briefing on COVID-19 – 11 March 2020*. World Health Organization. Retrieved from https://www.who.int/dg/speeches/detail/whodirector-general-s-opening-remarks-at-the-mediabriefing-on-covid-19--11-march-2020

Xiang, Y. T., Li, W., Zhang, Q., Jin, Y., Rao, W. W., Zeng, L. N., ... Hall, B. J. (2020). Timely research papers about COVID-19 in China. *The Lancet*, 395(10225), 684–685. doi:10.1016/S0140-6736(20)30375-5

CHAPTER 2

ONLINE TEACHING, LEARNING, AND ASSESSMENT DURING COVID-19: A CASE OF A MANAGEMENT FACULTY IN SRI LANKA

A. W. Janitha C. Abeygunasekera

ABSTRACT

Covid-19 pandemic has affected all sectors in the economy. Among them, education sector is one of the most influenced fields. This chapter presents a case of a faculty in a state university in Sri Lanka which underwent a transformation toward online teaching, learning, and assessment mode with the Covid-19 pandemic. The unexpected conversion to online mode impacted many parties, and among them, the lecturers and students were mostly affected within universities. The author explored the perception of students and lecturers on this unexpected compulsory transformation and identified how they perceive this new normal in teaching, learning, and assessment. In addition, the benefits and challenges faced, and the pre and post views on online experience were also studied. An online survey with students and a series of interviews with lecturers were exercised for data collection. The views that students have on online learning were different among the various study program levels, and the benefits and challenges faced by the different student groups also varied. Further, the lecturers had different perceptions on teaching the different level programs and subjects. These aspects are discussed in detail throughout the chapter, and at the end, suggestions for making the online mode more effective are presented.

Keywords: Online teaching; online learning; online assessment; Covid-19; higher education; Sri Lanka

INTRODUCTION

The Covid-19 pandemic affected the smooth functioning of all sectors of life. The education sector is one mostly affected (Bozkurt et al., 2020). All primary, secondary, and tertiary education sectors were influenced, and as per the World Bank reports, universities and other tertiary education institutions were closed in 175 countries by early April 2020, and 13% of the total student population was affected globally (World Bank Group, 2020). In Sri Lanka, the government decided to close all educational institutions from March 2020, including higher education institutions, due to Covid-19 pandemic (ADB, 2020).

With the closure of all academic institutions in countries, a major disruption was caused to teaching, learning, and research activities.

> The ad hoc nature of institutional closures continues to plague systems globally, as students, academic staff, and government officials grapple with the implications of these closures for their learning, teaching, research, innovation and education outcomes, and financial stability. (World Bank Group, 2020, p. 2)

As a result, the need for online education and learning became vital. A collapse in the sector cannot be tolerated because a collapse today will have a ripple effect for many future decades. Therefore, despite the issues of equity, infrastructure, broadband capacity, pedagogic capacity, and many other limitations, online delivery of teaching was initiated in many regions in the world (World Bank Group, 2020).

Similarly, in Sri Lanka, to minimize disruptions and potential damages to students' academic careers, online learning/teaching was introduced to the primary, tertiary, and higher education sectors at a large scale within a short period with the Covid-19 pandemic. Sri Lankan government and telecommunication organizations provided considerable high support for these initiatives.

When considering the tertiary education sector, the University Grants Commission (UGC), which is the supreme authority in the higher education sector in Sri Lanka, initiated discussions with the President and obtained approval for free internet access to use university web servers during the pandemic, from internet service providers in Sri Lanka. The existing Moodle-based learning management systems (LMSs) were used for this. The university web servers were connected to the Lanka Education and Research Network (LEARN) for online teaching and learning (ADB, 2020). Zoom was the most used platform during this period.

This chapter presents students' and lecturers' perceptions of converting the teaching, learning, and assessment modes to an online platform in a Management Faculty in a Sri Lankan university. The Management Faculty consists of eight departments offering eight special degrees and has undergraduate and postgraduate programs, with a proximate population of 3,000 students and 110 lecturers.

Online teaching and learning during pandemic periods are temporary shifts of the delivery mode to online. Mostly they are not well-designed nor well-planned compared to courses offered online in normal situations (Hodges, Moore, Lockee, Trust, & Bond, 2020). Before Covid-19 pandemic, the lecturers nor students expected any online delivery of courses and had to convert as it was compulsory. The focus of the author was to understand how the students and lecturers perceived this mandatory unexpected transformation. Studies that explore the perceptions on online teaching and learning exist (Ilgaz & Adanır, 2020; Rohman, Marji, Sugandi, & Nurhadi, 2020; Russo & Benson, 2005; Surani & Hamidah, 2020; Wallace, 2003; Young & Norgard, 2006); however, there are limited studies that had explored on developing country contexts during a pandemic situation (Bozkurt et al., 2020), where the conversion to online mode happens with less planning compared to non-pandemic situations. Further, this transformation to online mode was compulsory in the Sri Lankan context and in many other contexts as there was no other choice to minimize the negative disruption to the education sector.

Data were collected from a sample of lecturers and students in the selected Management Faculty using interviews and questionnaires to understand these phenomena in a developing country context. The chapter initially introduces online learning. Then it presents the background details on the transformation by the case organization together with data collection and analysis method. Next, the students' and lecturers' perceptions of online teaching and learning and the challenges the two groups faced when going online, and the changes in the views on online mode are discussed. After that, perceptions on online assessment are discussed, and finally, a list of proposals for the future success of online mode is presented.

ONLINE LEARNING

> Online learning is the latest in a succession of technology-based innovations in higher education ... most of these technologies undoubtedly enriched the process of tertiary teaching and learning, and some continue to do so, few if any have had the radical impact on higher education envisaged by early enthusiasts. (Curran, 2008, p. 27)

Despite the visible value of online learning (Darby & Lang, 2019), most universities do not use it much due to the challenges in initiating the process of going online. However, with the Covid-19, none of these challenges could be considered as there was no other option, and almost all universities went online. "What is the exact meaning of going online in an academic context?," is a question that needs an answer before moving further in the chapter.

With the term online learning, many other terms such as web-based learning, e-learning, computer-based learning, technology-based learning, emergency remote teaching are used, and more recently, the term blended online learning was added to the list. Though these terms are used interchangeably, they have different meanings. As the chapter uses the term online learning, the definition for that is provided next, together with the definition of a much broader term "online education," which covers online learning as well.

Singh and Thurman (2019) examined definitions on online learning and online education through a rigorous literature review and defined online learning as:

> learning experienced through the internet/online computers in a synchronous classroom where students interact with instructors and other students and are not dependent on their physical location for participating in this online learning experience. (p. 302)

Further, they defined online education as:

> education being delivered in an online environment through the use of the internet for teaching and learning. This includes online learning on the part of the students that is not dependent on their physical or virtual co-location. The teaching content is delivered online and the instructors develop teaching modules that enhance learning and interactivity in the synchronous or asynchronous environment.

BACKGROUND FOR GOING ONLINE

In the concerned university of this study, the vice-chancellor (VC) responded to the requirement of converting the teaching and learning into online mode by early March 2020. The VC started discussions with the responsible parties at the UGC and the internal parties of the university, such as deans, directors, rectors, heads of departments, centers, and units at the earliest possible. By the third week of March 2020, the decision was taken to initiate online teaching and learning for undergraduate programs. The UGC offered the facility for all university students to access the university and faculty web and proceed with their online learning activities free of any internet cost.

Apart from the plans to provide necessary free internet facilities through the university, the respective faculty websites were used to post encouraging messages to all students to boost confidence and determination to face the crisis. The main intention was to make them feel that they are being looked after by the university and the university is with them at all needed times.

With such decisions and facilities, the Management Faculty decided to start online learning and teaching for all undergraduate study programs as the first phase of the transformation process of the programs offered.

MANAGEMENT FACULTY GOING ONLINE

The decision taken at the VC level cascaded to the faculties, and the Management Faculty had its first online lesson to undergraduates in the third week of April 2020. Initially, one department started online lectures as they were prepared to it beforehand, with the guidance of the enthusiastic and proactive leader, who motivated the staff to prepare for going online as soon as the initial discussions on this transformation were reached at the university level. Within 2–3 weeks, all the eight departments converted to online mode. Gradually, all four years of the undergraduate study program were transformed into online mode, starting with the final year undergraduates. A main role was played by the heads of departments, and they carried out separate meetings with staff and students to plan and guide the process as well as to motivate them.

Other study programs offered by the faculty were converted to online mode after completing the semester that was ongoing for undergraduates at the point of closure of the universities. Step by step, all programs were changed to online, and the diplomas and higher diplomas were the last to go online. Before the second wave of the Covid-19, where the country was partially closed once again, the students were called to university year by year within a two-month period to conduct their end-semester examinations for the semesters for which teaching was completed online. The whole examination process was carried out adhering to the health and safety guidelines of Covid-19 regulations. However, with the second wave of Covid-19 pandemic, consideration was given to conducting end-semester examinations (summative assessments) also through online mode.

By this time, some of the other faculties in the same university had moved to pure online assessments, and the Management Faculty was doing online assessments only for continuous assessments. With the prevailing requirements for the continuation of online mode and the unexpected conditions in the world, Management Faculty was doing trial assessment rounds for selected undergraduate groups to explore the possibility of conducting pure online end-semester examinations. By the time of data collection for this study, the IT center in the faculty together with the dean, heads of departments in collaboration with lecturers, were discussing and experimenting on this conversion of assessments, and no concrete decision was reached.

The views of the lecturers and the students become vital in making decisions on change initiatives to study programs within faculties. Therefore, it is essential to identify and explore their perceptions on the changes before, during, and after such initiatives, which is one aim of this study. The following section presents the data collection and analysis of the study, followed by findings thereafter.

DATA COLLECTION AND ANALYSIS

The study used a mixed-method approach (Creswell, 2015). Lecturers and students were the respondent groups. Surveys and interviews were the main data collection methods. In developing the questionnaire and the semi-structured interview guide, four students and two lecturers were interviewed.

The respondents were recruited via convenience sampling and a total of 270 questionnaires were filled by the 4 groups of students (4.4% DBA students, 11.85% MBA students, 60% undergraduate students, and 23.7% diploma students; overall, 82% female and 18% male) and 17 lectures (71% female and 29% male) were interviewed using a semi-structured interview guide during the examination period.

The interview transcripts were coded inductively to identify the expected information. The data on the questionnaires were analyzed to determine averages, percentages, and rankings related to factors mentioned related to perceptions, benefits, challenges, and view changes.

PERCEPTIONS ON ONLINE TEACHING AND LEARNING
Students

As per the data, it was evident that the student views on online learning were different among various program levels (i.e., DBA, MBA, undergraduate, and diploma) (see Table 1).

Among the four student categories, doctoral students showed a completely different perception than others. The majority of the undergraduate students (86%), masters level students (91%), and diploma level students (89%) preferred online teaching mode compared to the physical classes whereas, the majority of the doctoral students (67%) disliked online teaching mode.

The reasons stated for preferring online mode by different student groups during the survey are summarized in Table 2.

Overall, the most mentioned reasons by most student groups are convenience due to studying from home or any other location at their comfort, time, and cost saving due to the elimination of traveling time in this mode. Comfortable environment of learning and the ease of managing home, work, and education with online mode were also frequently mentioned.

The reasons stated for not preferring online mode by different student groups during the survey are summarized in Table 3.

Undergraduates who disliked online teaching only stated three factors and those were mentioned by other groups also: (1) the inability to socialize with friends which will negatively impact the mental health of students (e.g., a student stated – "… 'we lost our University life,' this is the last year, and we could not do anything to recall and talk about later in our lives. No batch parties, trips, and hanging around with friends. It really affects our minds…"); (2) the issues and disturbances they face with the speed and bandwidth related issues in the network facilities; and (3) poor outcomes from the lecturers and students (e.g., a student stated – "both sides become ineffective. Teachers lose interest, and we too lose interest after some time. How hard they try to keep us up, when looking at the screen for 15–20 minutes, the mind starts roaming, sometimes feel like browsing internet or Facebook, and we miss some important things. … Because the mentality to listen to the recording is under the mind"). In addition to the above, the other three student groups stated the following factors: less direct interaction between

Table 1. Student Perceptions on Online Teaching and Learning (Survey).

Student Category	Prefer Online (%)	Not Prefer Online (%)
DBA	33	67
MBA	91	9
Undergraduate	86	14
Diploma	89	11

Table 2. Reasons for Preferring Online Teaching/Learning by all Student Groups.

Reason	DBA	MBA	Undergraduate	Diploma
Ease/convenience	x	x	x	x
Less costly (time and cost saving)	x	x	x	x
Comfortable environment when learning from home		x	x	x
Ease of managing time (ability to attend from any location)	x	x		x
Opportunity to learn within the home environment		x		x
Flexibility when studying from home		x		x
A safe environment for the learning process during pandemic situations		x		x
Ability to continue studies with this mode during pandemic situations			x	
Ability to listen to the recording many times and write notes			x	
Ease of managing office work	x			
Energy (physical) saving	x			

Table 3. Reasons for Not Preferring Online Teaching/Learning by all Student Groups.

Reason	DBA	MBA	Undergraduate	Diploma
Inability to socialize with friends will negatively impact the mental health of students	x	x	x	x
Issues and disturbances faced with the speed and bandwidth related issues in the network facilities	x	x	x	x
Poor outcomes from the lecturers and students	x	x	x	x
Less direct interaction between lecturers and students	x	x		x
Dullness when studying in front of a screen	x	x		x
Not having a feel of a real classroom atmosphere	x	x		x
Lack of enthusiasm for studying alone	x	x		x

students and lecturer; dullness when studying in front of a screen; and not having a feel of a real classroom atmosphere and lack of enthusiasm for learning alone.

However, all student groups were of the view that some portion of the lectures should be done physically.

Lecturers

Further, with the interviews with the lecturers, it was evident that the lecturers' perception on online teaching changes with the program and subject taught. Most lecturers (more than 80%) stated that doctoral-level students could not be catered with a purely online mode; this is quite like the doctoral students' views on learning online. The reasons mentioned were inability to build on rich conceptual discussions in online mode; inability to review progress of the ongoing research studies purely in online modes; and inability to ripe the benefits of discussions of invited groups of scholars during online sessions. Most lecturers (more than 90%) preferred online mode for other programs (e.g., a lecturer stated – "… can do with BBA courses, and may be others. But not for doctorates. You need a part of physical interactions within a class. Not only with the facilitator, even peer interactions and discussions are important at that level"). However, many (more than 60%) were concerned about the suitability of online mode for subjects of a quantitative nature such as accounting and statistics (e.g., a lecturer stated – "I don't agree that we can do everything online. How can you do a consolidation calculation online, a large analysis online ... nope, I don't think all subjects can be taught online").

The most mentioned reasons and benefits for preferring online teaching mentioned by lecturers include: the ability to manage lectures and commitments at home to a certain extent, with many lecturers having children at home who are also studying online (e.g., a lecturer stated – "we can do this at this level because it is flexible. Otherwise, how can we manage the other work"); savings of traveling time and cost (e.g., a lecturer stated – "I save almost 3 hours a day. It takes one and a half hours minimum for me to come to Colombo. During office hours it is more than that. Now, all that is saved, together with petrol"); flexible teaching times including late evenings which is not possible with a physical mode of teaching (e.g., a lecturer stated – "the students also prefer late evening lectures than daytime. Most masters courses, I ask to put after 5.30 p.m. Then I have the whole day to manage other things"); and the ability to shift lectures easily and quickly.

Amidst the benefits stated above, the students and lecturers face challenges as well.

CHALLENGES ON TEACHING AND LEARNING ONLINE

The varying challenges faced by these groups with the change to online mode can be divided as: (1) technical challenges and (2) other challenges. These are discussed next under the two respondent groups.

Students

The main technical challenges stated by the undergraduates (see Table 4) were: internet and connection problems; and difficulty to clearly see the visuals and slides when accessing the online session through mobile devices (phones) due to unavailability of computers/laptops (e.g., a student stated – "I don't have a computer. I log with my phone. Sometimes the letters in the power point slides are very small and can't see clearly. I can only listen in such instances"). The other student groups also mentioned two of the above: lack of data strength, coverage, and speed that disrupt the connectivity. In addition, they stated sudden power failures as a challenge (e.g., a student said – "it is common in our area to get 2–3 minutes power failures time to time. That is a huge problem. Some days I lose connection few times during a lecture and sometimes can't log in again for few minutes and I miss important discussions").

Most of these challenges are beyond the students' control as most students do not have a high financial capacity to resolve the issue. Especially among the undergraduates (30% of undergraduate respondents), it has been challenging for most of them as they are dependents. Most families are affected financially

Table 4. Challenges Faced with Online Teaching/Learning by all Student Groups.

Challenges	DBA	MBA	Undergraduate	Diploma
Technical challenges				
Internet and connectivity problems	x	x	x	x
Unavailability of computers/laptops resulting in a poor view of study material			x	
Sudden power failures	x	x	x	x
Other challenges				
Existence of younger siblings involved in online education			x	
Work–life balance – with online office work together with online studies	x	x		x
Costs in purchasing additional devices		x		x
Unavailability of servants for household chores during the pandemic period		x		x

during this period, and they are unable to prioritize internet connectivity and smart devices, among other basic needs, especially during this pandemic period.

Among the undergraduate level students, the existence of younger siblings involved in education is the only issue stated apart from the technical issues mentioned above. However, this is not a common issue, as only 15% of undergraduates noted this problem. The other student groups stated work–life balance, with online office work and online studies as a significant issue. Further, 30% of students who had children (studying online) faced specific difficulties with the requirement for several devices simultaneously. They had to purchase additional tablets/computers to manage this, which was another burden where most of them had pay-cuts. About 16% of the same group mentioned the unavailability of servants for household chores during this period as a challenge. The main reason for not having these issues among the undergraduates is that approximately 80% of them are unemployed and 100% are unmarried.

Despite the issues faced, most student groups prefer the online mode, and they prefer it to be recorded and shared with them to review later.

Lecturers

The main technical issues stated by the lecturers are disruptions to connectivity, logging in issues during peak hours due to network traffic, and lack of availability of devices at home (for lecturers with children).

The other issues mentioned are work–life balance (by 70%) with the spouses also working from home; high influence on personal life due to arranging the official meeting and discussions during late evenings (by 40%) (e.g., a lecturer stated "certainly this is going above the nose sometimes. I hate days with late evening meetings. It is very hard to put the little one to sleep on time when there is a meeting for me. … this is not only to me"); and unavailability of childcare facilities/support from servants for household chores during this pandemic period (36%) (e.g., a lecturer stated – "Day-care is closed, and I look after my two kids and have to do all chores and get ready for lecture. I didn't have a servant … now can't find one with this condition"). Few (15%) stated the unnecessary communication requirements with students during weekends and late evenings due to the inability to limit such discussions to office hours. Though students could call or email the lecturers before the pandemic also, with the move to online mode, the use of these communication modes has also increased rapidly (e.g., as stated by a lecturer – "now it is hard to find a day without 2–3 calls from students. Not only that, now I reply to many student emails during a day. I did not have such experience before").

Overall, the balance of work–life and online learning of parents with children is a significant challenge brought out by both lecturers and elderly students. The unavailability of childcare facilities/servants for household chores is also common.

CHANGE OF VIEW ON ONLINE TEACHING AND LEARNING

Within a short period, the initial perceptions of many lecturers and students on online mode have changed.

Students

A mixed result is seen among the different student groups. Some students who were reluctant to think of an online learning mode due to the lack of knowledge on how it happens and how they will face the change had changed their negative perceptions after following 3–4 weeks of online lectures (e.g., a student stated – "I did not know how zoom works. Our batch coordinator had some group meetings and discussed our issues and taught how it works. After some lectures, the fear went off"). The benefits they felt and experienced during this period and the indirect assurance they got about completing the degrees/diplomas within the stipulated periods have moved them toward the positive edge. However, the opposite was also evident; certain students who were with a very positive attitude had moved away from it due to experiencing a lower level of effectiveness during online lectures (e.g., a student stated – "… even though I expected that it was easy to learn online, it sometimes became boring and not really effective in some lectures").

According to the responses, none of the students were purely negative on online mode, nor were they strictly positive.

Lecturers

The perceptions on online teaching of 60% of the lecturers in the sample had changed from a positive scale to a negative scale between the point of initially teaching online and after continuing for nearly 6–7 weeks during this period. Most of them who initially perceived online teaching to be beneficial and easy had later changed their views. As identified through interviews, the reasons for the change of the positive perception to a negative one are the: felt ineffectiveness in certain instances; lack of responses from students, not being able to see the students, lack of interactions, etc. (e.g., a lecturer stated – "I thought students would be more interactive when we are online. But some days I had to force them to talk. ... you don't see them, and they don't talk; very disappointing sometimes. This made me to change my view"). Another fact is the change of environmental conditions exited when initiating online teaching after few weeks. The initial point of change occurred within a situation where a significant need for moving online existed. During that time, online schooling of children did not exist, and online office work of spouses was limited or not existed (e.g., a lecturer stated – "when we first started online, it was only me who had online work. But, now all except my mother is working online at home. The situation changes and my mind changed"). However, all these changes brought additional tasks that limited the time available for the preparation of online material and conduct of lectures which made them change their view.

PERCEPTIONS ON ASSESSMENT

Through assessments, we can gather information to make informed decisions about learners and inform them about their learning and performance (Black & Wiliam, 1998; Brookhart & Nitko, 2008). Generally, there are three types of assessments: (1) *diagnostic assessments*; (2) *formative assessments*; and (3) *summative assessments* (Larson & Lockee, 2014; Sterling, 2005).

The usual practice of the Management Faculty is having two main assessments: formative and summative. The assessments are designed at the beginning of every semester to continuously evaluate students during the semester and to evaluate them at the semester end through a written examination. During this pandemic period, the continuous assessment policy was flexed. Most lecturers who had not completed the continuous assessments at the time of closure were encouraged to convert their continuous assessments to online mode. Some revised their plans and designed the assessments afresh, and some twisted the already given assignments to enable students to do them using online resources.

However, the end-semester examinations were conducted without much flexibility. A series of end-semester examinations were completed physically adhering to safety guidelines by bringing students to the faculty cluster by cluster before closing the university with the second wave of Covid-19. However, due to the existing uncertain situation (at the time of data collection), discussions were ongoing in the faculty on converting the final examinations in the upcoming semesters into online mode; and was at the trial-and-error stage with few groups, and a final decision was not reached.

By the time of data collection for this study, the students and lecturers have experienced online assessments only for continuous assessments.

Students

About 80% of students preferred online assessments and presentations compared to in-class assessments and presentations. Most undergraduates preferring online presentations stated the reason as the possibility of hiding their emotions and nervousness, which was otherwise visible (e.g., a student stated – "I don't like to do presentations in front of the class. I get nervous. But now we did two online presentations, and I felt more comfortable"). All student groups except doctoral students stated their preference for online multiple-choice questions (MCQs) for continuous assessments, mid-semester exams, and quizzes. At the same time, 90% of them disliked the online final examinations. The reasons mentioned for the dislike were the speed of typing in the computer, connectivity issues, power failures, and the possibility of manipulations (e.g., a student stated – "most of us can't type very fast. If we get the finals online, then we will need more time. That won't happen so I don't think any of us like online end exams"). The doctoral students preferred online examinations with the concept of open-book examinations. However, they also raised the concern on the typing speed during examinations.

The need for adequately managing and facilitating online assessments was mentioned by many students. During the trial runs of online examinations, certain student groups have attempted to cheat, and this was a concern some of them raised (e.g., a student stated – "I hope you will not reveal my name ... before the online exam we planned how we can copy and decided to have a group chat on the phones. Screenshots of all answers were shared. But students who logged from the phone could not do this"). This had been happening in many institutes, and the examiners should consider such aspects as it further widens the gap between the students with resources and without resources.

Lecturers

The lecturers' views were compatible with the student views, and a majority (80%) of lecturers preferred online assessments only for continuous assessments and not for final examinations. Also, lecturers emphasized the need for face-to-face sessions during presentation evaluations as otherwise presentation skills cannot be evaluated (e.g., a lecturer stated – "it is very hard to evaluate them on presentation skills. We only can see the slide properly, and sometimes when the connection is not stable that creates more issues. Extra time is required, and students get disappointed"). Certain assessment methods such as MCQs and quizzes were accepted by a majority of lecturers as they can be managed easily to minimize cheating by having question banks and alternative papers.

The ease of online marking and auto-generation of marks of assessments were benefits of online assessments. This enables the quick release of results and time saving for lecturers.

WAY FORWARD

Based on this study, the following eight aspects are recognized as important areas to be focused on making teaching, learning, and assessments more effective during pandemic situations:

(i) *Planning* – The most common and preferred interaction method for teaching and learning is the physical presence (Baker & Woods, 2004; Coppola,

Hiltz, & Rotter, 2002). However, it is not feasible during pandemic situations, and therefore, online teaching and learning strategies need to be carefully implemented (Bozkurt et al., 2020; Hammond, 2005; Hulett, 2018). Pre-planning before pandemic situations with contingency plans should be developed to face unexpected moves to online mode.

(ii) *Motivating* – Encouraging the regular use of LMSs among students and lectures is necessary. Some LMSs such as Blackboard takes a commercial nature, and LMSs such as Moodle is open-source solutions. All these facilitate course administration and delivery through e-learning tools. Their features, such as upload of PowerPoint slides, audio files, video files, links to resources, assessments, online quizzes, grade books etc., need to be communicated to students and lecturers and motivate them to use them.

Most of the challenges faced by the students and lecturers were partially a result of the lack of use of information and communication technology (ICT) in society. Therefore, using ICT should be promoted among the community and enhance access to online libraries to make them conversant with these technologies.

(iii) *Equipping* – Both lecturers and students suggested providing the lecturers with additional infrastructure to facilitate the online sessions, especially for subjects with calculations. The whiteboards, cameras, and other teaching aids can be provided to them from universities or facilitate the purchase of them to use during online teaching to enhance the effectiveness of online learning.

Though most lecturers have access to infrastructure, most students do not. Authorities should consider providing laptops and internet facilities to all university students in the longer term to enable online mode of teaching and learning continuously even in the future (Pete & Soko, 2020). A laptop can be provided to all students registering to universities with an agreement for repaying the cost once they are employed after graduation. This cannot be done overnight; however, authorities can initiate mechanisms to provide new equipment with a plan.

(iv) *Training* – Training for online course design and teaching is also essential (Lloyd, Byrne, & McCoy, 2012; Martin, Budhrani, Kumar, & Ritzhaupt, 2019; McGee, Windes, & Torres, 2017) as it is a different art compared to preparing for physical face-to-face lectures. Such training can be organized at the university level for lecturers.

(v) *Blending* – Blended learning is a concept that gained attention, and it is not merely teaching online. In addition to blended learning, "blended online learning" which is an emerging variation of blended learning, need to be promoted because "blended online learning adds synchronous online learning via web conferencing to enhance otherwise asynchronous online courses" (Fadde & Vu, 2014, p. 33). The authorities can take responsibility for this. In doing so, firstly, the lecturers can be trained and informed on the methods and tools for blended learning and blended online learning.

(vi) *Quality* – The current focus during this pandemic period focuses more on the adoption of online teaching/learning mode. While promoting the adoption, maintenance, and improvement of the quality is also essential. As stated by Dhawan (2020, p. 7), "online learning is emerging as a victor ludorum amidst this chaos. Therefore, the quality enhancement of online teaching–learning is crucial." And Chaloux and Miller (2014, p. 10) emphasize the role of leadership and faculty in creating quality as: "ensuring quality in this area means that leaders must involve their organization in a variety of functions, from instructional design to faculty development, assessment, and retention, and other factors that reflect learning outcomes." In addition, clear policies and standards for online courses are also paramount for maintaining quality (Lloyd et al., 2012). Thus, responsible authorities should focus on the promotion and stabilization of online mode and enhance its quality. Otherwise, the effectiveness of online mode may not be sufficient for it to sustain in the long term.

(vii) *Ethics* – Minimizing attempts of cheating during assessments is another aspect that needs attention. In traditional terms, cheating is copying from another student. However, in the online mode, even using the internet while answering questions is considered cheating (Ko & Rossen, 2010). To minimize cheating, the use of a proctor (Bedford, Gregg, & Clinton, 2009), installing lockdown browser programs that limit the ability to surf the internet (Cluskey, Ehlen, & Raiborn, 2011), etc., can be used.

(viii) *Equality* – As stated by the World Bank Group (2020, pp. 8–9), "students without access or the resources to afford the technology are being left behind. Student with learning challenges are being left behind. Students with disabilities are being left behind." Therefore, to minimize such disparities in the future, responsible authorities should focus on equality when making policies and procedures.

REFERENCES

ADB. (2020). Online learning in Sri Lanka's higher education institutions during the COVID-19 pandemic. Retrieved from https://www.adb.org/publications/online-learning-sri-lanka-during-covid-19. Accessed on November 10, 2020.

Baker, J. D., & Woods, R. H. (2004). Immediacy, cohesiveness, and the online classroom. *Journal of Computing in Higher Education*, *15*, 133–151.

Bedford, W., Gregg, J., & Clinton, S. (2009). Implementing technology to prevent online cheating: A case study at a small southern regional university (SSRU). *Journal of Online Learning and Teaching*, *5*(2), 230–238.

Black, P., & Wiliam, D. (1998). Inside the black box: Raising standards through classroom assessment. *Phi Delta Kappan*, *80*(2), 139–148.

Bozkurt, A., Jung, I., Xiao, J., Vladimirschi, V., Schuwer, R., Egorov, G., ... & Paskevicius, M. (2020). A global outlook to the interruption of education due to COVID-19 pandemic: Navigating in a time of uncertainty and crisis. *Asian Journal of Distance Education*, *15*(1), 1–126.

Brookhart, S. M., & Nitko, A. J. (2008). *Assessment and grading in classrooms*. Upper Saddle River, NJ: Pearson Education.

Chaloux, B., & Miller, G. E. (2014). E-learning and the transformation of higher education. In G. Miller, M. Benke, B. Chaloux, L. C. Ragan, R. Schroeder, W. Smutz, & K. Swan (Eds.), *Leading the e-learning transformation of higher education* (pp. 3–22). Sterling, VA: Stylus.

Cluskey, G. R., Jr, Ehlen, C. R., & Raiborn, M. H. (2011). Thwarting online exam cheating without proctor supervision. *Journal of Academic and Business Ethics*, *4*, 1–7.

Coppola, N. W., Hiltz, S. R., & Rotter, N. G. (2002). Becoming a virtual professor: Pedagogical roles and asynchronous learning networks. *Journal of management information systems*, *18*(4), 169–189.

Creswell, J. W. (2015). *A concise introduction to mixed methods research*. Thousand Oaks, CA: SAGE.

Curran, C. (2008). Online learning and the university. In W. Bramble & S. Panda (Eds.), *Economics of distance and online learning* (pp. 38–63). New York, NY: Routledge. https://doi-org.ezp01.library.qut.edu.au/10.4324/9780203892985

Darby, F., & Lang, J. M. (2019). *Small teaching online: Applying learning science in online classes*. Newark, NJ: John Wiley & Sons, Incorporated.

Dhawan, S. (2020). Online learning: A panacea in the time of COVID-19 crisis. *Journal of Educational Technology Systems*, *49*(1), 5–22.

Fadde, P. J., & Vu, P. (2014). Blended online learning: Benefits, challenges, and misconceptions. In P. R. Lowenthal, C. S. York, & J. C. Richardson (Eds.), *Online learning: Common misconceptions, benefits and challenges* (pp. 33–48). New York, NY: Nova Science Publishers.

Hammond, M. (2005). A review of recent papers on online discussion in teaching and learning in higher education. *Journal of Asynchronous Learning*, *9*(3), 9–23.

Hodges, C., Moore, S., Lockee, B., Trust, T., & Bond, A. (2020). The difference between emergency remote teaching and online learning. *Educause Review*, *27*, 1–12.

Hulett, M. (2018). *Online teaching strategies and best practices from the perspectives of effective community college online instructors: A phenomenological study*. Ann Arbor, MI: ProQuest Dissertations Publishing.

Ilgaz, H., & Adanır, G. A. (2020). Providing online exams for online learners: Does it really matter for them?. *Education and Information Technologies*, *25*(2), 1255–1269.

Ko, S., & Rossen, S. (2010). *Teaching online: A practical guide* (3rd ed.) New York, NY: Routledge.

Larson, M. B., & Lockee, B. B. (2014). *Streamlined ID: A practical guide to instructional design*. New York, NY: Routledge.

Lloyd, S. A., Byrne, M. M., & McCoy, T. S. (2012). Faculty-perceived barriers of online education. *MERLOT Journal of Online Learning and Teaching*, *8*(1), 1–12.

Martin, F., Budhrani, K., Kumar, S., & Ritzhaupt, A. (2019). Award-winning faculty online teaching practices: Roles and competencies. *Online Learning*, *23*(1), 184–205.

McGee, P., Windes, D., & Torres, M. (2017). Experienced online instructors: Beliefs and preferred supports regarding online teaching. *Journal of Computing in Higher Education*, *29*(2), 331–352.

Pete, J., & Soko, J. J. (2020). Preparedness for online learning in the context of Covid-19 in selected Sub-Saharan African countries. *Asian Journal of Distance Education*, *15*(2), 37–47.

Rohman, M., Marji, D. A. S., Sugandi, R. M., & Nurhadi, D. (2020). Online learning in higher education during Covid-19 pandemic: students' perceptions. *Journal of Talent Development and Excellence*, *12*(2s), 3644–3651.

Russo, T., & Benson, S. (2005). Learning with invisible others: Perceptions of online presence and their relationship to cognitive and affective learning. *Educational Technology and Society*, *8*(1), 54–62.

Sterling, D. R. (2005). Assessing understanding. *Science Scope*, *28*(4), 33–37.

Surani, D., & Hamidah, H. (2020). Students perceptions in online class learning during the Covid-19 pandemic. *International Journal on Advanced Science, Education, and Religion*, *3*(3), 83–95.

Singh V., & Thurman A. (2019) How many ways can we define online learning? A systematic literature review of definitions of online learning (1988–2018). *American Journal of Distance Education*, *33*(4), 289–306.

Wallace, R. M. (2003). Online learning in higher education: A review of the research on interactions among teachers and students. *Education, Communication & Information*, *3*(2), 241–280.

World Bank Group. (2020). The COVID-19 crisis response: Supporting tertiary education for continuity, adaptation, and innovation. Retrieved from https://www.worldbank.org/en/topic/edutech/brief/lessons-for-education-during-covid-19-crisis-guidance-notes. Accessed on November 10, 2020.

Young, A., & Norgard, C. (2006). Assessing the quality of online courses from students' perspective. *Internet and Higher Education*, *9*(2), 107–115.

CHAPTER 3

PREPAREDNESS OF STUDENTS FOR FUTURE TEACHING AND LEARNING IN HIGHER EDUCATION: A BANGLADESHI PERSPECTIVE

M. Mahruf C. Shohel, Md. Ashrafuzzaman,
Atm Shafiul Alam, Arif Mahmud,
Muhammad Shajjad Ahsan and Md Tariqul Islam

ABSTRACT

The COVID-19 pandemic has had a significant impact on higher education (HE) across the globe, including in Bangladesh. The Bangladeshi HE system is going through an abrupt transition and transformation to cope with the crisis. This chapter is based on data collected from teachers and students of Bangladeshi public and private HE institutions regarding teaching and learning during the COVID-19 lockdown. In Bangladesh, some universities switched to online distance teaching and learning quickly during this period, and others lagged behind in this regard. Teachers and students from both groups of public and private universities participated in the study, including those who attended online teaching and learning activities and those who did not participate. This chapter highlights both teachers' and students' perspectives regarding students' future preparedness for participating fully in the changing landscape of HE, especially technology-enhanced teaching and learning. Understanding these perspectives of teachers and students is important to address the digital divide and social justice issues in the policy and practice. Within the HE sector in Bangladesh, it is especially vital while transforming its education system and adapting emerging technologies to address the challenges of education in future emergencies.

Keywords: Students' preparedness; COVID-19; online distance teaching and learning; higher education; policy and practice; digital divide; social justice; emerging technologies; digital transformation; Bangladesh

INTRODUCTION

At all levels of education, the COVID-19 pandemic has triggered vast disruptions in teaching and learning (Liguori & Winkler, 2020; Shohel et al., 2022). According to UNESCO (2020), as many as 1.5 billion students in nearly 200 countries have been affected by school closures at the local or national level, representing approximately 90% of the global student population. However, in the context of higher education (HE), traditional classroom teaching is gradually being replaced by online teaching by many higher educational institutions (HEIs) due to the COVID-19 pandemic (Shohel et al., 2021b). In several nations, students and teachers have been forced to experience a hasty migration from conventional classrooms to online classes without ample time to adapt to these changes (Mittal, 2020; Sykes, 2020). Thus, it has become challenging for both teachers and students since they have had to adapt to distance learning via e-learning platforms that are entirely different from face-to-face learning (Kunwar, Poudel, & Shrestha, 2020). The COVID-19 pandemic highlights the need to use online models and applications to achieve the learning goals (Schneider & Council, 2020; Verawardina et al., 2020). It requires significant actions related to learning model policy, and this pandemic is an enormous challenge to education systems globally (Daniel, 2020). However, it is unexplored whether this transition produces positive results for students' academic attainments or not in the context of Bangladesh.

One of the characteristics of HE is that it is self-regulated based on the students' needs, where students have active roles in regulating and managing their learning process (Jones, 2019). Online distance teaching and learning (ODTL) allows students to play a more active role in their education. It focuses on personalization, including adjusting to the level of learners' skills and managing knowledge resources as mutual support (Berry & Kitchen, 2020). ODTL combines some of the best aspects of conventional learning (face-to-face) and online ICT-based learning in a complementary way (Wargadinata et al., 2020).

According to studies conducted on various subjects, there is a nexus between student engagement and academic performance (Delfino, 2019; Lee, 2014; Lei, Cui, & Zhou, 2018). Moreover, effective pedagogy is necessary to engage students and satisfy their needs to belong to educational environments (Osterman, 2000). An engaging learning environment plays a vital role in achieving learning outcomes. Face-to-face contact, peer participation, faculty input, and the absence of culture are frequently missing in many online courses. For learning and fostering student satisfaction, the engagement of the learner is essential. There are online teaching techniques that could increase students' sense of interaction (Mitchell, 2014). Moreover, a strong network, internet access, a smart device or computer, a friendly atmosphere, and technical skills are essential for an engaging online teaching–learning environment (Murillo & Jones, 2020). The situation requires all educational institutions to take precautions so that the COVID-19 pandemic does not cause wider disruption. Most importantly, innovation in learning is necessary to maintain the development of global education (Verawardina et al., 2020).

THE CHANGING LANDSCAPE OF HE

There has been an unprecedented development of new technologies, which have expanded exponentially in all areas of the modern world during recent decades (Chima & Gutman, 2020). Digital technologies have created endless opportunities to accelerate every aspect of human progress that could change societies and individuals for good (Kelly, 2010). The justification for incorporating technology within HE practice has been argued for many years. It has been recently strengthened by evidence that, for the first time in history, young people have adopted technology as part of their youth culture and identities before their parents and teachers (Boyd, 2014; Ito et al., 2010; Montgomery, 2007). Nevertheless, the radical transformation of HE has not lived up to the promise of reality. It has been suggested that the technological transformation is only slowly impacting HEIs and that it has yet to deliver on the promise of revolutionizing education and developing the knowledge economy, despite substantial investment in digital infrastructure (Younie & Leask, 2013).

Nevertheless, Sheely (2008) indicates that young people are generally more tech-savvy than previous generations (Bennett & Maton, 2010; Ofcom, 2012); that we exist in a remarkable historical moment observing the rapid embracing of social media and media production (Ito et al., 2010); and that technology is a fundamental part of young people's lives and identities (Jukes, McCain, & Crockett, 2010; Takahashi, 2011). Students of HEIs have adopted new technologies with tremendous vigor, responding to structures that can be personalized and controlled by themselves. This modern, immersive technology allows young people to be in daily touch with their social networks; discover and communicate their personalities and innovative ideas; explore information instantaneously; and promote mobility and individuality (Boyd, 2014; Montgomery, 2007). With young people's unique technological learning behaviors, this generation does not just want lectures during teaching and learning activities but favors experiential learning with instant feedback. Young people seek to collaborate with their peers to make decisions through functioning at high speed and multitasking in their own time utilizing technology-based learning resources (Dede, 2005; Oblinger & Oblinger, 2005; Prensky, 2011; Tapscott, 2009). Consequently, emerging technologies have become more widespread in contemporary HE classrooms. Though technology has been a common addition to many lecture halls and classrooms over the last decade, HEIs have been reluctant to absorb the creative use of digital technology to change teaching and learning, particularly in developing countries around the world (Conole et al., 2006; Crowne, 2009; Cuban, 1986; Dede, 2005; Godwin-Jones, 2015; Kolo & Breiter, 2009; Luckin et al., 2012; Papert, 1996; Walker & Shepard, 2011).

The progressive outbreak of the COVID-19 pandemic has posed a major challenge and transformation to the HE landscape (Mseleku, 2020). HEIs have been forced to close and look for alternative teaching and learning approaches through digital learning environments (Shohel et al., 2021; Simamora, 2020). Due to social distancing measures, HEIs worldwide have been pushed to experiment with e-learning as an alternative to traditional face-to-face learning (Demuyakor, 2020; Ratten, 2020; Raaper & Brown, 2020). This is particularly true for all education systems, and the global pandemic has forced HEIs around the world to use new and existing technologies with underlying intentions to revolutionize learning and teaching and embrace progress (United Nations, 2020). Universities have quickly adopted new ways of teaching and learning in response to the current crisis, with changes to online education, new forms of rubrics, assessment and evaluation strategies, and creative digital communication technologies all evident (Clow, 2020; Clune, 2020; Lederman, 2020).

THE CONTEXT OF HE IN BANGLADESH

There are four types of HEIs in Bangladesh: public universities, private universities, international universities, and affiliated colleges and institutes. Bangladesh had only seven public universities until 1990. In the early 1990s, new public universities such as Shahjalal Science and Technology University, Khulna University, National University, and Bangladesh Open University (BOU) were established. In 1992, the Private Universities Act 1992 opened the door for private universities to start their journey in Bangladesh, and this act was replaced by the Private University Act 2010. Currently, there are a total of 156 universities in Bangladesh, of which 46 are public universities and 107 private universities, and there are also three 3 international universities in Bangladesh (University Grants Commission of Bangladesh (UGC), 2020). There are many other colleges (1,862), both public (283) and private (1,579) which provide HE in Bangladesh. There are also madrasahs (234 kamil madrasahs including three public ones) that provide HE, mainly in the theology discipline (BANBEIS, 2018).

The HE facilities of the public universities are spread over the entire country so that students of different regions can receive HE without the commute. Thus, at least one public university exists in all the administrative divisions of the country (Monem & Baniamin, 2010). HEIs improvement issues, especially under the quality assurance banner, are a recent concern in education systems worldwide (Carlson, 2009).

In Bangladesh, the quality of education remains a serious issue because of the rapid growth of private HEIs and the increase in HE's enrollment during the last two decades.

Open and distance learning or blended learning, in particular technology-enhanced learning, has not been popularly promoted and practised as there is a belief that face-to-face and distance learning does not have the same quality (Jameel & Rea, 2020) (the former being more valued). Therefore, apart from the BOU and newly established Bangabandhu Sheikh Mujibur Rahman Digital University, Bangladesh, all other HEIs mainly continued with the traditional face-to-face approach in teaching and learning. The traditional "norm" of the delivery of teaching and learning in Bangladeshi HEIs does not require either universities/colleges or students to be well-equipped with technologies. However, information and communication technology (ICT) has been adapted by some faculties for teaching and learning in Bangladesh since the late 1980s in mainstream HE, that is, computer technology, including using PowerPoint presentations.

During the COVID-19 pandemic, the most common response from HEIs has been to shut down campuses and cancel all physical classes and meetings (Berezhna & Prokopenko, 2020; Ratten, 2020). Like many other countries, the government of Bangladesh decided to close educational institutions as part of preventive measures against the spread of Coronavirus by maintaining social distancing (Dutta & Smita, 2020). Accordingly, all HEIs of Bangladesh either postponed or canceled all campus events such as physical classes, graduation ceremonies, workshops, conferences, sports (both intra- and inter-universities), cultural events, and other activities, including student accommodations. There has been a mixed response to the sudden transition of teaching and learning into the complete online mode, with some hailing the move as a welcome drive toward pushing Bangladesh into the digital era. In contrast, others argue that the move to e-learning has marginalized many people increasing economic and social inequality, with many students facing "systematic" or "structural" discrimination if they are to stay out of online learning activities due to their socio-economic status (SES) and other factors (Shohel et al., 2021a).

To ensure the continuity of education, universities started to run virtual classes via online platforms such as Zoom, Google Classroom, Microsoft Teams, and other conferencing tools (Anwar & Fuad, 2020; UNICEF, 2020). However, as ODTL has its own set of challenges, Bangladeshi universities have faced a variety of challenges in continuing ODTL. Owing to a lack of access to laptops and smartphones, inability to afford internet packages, and power supply disruptions, a substantial number of students are unable to attend the online classes (Barura, 2020; Emon, Alif, & Islam, 2020; Nath, Chowdhury, & Nath, 2020; Uddin, 2020; Wadud, 2020). To reduce the gap, the UGC, the nation's top regulatory body for HE, sent letters to 43 public universities on 6 August 2020 requesting lists of poor students who did not have smartphones and needed financial assistance (Kamruzzaman, 2020). Moreover, prompt response to this emergency further complicated the lack of formal training, with academics quickly transitioning to online teaching, including lab, practicum, and assessment (Kidd & Murray, 2020).

RESEARCH METHODOLOGY

Research is a continuous process, and therefore, research in continuous times requires widening the methodological imaginations and making choices as it progresses (Gray, 2004). However, this chapter is based on an empirical study which used multiperspectival design and interpretative phenomenological analysis techniques (Larkin, Shaw, & Flowers, 2019).

Design

This study was designed as a mixed-methods interpretative study (Creswell, 2003) through a progressively focusing research methodology, which could be termed as "convergent parallel" (Creswell & Plano-Clark, 2011). This chapter is mainly based on qualitative data from the online questionnaire surveys with teachers and students during the first phase of a research project to explore teaching and learning practice in HE in Bangladesh during the COVID-19 lockdown.

Sampling

For the first phase of the study, teachers in Bangladeshi HEIs, especially universities, were chosen as participants. Purposive sampling was followed to reach the research participants from both public and private universities. Following the UGC's website, the teachers' available email addresses from public and private universities were collected from individual university websites, and they were invited to participate in the survey.

Data Collection

Data were collected during the first stage of the national lockdown from June to August 2020. During the first and second phases of the study, country-wide campaigns were run to collect data from teachers and students using two separate online-based questionnaires. In each questionnaire, there were five open-ended questions for the research participants. This chapter presents qualitative data derived from these open-ended questions.

For the teachers' perspectives part, a total of 12,468 email addresses were collected, and email invitations were sent (11,649 delivered and 819 bounced back) to participate in the survey. Within an 8-week window, 525 survey responses were received, and 23 responses were excluded due to the validity and quality of the responses, including not fulfilling the criteria. Finally, after cleaning the data, 502 responses were accepted for analysis. Among the participants, 274 (54.6%) were from the public, and 228 (45.4%) were from the private HEIs as summarized in Table 1.

Table 1. Teacher Outreach and Responses.

	Public University Teachers	Percentage (%) of Outreach and Responses	Private University Teachers	Percentage (%) of Outreach and Responses	Total
Email sent	7,523	60.34	4,945	39.66	12,468 (*delivered* 11,649)
Email bounced	449	54.82	370	45.18	819
Responded	291	55.40	234	44.60	**525**

Table 2. Total Number and Percentage of Male and Female Respondents.

	Total	Percentage (%)
Male	367	73.1
Female	124	24.7
Preferred not to say	3	0.6
No answer	8	1.6
Total	502	100

Among the respondents, 367 (73.1%) were male, and 124 (24.7%) female, 3 (0.6%) preferred not to say about their gender, and 8 (1.6%) did not respond to this question (Table 2).

For students' perspectives, the snowball sampling technique was used channeling through the teachers who attend the teachers' survey. At the first stage, teachers were requested to forward the invitation email to their students. Then students who had already participated in the students' survey were asked to send the invitation email to their friends. Again, within an 8-week window, a total of 786 survey responses were received.

Data Analysis and Interpretation

For this chapter, qualitative data from the survey are used by pre-processing and analyzing mostly manually (with a part of the analysis being processed semi-autonomously using Microsoft Excel). Thematic analysis was used to analyze all the qualitative data in this research. This approach to analysis involves the identification, coding, and analysis of patterns within the data (Boyatzis, 1998). A thematic approach was taken to analyze the data, based on its broadest definition as "a method for identifying, analysing and reporting patterns (themes) within data" (Braun & Clarke, 2006, 2012). The thematic analysis allows for contextual information to be taken into account (following Braun and Clarke's definition of a "contextualised" thematic analysis). Acknowledging factors arising from the context is particularly important for this research as it focuses on exploring the experiences of staff and students in HE in Bangladesh. The initial stage of analysis was the familiarization of the data. The next step consisted of coding and analyzing the data. This phase involved working systematically through the open-ended answers in the survey and creating preliminary codes. As such, the preliminary codes represented broad elements of the raw data that could be evaluated in a meaningful way (Boyatzis, 1998). Codes that had similar meanings to each other were combined into potential themes and sub-themes with subsequent repetition of the coding procedure to ensure that all data were coded and grouped accordingly. The themes were further reexamined to ensure that they were coherent and logical. The open-ended survey responses were also revisited to ensure that an accurate representation was provided by the analysis. The final step of the analysis included assembling the results into a written evaluation.

Upon accumulating the themes and categories of the qualitative data, it is expected to increase the understanding of the phenomenon leading to broadening the explanation of theoretical or practical importance. Although this chapter is mainly dedicated to exploring the values, meanings, beliefs, thoughts, experiences, and feelings of teachers and students who reflect on their teaching and learning experience during the first phase of the COVID-19 lockdown, interpretation has been made of what they have expressed in their responses.

Ethical Consideration

Consent was obtained from the participants at the beginning of the survey. Throughout the research process, information has been handled with special care to make the data management secure and to keep personal information provided entirely confidential. We are using the data anonymously here in this report. This ethical consideration will be followed in any future use of the data. However, the participants have the right to withdraw at any time during the research. The academic ethical guidelines (British Educational Research Association (BERA), 2018; British Psychological Society (BPS), 2018) have been followed throughout the research process to ensure confidentiality, anonymity, and the right to withdraw from the study.

Data were electronically stored, and personal information was excluded before processing the data for analysis by the lead researcher. Only a cleaned dataset without any personal information was shared with the other team members for analysis and interpretation. Safeguarding for confidentiality and anonymity has been ensured throughout the process of collecting, sharing, analyzing, and presenting data.

FINDINGS: TEACHERS' AND STUDENTS' PERSPECTIVES

The following themes were derived from the data collected which reflect teachers' and students' view regarding students' preparedness for ODTL during the first lockdown to maintain social distancing due to the unprecedented situation created by the COVID-19 pandemic. A number of themes were derived and categorized according to the survey responses before moving on to a discussion of the possible impacts and potential ways forward toward the preparedness of online teaching and learning in the HE context in Bangladesh.

Training Needs for Students and Staff on Online Teaching and Learning

The importance of training students for participating in online education is prominent in the data collected from the teachers. They suggested that the trained teachers introduce the students to different teaching and learning technologies and their applications. The most important thing for teachers, in this aspect, is to inspire their students for technological adaptation and integration in the teaching and learning processes. According to teachers, students would never be encouraged to participate in new learning activities without any positive motivation or initiatives. To develop motivation among the students, a national-level campaign through radio, television, newspapers, and other social media platforms are also suggested by the teachers. They think that a positive attitude about digital and distance education throughout the country might be created. Moreover, teachers also stressed the need to ensure students' hands-on learning ability of such new technological and digital knowledge and skills. In their responses, students who are new to online learning or have doubts about the quality and effectiveness of online education were reluctant to participate in emergency remote teaching and learning (ERTL). However, they need preparation to use cutting-edge technologies and change their mindsets to succeed in this transition and transformation of teaching and learning. Accordingly, almost all participants think that adequate training on technological tools and techniques for online education must be provided to both teachers and students as an initial preparation before adapting ODTL in HE.

Consensus about ODTL

There was disagreement among teachers about implementing an "online education" system at the beginning of the COVID-19 crisis in Bangladesh. Most teachers were not entirely familiar with the "online pedagogies" as it is not the norm in the country's HE sector to teach online apart from two public universities. Hence, most teachers strongly supported organizing training programs for adopting digital technologies and contents for teaching and learning. In this case, they suggested that the training should be administered by the Institutional Quality Assurance Cell (IQAC) or the respected body that oversees university's management or the UGC, which oversees the HE sector of Bangladesh.

Differences have been noticed among teachers' opinions regarding the training venue and frequencies. Some of the respondents suggested providing the training within the university campuses using their resource personnel, while others have focused on providing this training through an online platform and/or using third parties. While talking about the training duration, many teachers felt that a continuous training program would be most appropriate rather than a single training program. The rationale behind "continuous training" was including inductions of new and emerging technologies and applications. Therefore, they believe that continuous and repeated training programs will help to orient students to the new working environment and adapted technologies for teaching and learning. Also, students who are weak in adapting the new knowledge or skills would benefit from being able to attend training sessions more than once.

The respondents took different approaches on the issue of prospective training providers. Most of the faculties suggested that the information technology (IT) experts of the computer science and engineering department, or the technical staff of ICT sections of the university can offer the required training to the broader student community. A few respondents have suggested that training should be provided by foreign experts.

Most of the teachers were in favor of making training videos or training materials. A difference of opinion was noticed among the respondents regarding disseminating the training materials. Those who did not support training through online platforms alone, thought that students should be allowed to be physically present during their training before attending demo "online classes." They believed this would help students in learning new skills. Some advocated providing training in small groups without including many students in training sessions. Due to this pandemic, maintaining social distance is crucial. Therefore, training in small groups would allow trainers and trainees (students) to keep themselves safe. Additionally, smaller groups would also let learning be more interactive and, therefore, more effective. Moreover, some of the respondents asked for training materials/videos in Bengali, along with English.

Developing Digital Contents and Making Them Available for Students on Online Platforms

Many teachers pointed out that the biggest challenge of the transformation of traditional face-to-face teaching to online distance teaching is to create digital contents. In their views, online education will never be successful unless all the materials of the modules are readily available in digital formats and uploaded to the online platforms (i.e., VLE such as Blackboard, Canvas, Moodle, etc.). Specifically, some teachers think that developing the e-book collections of all the texts and reference books and other journals and archival materials is crucial. Without developing a rich and user-friendly e-library support system, ODTL will never be effective and attractive for both teachers and students.

Technical and Technological Capacity Building

Many teachers have suggested acquiring all the supportive technologies required for the implementation of online education. On the one hand, some have proposed customizing or modifying the hardware and software available in the markets to suit their students' needs. Moreover, another important recommendation is to use multiple technologies to achieve the desired results without relying on a single technology. It has been observed that the teachers have given more importance to ensure conducive learning environments to enhance productivity of students and assisting their students with their needs. Nonetheless, one basic yet mandatory requirement for students in online education is to have a smart device with an internet connection based on which students communicate and interact with teachers and peers, take part in assessments in the form of quizzes, exams, assignments, etc.

Many teacher respondents state that their students struggle to acquire such basic resources (a smart device with internet connectivity) to join online activities.

Access to the Internet at an Affordable Cost and Fund Allocation for Online Education

As mentioned earlier, having internet connectivity is one of the mandatory basic needs in online education. Despite the fact that mobile broadband is not available in many remote places in the country, mobile data are moderately expensive, and many students cannot afford to buy the high-cost mobile data package due to their financial conditions. Most respondents have strongly emphasized that the cost of internet data should be reduced overall. Both students and academics should be offered mobile broadband at a reduced price if not freely available. In this case, the government can take the initiative to negotiate with the telecom authority to settle the cost of the internet data for students and academics.

The opening move of online training and online education will not be realized unless adequate financial support is available. That is why some teachers have emphasized the need for financial support from the government to do the online training and purchase the appropriate tools for students' success. Financial assistance is required for those teachers and students who are financially not solvent enough to buy internet data or digital gadgets. Above all, setting up digital and technological capacities would require an additional budget in every institution.

SES Diversity and Lack of Logistic Facilities in Remote Areas

Based on the survey, it is identified that there is a huge gap between high and low socio-economic status (SES) students when it comes to online education that relies on well-equipped resources and internet access. Many students simply cannot attend online lessons because they cannot afford to buy devices and internet services, nor do they have a good environment at home. This leads to a violation of inclusive education policy (i.e., to embrace all learners with equitable access and participation), and many students may drop out of HE due to the SES diversity in their learning needs.

According to the survey, many students simply do not have access to such basic facilities such as the availability of internet, electricity, and other basic needs to attend the online lessons. One student mentioned that:

> [...] There's another problem which is a network problem. Proper mobile networks do not cover many places in our country. For my personal experience, I go to open fields or rooftop during any online activity. If rains come, then it would be so difficult to continue online activity ....

Students often fail to cope with lectures due to inadequate network coverage, and the lessons become tiresome and hard to get along with once lecture flow is interrupted.

Issues of Curriculum, Assessments, Student Engagement, and Interactivity

The ODTL system is a "two-way and participatory" process, which is largely absent in the pedagogical practice of many disciplines. According to student participants' feedback, online classes are less interactive and less effective. This can probably be reiterated because neither students nor teachers are adequately trained with the online teaching and learning strategies, or the teacher may fail to adapt to the required standards. A well-designed curriculum can provide opportunities to innovate, raise standards, and most importantly, excite and inspire learners and educators, leading to an excellent learning experience. Many students highlighted that the current curriculum in some disciplines is not suitable to deliver online and must be adjusted accordingly.

DISCUSSION

Findings of the study and literature showed that due to the COVID-19 pandemic, traditional teaching and learning has changed from face-to-face classes to online classes (Dutta & Smita, 2020). The active involvement of the stakeholders and the successful training of both teachers and students can ensure the successful transition of conventional teaching and learning approaches into ODTL. In Bangladesh, teachers are often underprepared to deploy content and use online teaching and learning methods. Moreover, ODTL is not yet common practice for many teachers and students in this country, and for this reason, they have mostly advocated to organize training for both students and teachers. While most teachers are active in online activities, mainly engaging in social media and other communication tools, many have not taught online before this crisis. In this situation, World Bank (2020) recommended that there should be training for teachers on how to teach remotely, that is, tailoring the training to allow each teacher to define their plan for content, goals, and learning assessment within the new modality.

During the transitional period, support is needed for students to be accustomed to the online pedagogies and learning materials in the digital forms, including open educational resources. Many teachers would need to revisit teacher-centered pedagogies and introduce more efficient student-centered learning methods (Borup, Graham, & Drsydale, 2013). While there are many materials available online, there is little on-demand technical and pedagogical support available for them. However, it is essential to make continuous professional development programs for teachers and students to provide training on digital skills. Mittal (2020) also said that the development and training of staff and teachers for online teaching and learning pedagogy through extensive capacity-building programs would go a long way toward improving the quality of online teaching and learning.

Many teachers have pointed out that producing interactive content is the greatest challenge facing the transition to online education. Unless all the materials in the modules are readily available in digital format and submitted to online platforms, which often takes time to develop, online education will never be successful. It is particularly important to establish e-book collections of all essential texts and reference books and relevant journal articles and archival materials as currently there is a lack of a rich and user-friendly support framework for e-library access throughout the country.

Mladenova, Kalmukov, and Valova (2020) suggest that teachers should be given enough time to adapt their existing teaching and examination materials and develop new ones suitable for e-learning and e-examination. In this study, most respondents also recommended to acquire all the supportive technology required to implement online education. Moreover, many others have concentrated on customizing or changing the hardware and software available to meet their own needs in the markets. Several participants also suggest that various alternative technologies can be used without relying just on a single technology to produce the desired results.

Students' training needs are paramount to make ODTL effective and attractive, if they are to be efficient in using emerging technologies and change their mindset to be self-regulated learners in the twenty-first century's digitized education future. Everitt, Neary, Delgardo, and Clark (2018) stated that personal guidance for students impacts their effectiveness in self-awareness and self-esteem, career readiness and decision-making, and improved attendance and attainment. Most of the teachers said that trained teachers would be able to introduce learning technologies to their students. The most important thing, in this case, is to inspire students to change their mindset toward the value and importance of ODTL, especially in the context of emergency. However, positive motivation would encourage students to participate in new learning activities.

A national-level campaign through television and other social media platforms should be initiated to create a positive attitude about online education within the country's wider student communities. Moreover, teachers also stressed the need to ensure students' hands-on learning ability of such new skills. In the context of switching to emergency remote learning, World Bank (2020) reported that many, if not most, students are not experienced as formal online learners as they are mostly educated through traditional face-to-face teaching and learning methods. Students face difficulties that lead to disappointment with their academic experience, although they may be quick to adapt. To improve teaching, student feedback can be leveraged, but feedback can also risk revealing grievances that are difficult to handle.

In Bangladesh, public HEIs mostly depend on the government for their budget. Therefore, the opening move for online training and education will not be realized unless adequate financial support is available from the government or other sources. That is why some teachers and students have proposed adequate financial support for online training to prepare students to make this transition smooth and prepare them for future emergencies. In their views, it is also essential to give financial assistance to those teachers and students who are financially not solvent enough to buy internet data or digital gadgets. Above all, setting up digital technological capacity would require an additional budget in every institution, especially to develop their infrastructure suitable for delivering ODTL. However, studies suggest that for most educational institutions (including secondary and high schools), the COVID-19 pandemic appears to have provided the impetus to initiate a large-scale digital transformation, which will continue to evolve in post-COVID or new-normal times. There is enormous support needed from both the government and society toward digitizing and adapting all teaching materials and providing students from low-income families with high-speed internet and the necessary devices (Mladenova et al., 2020; World Bank, 2020).

Ensuring equal learning environments for all students, in general, is expected to deliver an inclusive education. However, both students and teachers do not have adequate resources, for example, broadband connectivity and smart devices, at home, which is especially true for the most remote and deprived areas. The digital divide between and within countries remains strong. For the massive load that is coming, international bandwidth and local server (and hosting/data storage) capability are not planned (World Bank, 2020). Most respondents, both teachers and students, think that many students struggle to acquire essential resources (a smart device with internet connectivity) to join online activities.

Gaebel (2020) stated that this abrupt and disruptive change to remote education varied by scale, models of governance, and variations in disciplines. It is typically more difficult for big, comprehensive organizations to establish an institutional approach. However, different units with a HEI, that is, faculties and departments might have their teaching and learning policy as to what methods and tools they should use depending on the governance model they follow. There is a wide belief among teachers and students that disciplines that require lab work, practical experience, and external collaboration are more challenging to teach remotely.

However, many universities have taken no action to find and provide an alternative way to offer their students learning opportunities for laboratory work and evaluations with online education. Therefore, adopting new and alternative modes of providing hands-on laboratory work to produce high-quality engineers and scientists is important. For example, universities could support initiatives to encourage international education equipment suppliers to arrange individualized take-home lab kits like Chapman University's Schmid College of Science and Technology delivers microbes, test tubes, and more to support science students at home. This equipment will be loaned to students for the duration of the semester, and they will be responsible for returning it (Buckley, 2020). World Bank (2020) advocates that:

> Education leaders and stakeholders must seek and produce evidence from the learning sciences while embracing technological innovations, to ensure this push to change the delivery of teaching to online platforms delivers on the promise of learning and skills development. Such changes must be studied for efficacy and to understand best what works and does not and for whom. To date, most online learning approaches do not have comparable evidence-based foundations, and this should be concerning enough to drive investments in the science of teaching and learning. (p. 9)

Students' readiness to attend online courses is one of the major issues (Hung, Chou, Chen, & Own, 2010). This survey's analysis has also identified that students who are new to or suspicious of online education need preparation and the right mindset to succeed. Accordingly, almost all participants think that adequate training on tools and techniques for online education must be provided to both teachers and students as an initial preparation before introducing an online education. The lack of proper capability and mindset for participating in online teaching and learning is a great challenge in Bangladesh. People often have a fixed mindset about the quality and effectiveness of online education. Most people think that online education is of less value in preparing for future career opportunities. Mittal (2020) reported that:

> the availability of technical infrastructure for imparting online education varies over the length and breadth, creating a digital divide and a sense of inequity in the minds of the students.

Since students are not used to online education systems, the use of technologies (being in front of computer monitors) for a long time is frustrating. It may cause other mental and physical illnesses such as stress and back pain. Similarly, Mittal (2020) stated that adopting complete online learning is also becoming a health hazard for students in terms of obesity, sleep disturbances, spinal problems, anxiety, and depression. Erasmus Student Network (ESN) (2020) reported that, as a consequence of the COVID-19 pandemic, students faced many difficulties in their everyday lives, apart from those previously mentioned. Students were faced with mental health challenges at these times, such as the feeling of anxiety, social isolation, and loneliness.

This is a result of the lack of institutional initiatives in the use of IT for supporting students in HE. According to the students' survey, many students conclude that their university cannot develop the right infrastructure to offer online classes. Mittal (2020) stated that accessibility of the technological infrastructure, accessibility of the institute, capacity building for teachers, and distance learning competencies, including equipment and student networks, are the key factors driving this change. Due to a lack of technological infrastructure, HEIs, especially in low- and middle-income countries, have not moved entirely online. However, it is expected that the forced digital transformation in education due to the COVID-19 pandemic will continue to be an integral part of post-COVID or new-normal education. Therefore, it becomes essential that careful planning be put in place as new challenges emerge to continue offering quality education in the new academic year.

THE RELEVANCE OF CURRICULUM, PEDAGOGIES, AND ASSESSMENTS

The relevance of changing the curriculum to fit with the new situation is a significant task for every HEI. Therefore, the country needs to adopt new and alternative ways of delivering hands-on laboratory work to produce high-quality engineers and scientists. For example, universities could use initiatives to encourage international education equipment suppliers to arrange individualized take-home lab kits. Additionally, STEAM (Science, Technology, Engineering, Arts and

Mathematics) students are often required to attend practical sessions or laboratory works, and universities usually offer the needed resources such as specialized hardware and software, which must be available in the on-campus laboratory environment and be accessible remotely if possible. However, with online education, many universities have not taken any initiatives to achieve such learning outcomes. On the contrary, other universities offer an alternative way of providing the learning opportunities of lab-based works and assessments to their students (Alam, Lau, Oh, & Chai, 2020).

In the context of HE in Bangladesh, many disciplines do not use technologies widely, and many students from those disciplines are not competent enough to use computers and other associated technologies. On the contrary, the competency of basic technological literacy is essential. Moreover, many of the "tools and techniques" used for online education are unknown to many students and even many teachers, as most universities teach traditionally. There is a significant lack of technical skills of both teachers and students for adapting to online education. Thus, online education's effectiveness will be uncertain if it is suddenly introduced without the provision of adequate training.

Since online distance learning has many challenges, one of many important aspects is developing or adapting multiple alternative approaches for online education. For example, some students can choose a synchronized model, and others can choose an asynchronized one for the same curriculum content, which will be both teacher and student friendly. However, online assessment is vague to many students because teachers do not provide clear instructions about the assessments and their formats. As mentioned earlier, STEAM students usually require gaining hands-on experience through laboratory works, and the assessment of laboratory works is a great challenge (Alam et al., 2020). At the same time, many teachers have adapted alternative assessment techniques ranging from no exams to take-home and open-book exams to digitally invigilated exams. Many teachers have adapted quizzes with strict "time-bound" features for formative assessments (Martin et al., 2019) and generated the same quiz questions visible to every student in random order.

Preparedness of Students for Future HE and Employability

Education has been a powerful tool to combat unemployment and the precariousness of employment, and this connection between HE and employment was strengthened after the Great Recession (Pompei & Selezneva, 2019). Clearly, a person's education level is not the only attribute that makes them well-matched for a job. Formal education is becoming less useful to anticipate the specific skills that will be needed in the near future in jobs that sometimes are not yet created (Pardo-Garcia & Barac, 2020). HEIs response to developing employability among students has principally centered on providing opportunities to develop employability skills by embedding them within the curriculum or bolting them on to the curriculum (Gracia, 2009). Youth unemployment and underemployment have sadly reached critical levels and are expected to continue rising.

Many employers are unable to find enough employees with the skills they need to expand their business. The links are often missing between universities and local business organizations to support the local economy (Zaring, Gifford, & McKelvey, 2019). There is an urgent need to forge deeper ties between academia and industry, education and skills, theory and practice, and supply and demand to fight the employability crisis. The low functioning of the 3 Es of education, employment, and employability has resulted in growth not being translated into sustained poverty reduction in many Asian countries (Sabharwal, n.d.).

HE operates within an increasingly knowledge-driven economy, characterized by rapid obsolescence of technical and practical skills. Economic and political forces allied with policy drives to widen access and increase participation rates have directed university attention to the competitive mass production of flexible, creative, and employable graduates catalyzing an increasing focus on a discourse of employability within the sector (Gracia, 2009).

HE, as illustrated by Moreland (2006), should pay more attention to employability and entrepreneurship. First, due to the impact of globalization, rapid change is happening in every sphere of life through innovations and adaptations. A global environment implies that students should be more independent, able to adapt to innovations, work in groups, take responsibility, have attitudes to sustain and renew their abilities, and be reflexive (thinking about experiences and perspectives to understand them better and respond with learning and behavioral changes). Second, the recruiting of university graduates has social advantages. Through enhancing students' employability skills, HEIs will contribute to their high-level skills and understanding of workplaces and professional practice, even though those jobs do not need a graduate person. Third, government policy and the promotion of self-employment are required. Students at university can be unaware of the benefits of being self-employed. For several decades, entrepreneurship education and training have been a rapidly growing, if diverse, area, and has become a prominent feature in the curricula of not only business schools but also other sections of HEIs (Katz, 2003; Kuratko, 2005). Consequently, broadening education in innovation and entrepreneurship aligns with expectations about the need for society to encourage entrepreneurship as a key driver of economic development and increased jobs (Greene & Saridakis, 2008).

There are different ways in which HEIs try to improve employability: (1) improvements in the curricula (inviting employers, use of ICT, languages, tutorials to help students adapt to university, and double degrees); (2) teaching of business protocols (training in personal attributes such as decision-making or problem-solving, training in such interpersonal skills as teamwork or communication skills, and training for entrepreneurship and self-employment including how to create business plans); (3) job matching (job search forums, practical work experience, and internships); and (4) learning from the experience of university alumni (activities with alumni, students' visits to alumni's companies, and occupational observatory) (Caballero, Vázquez, & Quintás, 2015 cited in Pardo-Garcia & Barac, 2020).

In the post-2015 era, the Sustainable Development Goals recognize that quality growth and jobs should be central to a new development framework beyond 2015. Goal 8 proposes to "promote sustained, inclusive and sustainable economic growth, full and productive employment, and decent work for all" (UN, 2014). Education systems are accused of not providing the people who pass through them with the skills that a globalized knowledge-based economy demands. These skills include sophisticated literacy and numeracy skills, problem-solving skills, reflection, emotional intelligence, critical/independent thinking, and communication skills (Erling, 2015).

The COVID-19 epidemic has had a major impact on education (Impey, 2020; Oyedotun, 2020; Shohel et al., 2021a; Shohel et al., 2022) and employability (Sato et al., 2021). Many global sectors and systems, including education, healthcare (Peng, Xu, & Li, 2020), job market, agriculture, industry (Assocham, 2020; Sato et al., 2021), business and socio-economic systems (Nicola et al., 2020), have been severely impacted by the outbreak, potentially resulting in workplace changes. Since the epidemic began, for example, individuals and organizations have undergone significant changes such as social distancing and remote work environments (Angelucci et al., 2020). Employers' expectations of employees should vary before and after the pandemic, requiring graduates to train for the new normal's necessary skill sets (Buheji & Buheji, 2020).

Digital Transformation of Life and Future of HE

Digital technologies are changing the lives, company, and culture of human beings. Digital transformation, which can enable new services and provide new opportunities for innovation and entrepreneurship, is mostly affected by HE systems and institutions. Schools and the education of children should undergo an extensive digital transformation to meet the needs of the young generation and their digitized future. The COVID-19 pandemic has suddenly and abruptly forced schools and education to engage in such a transformation (Iivari, Sharma, & Ventä-Olkkonen, 2020).

HEIs that adopt digital technologies can become drivers of their ecosystems for growth and development (OECD/European Union, 2019). The rapid growth and spread of digital technologies are leading to change in every part of people's lives, businesses, and society. Digital transformation is "a process that aims to improve an entity by triggering significant changes to its properties through combinations of information, computing, communication, and connectivity technologies" (Vial, 2019, p.118). Digital transformation is the product of digitization and digitalization of economies and communities (OECD, 2019). Intrinsically, the digital transition is related to what has been described as the "fourth industrial revolution" (Schwab, 2016): a mechanism in which digital technologies shape society's future and economic growth in a way comparable to the first industrial revolution's case of steam power. Digital transformation involves several digital technologies, from 5G to artificial intelligence, big data, Internet of Things, and Blockchain. These technologies form an ecosystem through which future economic and social changes will arise (OECD, 2019).

Universities remain the founding pillar of HE and they are the necessary lens for envisioning its future. Despite the impact of the COVID-19 and the havoc it may wreak on its modus operandi, the current practice should not underestimate or forget the resilience universities have shown throughout human history. Though HE will never be the same as it has gone through a huge experiment with this health emergency, universities are now engaged across the globe in the most extensive and most revolutionary technology-enabled pedagogical changes. This is a paradigm shift that will potentially shape the future course of campus life and the way people perceived HE. HEIs are making sweeping changes in a brief period to adjust to the situation (Lamagna & Mazumder, 2020). More broadly, academics and individuals involved in or with HEIs are becoming more aware of these needs for changes and changing mindset to adapt to the changes in practice.

The COVID-19 pandemic has kept a sign on every sphere of life and changed everything, and people have been forced to think about the future differently. Therefore, new and more pressing goals are added as priorities in personal, professional, and societal levels. As a result of seeking alternative learning opportunities, several massive open online course (MOOC) platforms have taken advantage of the virtual transition and digital transformation. They offered their online courses free of charge, as a temporary alternative to all students lacking continuity of university activities. However, contents and learning material are becoming better as being saved in a learning management system and spread through a global online program management. Therefore, HEIs are now in a virtual learning transition and they should refocus, emphasize, and generate a proactive and collaborative attitude to enhance the capacity for teaching and learning and support their students to adapt to the changes in practice (Martin-Barbero, 2020).

Several alternative education models have emerged over the last decade. MOOCs, bootcamps, "learn now-pay later" education, nanodegrees, and alternative credentialing have now cycled through one or more business model changes in their pursuit of sustainability. However, university leaders are "looking" at potential models. Most currently see technology as something that can quickly boost student engagement and improve the overall learning experience (Digital Transformation in Higher Education, 2017).

IMPLICATIONS

This study undoubtedly proved that Bangladesh has not been prepared for emergency remote teaching and learning including using emerging technologies for online education. There is a long way to go to embrace the situation and make a transition to the fourth industrial revolution and twenty-first century's HE policy and practice. Changes at the policy level are vital if practice is to change in line with policy. There should be priority given at national and institutional levels to developing an infrastructure which would support technological adaptation for HE delivery by addressing equity and equality, in order to reduce the digital divide and ensure social justice.

Traditionally, private universities have excelled in competitive marketing, and public universities have not been as successful in this competition. This is because of job security at public universities where faculty positions are secure through their permanency, as a result of which staff are reluctant to embrace changes needed to serve the needs of the students. Therefore, it has been found that many public university teachers were opposing classes online. The UGC have stated that it has been directed to conduct online classes since July 2020. The differences between the universities' capacity and teachers' capability in online education has, however, prevented them from being able to uphold the UGC direction. It is also clear that public university students have less access to resources and materials like the technologies needed for their online education, thus making it hard for their institutions to follow the UGC direction.

Although there is a lack of exact data, it is assumed that public universities' online education implementation is approximately 60% when this chapter was written. To be able to implement this emergency remote online education fully, the government's intervention needs to be answered. Therefore, a policy question is made as to whether this emergency remote online education system should be compulsory or spontaneous. Most say it should be made mandatory, and some advocate penalties for any teacher or student who does not want to be involved in the new education delivery system. Democratically, the government could never force an academic community; instead, they should make motivational programs, infrastructure development, and resource allocation.

FUTURE DIRECTION

Historically, suspending academic activities at universities has been a norm in Bangladesh, due to political turmoil and natural calamity. Many times, academic activities were suspended in leading public universities, and students were deprived of having alternatives to continue their education. Months after months, universities were closed mostly due to breaking out of fights between different student wings of political parties. However, under emergency circumstances, the online education delivery system will help the academic community to continue providing education and supporting students to complete their ongoing academic programs in due course. Therefore, online education delivery could easily become an alternative to provide emergency remote education during an unprecedented or unpredictable times. In that case, the Bangladeshi migrant community that teaches outside of Bangladesh will also contribute to online courses through knowledge sharing, curriculum development, online lectures, and other pedagogical and research activities.

However, the key challenges and weaknesses in emergency remote online teaching and learning are a lack of training, infrastructure, devices, and digital content, along with insufficient internet access and the digital divide.

- Many students lack the skills necessary to use emerging technologies for educational purposes, and they are unfamiliar with online pedagogical approaches, tools and techniques. The need for technical skill sets may be one of the reasons for negative attitudes toward the shift to emergency remote online teaching and learning. As an outcome, it is crucial to provide students with the required training, especially in the use of technology.
- The respondents stressed the importance of ensuring technological facilities such as computers or smart devices for students, internet connectivity, and adequate internet speed. These three resources are needed for students to have a successful online class.

Moreover, since internet coverage is not available everywhere and mobile operators strategically deploy their coverage in hotspots only, the pandemic is an excellent opportunity for the government to impose conditions on mobile operators to expand their coverage throughout the country. Four key points to note for internet connectivity in Bangladesh are as follows:

- The mobile broadband coverage is noticeably low throughout the country resulting in many students being out of the network coverage and hence no access to the online lessons.
- The cost of mobile data is excessively high, and there is no incentive to students and teachers for educational purposes except three or four universities. It is not affordable to many which is resulting in the disruption of online education activities.
- The internet speed is not up to the level that can support bandwidth-hungry educational applications (e.g., video conferencing, real-time learning activities for a large group of students); in other words, it is not fit for the purpose – so the government must encourage operators to mass deploy new generation technologies such as 4G/5G networks.
- The availability of emerging technologies is important for the delivery of online education. Many students are impoverished and live in remote areas with lack of devices and limited or no internet access. Finally, the government, universities, colleges, or private organizations should set aside a specific budget to assist financially disadvantaged students.

CONCLUSION

Higher education is all about self-administered learning journeys where teachers facilitate, and students take active roles to bridge their knowledge gap and develop their transferable skills for their future careers. The unprecedented COVID-19 lockdown period was a wake-up call for HEIs, educators, and students alike to place less importance on physical attendance in the classroom as the only way to gain formal accredited qualifications. Instead, viable alternatives should be explored and held up as examples of how the future of HE could be developed. This, in turn, could go a long way to helping address the skill development issue for students in the HE system and to be prepared for education in emergencies in the future.

In the process of ERTL or ODTL, the connect–communicate–create strategy does not work as many teachers and students do not have the skills to use required technologies and have limited or no access to technologies and the internet. Emerging technologies could be the vehicles for transforming teaching, learning, and research within the fast-changing digitized world. A burning question remains unanswered for many teachers: *how should students be supported to develop their study and technology know-how skills in a resource-constrained environment for teaching and learning in HE settings?* At the same time, it is imperative to ensure that students are helped to achieve the required technological fluency to prevent educational inequalities and exclusion. In reality, student success depends on the ownership of their learning and how they involve themselves as the co-creators of knowledge and skills, thus ensuring that future generations are equipped with the technological literacies fit for any future time of crisis.

REFERENCES

Alam, A. S., Lau, E., Oh, C., & Chai, K. K. (2020). An alternative laboratory assessment approach for multimedia modules in a transnational education (TNE) programme during COVID-19. In *2020 Transnational Engineering Education using Technology (TREET)* (pp. 1–4). IEEE doi:10.1109/TREET50959.2020.9189756.

Angelucci, M., Angrisani, M., Bennett, D. M., Kapteyn, A., & Schaner, S. G. (2020). *Remote work and the heterogeneous impact of Covid-19 on employment and health* (No. w27749). National Bureau of Economic Research, Cambridge, MA. https://doi.org/10.3386/w27749

Anwar, S. B., & Fuad, N. (2020). Remote learning, a remote possibility. *Dhaka Tribune*. Retrieved from https://www.dhakatribune.com/climate-change/2020/06/27/remote-learning-a-remote-possibility

Assocham. (2020). COVID-19 impact on Indian industry. Voice of the Indian Industry. Retrieved from https://www.assocham.org/userfiles/industry.pdf

BANBEIS. (2018). Pocket book on Bangladesh education statistics 2017. Retrieved from http://lib.banbeis.gov.bd/BANBEIS_PDF/Pocket%20Book%20on%20Bangladesh%20Education%20Statistics%202017.pdf

Barura, A. (2020). The impact of COVID-19 pandemic: Education sector of Bangladesh. BIPSS Commentary. Bangladesh Institute of Peace and Security Studies. Retrieved from http://bipss.org.bd/pdf/The%20impact%20of%20COVID-19%20Pandemic-Education%20sector%20of%20Bangladesh.pdf

Bennett, S., & Maton, K. (2010). Beyond the 'digital natives' debate: Towards a more nuanced understanding of students' technology experience. *Journal of Computer Assisted Learning, 26*, 321–331. doi:10.1111/j.1365-2729.2010.00360.x. Retrieved from https://www.researchgate.net/publication/229660413_Beyond_the_'Digital_Natives'_Debate_Towards_a_More_Nuanced_Understanding_of_Students'_Technology_Experiences

Berezhna, S., & Prokopenko, I. (2020). Higher education institutions in Ukraine during the coronavirus, or COVID-19. Outbreak: New challenges vs new opportunities. *Revista Romaneasca pentru Educatie Multidimensionala, 12*, 130–135. https://doi.org/10.18662/rrem/12.1sup2/256

Berry, A., & Kitchen, J. (2020). The role of self-study in times of radical change. *Studying Teacher Education, 16*(2), 123–126.

Borup, J., Graham, C., & Drsydale, J. (2013). The nature of teacher engagement at an online high school. *British Journal of Educational Technology, 46*(5), 793–806.

Boyatzis, R. E. (1998). *Transforming qualitative information: Thematic analysis and code development.* Thousand Oaks, CA: Sage Publications.

Boyd, D. (2014). *It's complicated: The social lives of networked teens.* New Haven, CT: Yale University Press.

Braun, V., & Clarke, V. (2006). Using thematic analysis in psychology. *Qualitative Research in Psychology, 3*(2), 77–101.

Braun, V., & Clarke, V. (2012). Thematic analysis. In H. Cooper, P. M. Camic, D. L. Long, A. T. Panter, D. Rindskopf, & K. J. Sher (Eds.), *APA handbook of research methods in psychology, Vol. 2: Research designs: Quantitative, qualitative, neuropsychological, and biological* (pp. 57–71). Washington, DC: American Psychological Association.

British Educational Research Association (BERA). (2018). *Ethical guidelines for educational research* (4th ed.). London: British Educational Research Association.

British Psychological Society (BPS). (2018). *Code of ethics and conduct.* Leicester: British Psychological Association.

Buckley, S. (2020). *At-home lab kits and supplies enhance remote science instruction at Chapman.* Chapman University. Retrieved from https://news.chapman.edu/2020/09/01/at-home-lab-kits-and-supplies-enhance-remote-science-instruction-at-chapman/

Buheji, M., & Buheji, A. (2020). Planning competency in the new normal – Employability competency in post-COVID-19 pandemic. *International Journal of Human Resource Studies, 10*(2), 237–251. https://doi.org/10.5296/ijhrs.v10i2.17085

Carlson, B. (2009). School self evaluation and the 'critical friend' perspective. *Educational Research and Reviews, 4*(3), 078–085.

Chima, A., & Gutman, R. (2020). What it takes to lead through an era of exponential change. *Harvard Business Review.* Retrieved from https://hbr.org/2020/10/what-it-takes-to-lead-through-an-era-of-exponential-change

Clow, D. (2020, March). *What should universities do to prepare for COVID-19 coronavirus?* (Vol. 2). London: Wonkhe. Retrieved from https://wonkhe.com/blogs/what-should-universities-do-to-prepare-for-covid-19-coronavirus/. Accessed on June 4, 2020.

Clune, A. (2020, March). *Using technology to cope with Covid-19 on (or off) campus* (Vol. 13). London: Wonkhe. Retrieved from https://wonkhe.com/blogs/using-technology-to-cope-with-covid-19-on-or-off-campus/. Accessed on June 4, 2020.

Conole, G., de Laat, M., Dillon, T., & Darby, J. (2006). *LXP: Student experience of technologies.* Bristol: JISC. Retrieved from http://www.jisc.ac.uk/whatwedo/programmes/elearning_pedagogy/elp_learneroutcomes.aspx. Accessed on November 20, 2020.

Creswell, J. W. (2003). *Research design: Qualitative, quantitative and mixed methods approaches* (2nd ed.). London: Sage Publications.

Creswell, J. W., & Plano-Clark, V. L. (2011). *Designing and conducting mixed methods research.* London: Sage Publishing.

Crowne, S. (2009). Opening address during the harnessing technology: Building on success national conference on Wednesday, 2nd of December. Retrieved from http://news.becta.org.uk/display.cfm?resID=41399. Accessed on November 12, 2020.

Cuban, L. (1986). *Teachers and machines: The classroom use of technology since 1920.* New York, NY: Teachers College Columbia University.

Daniel, S. J. (2020). Education and the COVID-19 pandemic. *Prospects, 49,* 91–96. https://doi.org/10.1007/s11125-020-09464-3. Retrieved from https://link.springer.com/content/pdf/10.1007/s11125-020-09464-3.pdf

Dede, C. (2005). Planning for neomillennial learning styles. *Educause Quarterly, 28*(1), 7–12 USE Retrieved from http://www.educause.edu/educatingthenetgen/5989. Accessed on October 31, 2020).

Delfino, D. A. P. (2019). Student engagement and academic performance of students of Partido State University. Retrieved from https://files.eric.ed.gov/fulltext/EJ1222588.pdf

Demuyakor, J. (2020). Coronavirus (COVID-19) and online learning in higher institutions of education: A survey of the perceptions of Ghanaian international students in China. *Online Journal of Communication and Media Technologies, 10*(3), e202018.

Digital Transformation in Higher Education. (2017). Navitas Ventures. Retrieved from https://www.navitasventures.com/wp-content/uploads/2017/08/HE-Digital-Transformation-_Navitas_Ventures_-EN.pdf

Dutta, S., & Smita, M. K. (2020). The impact of COVID-19 pandemic on tertiary education in Bangladesh: Students' perspectives. *Open Journal of Social Sciences, 8*, 53–68. https://doi.org/10.4236/jss.2020.89004

Emon, E. K. H., Alif, A. R., & Islam, M. S. (2020). Impact of COVID-19 on the institutional education system and its associated students in Bangladesh. *Asian Journal of Education and Social Studies, 11*(2), 34–46. doi:10.9734/ajess/2020/v11i230288

Erasmus Student Network (ESN). (2020). JOINT PAPER: IAU AND ESN: COVID-19 impact on higher education: Institutional and students' perspectives. Retrieved from https://www.iau-aiu.net/IMG/pdf/joint_paper_iau_and_esn_-_institutional_and_students_perspectives_of_covid-19_impact_on_higher_education.pdf

Erling, E. J. (2015). The relationship between English and Employability in the Middle East and North Africa, British Council. Retrieved from https://www.britishcouncil.jo/sites/default/files/en-the_relationship_between_english_employability_in_mena_research.pdf

Everitt, J., Neary, S., Delgardo, M. A., & Clark, L. (2018). *Personal guidance. What works?*. London: The Careers & Enterprise Company.

Gaebel, M. (2020). European higher education in the COVID-19 crisis. *European University Association, Regional/national perspectives on the impact of COVID-19 on higher education*. Paris: International Association of Universities. Retrieved from https://eua.eu/downloads/publications/briefing_european%20higher%20education%20in%20the%20covid-19%20crisis.pdf

Godwin-Jones, R. (2015). The evolving roles of language teachers: Trained coders, local researchers, global citizens. *Language, Learning & Technology, 19*(1), 10–20.

Gracia, L. (2009). Employability and higher education: Contextualising female students' workplace experiences to enhance understanding of employability development. *Journal of Education and Work, 22*, 301–318.

Gray, D. E. (2004). *Doing research in the real world* (4th ed.). London: Sage Publications.

Greene, F. J., & Saridakis, G. (2008). The role of higher education skills and support in graduate self-employment. *Studies in Higher Education, 33*(6), 653–672. doi:10.1080/03075070802457082

Hung, M., Chou, C., Chen, C., & Own, Z. (2010). Learner readiness for online learning: Scale development and student perceptions. *Computers & Education, 55*, 1080–1090.

Iivari, N., Sharma, S., & Ventä-Olkkonen, L. (2020). Digital transformation of everyday life – How COVID-19 pandemic transformed the basic education of the young generation and why information management research should care?. *International Journal of Information Management, 55*, 102183. https://doi.org/10.1016/j.ijinfomgt.2020.102183

Impey, C. (2020). Coronavirus: Social distancing is delaying vital scientific research. *The Conversation*. Retrieved from http://theconversation.com/coronavirus-social-distancing-is-delayingvital-scientificresearch-133689

Ito, M., Baumer, S., Bittanti, M., boyd, D., Cody, R., Herr-Stephenson, B., ... Tripp, L. (2010). *Hanging out, messing around, and geeking out*. Cambridge, MA: The MIT.

Jameel, R., & Rea, H. R. K. (2020). The lessons of online learning. *The Daily Star*. Retrieved from https://www.thedailystar.net/shout/news/the-lessons-online-learning-1958629

Jones, J. A. (2019). Scaffolding self-regulated learning through student-generated quizzes. *Active Learning in Higher Education, 20*(2), 115–126.

Jukes, I., McCain, T., & Crockett, L. (2010). *Understanding the digital generation: Teaching and learning in the new digital landscape*. Kelowna: 21st Century Fluency Project co-published with CORWIN, a SAGE company.

Kamruzzaman, Md. (2020). *Bangladesh to give phone loans to pupils amid lockdown*. Anadolu Agency. Retrieved from https://www.aa.com.tr/en/asia-pacific/bangladesh-to-give-phone-loans-to-pupils-amid-lockdown/1971859

Katz, J. A. (2003). The chronology and intellectual trajectory of American entrepreneurship education 1876–1999. *Journal of Business Venturing, 18*, 283–300. doi:10.1016/S0883-9026(02)00098-8

Kelly, K. (2010). *What technology wants*. London: Viking Penguin Ltd. Retrieved from https://nebula.wsimg.com/fb88fd2e75ed5e26e53082aab6aa26ee?AccessKeyId=39A2DC689E4CA87C906D&disposition=0&alloworigin=1

Kidd, W., & Murray, J. (2020). The Covid-19 pandemic and its effects on teacher education in England: How teacher educators moved practicum learning online. *European Journal of Teacher Education, 43*(4), 542–558. doi:10.1080/02619768.2020.1820480

Kolo, C., & Breiter, A. (2009). An integrative model for the dynamics of ICT-based innovations in education. *Digital Culture & Education, 1*(2), 89–103.

Kunwar, R., Poudel, K. K., & Shrestha, A. K. (2020). Online education as a new paradigm for teaching and learning in higher education in Nepal: Issues and challenges. *Global Scientific Journal, 8*(8), 208–217.

Kuratko, D. F. (2005). The emergence of entrepreneurship education: Development, trends, and challenges. *Entrepreneurship Theory and Practice, 29*, 577–597. doi:10.1111/j.1540-6520.2005.00099.x

Lamagna, C. Z., & Mazumder, D. C. L. (2020). Transformation in higher education (HE) learning. Retrieved from https://bbf.digital/transformation-in-higher-education-he-learning

Larkin, M., Shaw, R., & Flowers, P. (2019). Multiperspectival designs and processes in interpretative phenomenological analysis research. *Qualitative Research in Psychology, 16*(2), 182–198.

Lederman, D. (2020, April), Evaluating teaching during the pandemic. *Inside Higher Ed* (Vol. 8). Retrieved from https://www.insidehighered.com/digital-learning/article/2020/04/08/many-colleges-are-abandoning-or-downgrading-student-evaluations. Accessed on June 4, 2020.

Lee, J. S. (2014). The relationship between student engagement and academic performance: Is it a myth or reality?. *The Journal of Educational Research, 107*(3), 177–185. https://doi.org/10.1080/00220671.2013.807491

Lei, H., Cui, Y., & Zhou, W. (2018). Relationships between student engagement and academic achievement: A meta-analysis. *Social Behavior and Personality, 46*(3), 517–528. https://doi.org/10.2224/sbp.7054

Liguori, E., & Winkler, C. (2020). From offline to online: Challenges and opportunities for entrepreneurship education following the COVID-19 pandemic. *Entrepreneurship Education and Pedagogy, 3*(4), 346–351. https://doi.org/10.1177/2515127420916738

Luckin, R., Bligh, B., Manches, A., Ainsworth, S., Crook, C., & Noss, R. (2012). Decoding learning: The proof, promise, and potential of digital education. NESTA. Retrieved from http://www.nesta.org.uk/library/documents/DecodingLearningReport_v12.pdf. Accessed on November 1, 2020.

Martin, F., Ritzhaupt, A., Kumar, S., & Budhrani, K. (2019). Award-winning faculty online teaching practices: Course design, assessment and evaluation, and facilitation. *The Internet and Higher Education, 42*, 34–43.

Martin-Barbero, S. (2020). COVID-19 has accelerated the digital transformation of higher education. World Economic Forum. Retrieved from https://www.weforum.org/agenda/2020/07/covid-19-digital-transformation-higher-education/

Mitchell, A. (2014). Online courses and online teaching strategies in higher education. *Creative Education, 5*, 2017–2019. Retrieved from http://www.scirp.org/journal/ce

Mittal, P. (2020). Impact of Covid-19 on higher education in India. In *Regional/national perspectives on the impact of COVID-19 on higher education*. Paris: International Association of Universities. Retrieved from https://iau-aiu.net/IMG/pdf/iau_covid-19_regional_perspectives_on_the_impact_of_covid-19_on_he_july_2020_.pdf

Mladenova, T., Kalmukov, Y., & Valova, I. (2020). Covid 19 – A major cause of digital transformation in education or just an evaluation test. *TEM Journal, 9*(3), 1163–1170.

Monem, M., & Baniamin, H. M. (2010). Higher education in Bangladesh: Status, issues and prospects. *Pakistan Journal of Social Sciences (PJSS), 30*(2), 293–305.

Montgomery, K. C. (2007). *Generation digital: Politics, commerce, and childhood in the age of the Internet*. Cambridge, MA: The MIT Press.

Moreland, N. (2006). Entrepreneurship and higher education: An employability perspective. *Learning and employability, Series one.* York: The Higher Education Academy. Retrieved from https://www.qualityresearchinternational.com/esecttools/esectpubs/morelandentrpreneur.pdf

Mseleku, Z. (2020). A literature review of E-learning and E-teaching in the era of Covid-19 pandemic. *International Journal of Innovative Science and Research Technology*, 5(10), 588–597.

Murillo, A., & Jones, K. M. L. (2020). A "just-in-time" pragmatic approach to creating quality matters-informed online courses. *Information and Learning Sciences*, 121(5/6), 365–380. https://doi.org/10.1108/ILS-04-2020-0087

Nath, J., Chowdhury, A. F., & Nath, A. K. (2020). Analyzing COVID-19 challenges in Bangladesh. *Preprints* 2020, 2020070129, doi:10.20944/preprints202007.0129.v1

Nicola, M., Alsafi, Z., Sohrabi, C., Kerwan, A., Al-Jabir, A., Iosifidis, C., ... Agha, R. (2020). The socio-economic implications of the coronavirus pandemic (COVID-19): A review. *International Journal of Surgery*, 78, 185–193.

Oblinger, D. G., & Oblinger, J. L. (2005). *Educating the net generation.* Washington, DC: EDUCAUSE. Retrieved from http://www.educause.edu/books/educatingthenetgen/5989

OECD. (2019), *Going digital: Shaping policies, improving lives.* Paris: OECD Publishing. https://doi.org/10.1787/9789264312012-en

OECD/European Union. (2019). Digital transformation and capabilities. In *Supporting entrepreneurship and innovation in higher education in Italy*. Paris: OECD Publishing. Retrieved from https://www.oecd-ilibrary.org/docserver/6cc2e0a5-en.pdf?expires=1606163274&id=id&accname=guest&checksum=78BCECE59B12D80D4291F6FDD3080A0B

Ofcom. (2012). Children and parents: Media use and attitudes report. Retrieved from http://stakeholders.ofcom.org.uk/binaries/research/media-literacy/oct2012/main.pdf. Accessed on November 4, 2020.

Osterman, K. F. (2000). Students' need for belonging in the school community. *Review of Educational Research*, 70(3), 323–367.

Oyedotun, T. D. (2020). Sudden change of pedagogy in education driven by COVID-19: Perspectives and evaluation from a developing country. *Research in Globalization*, 2, 100029. https://doi.org/10.1016/j.resglo.2020.100029

Papert, S. (1996). *The connected family: Bridging the digital generation gap.* Atlanta, GA: Longstreet Press.

Pardo-Garcia, C., & Barac, M. (2020). Promoting employability in higher education: A case study on boosting entrepreneurship skills. *Sustainability*, 12(10), 4004. doi:10.3390/su12104004

Peng, X., Xu, X., & Li, Y. (2020). Transmission routes of 2019-nCoV and controls in dental practice. *International Journal of Oral Science*, 12(1), 9.

Pompei, F., & Selezneva, E. (2019). Unemployment and education mismatch in the EU before and after the financial crisis. *Journal of Policy Modeling*, 43(2), 448–473.

Prensky, M. (2011). *Teaching digital natives: Partnering for real learning.* Thousand Oaks, CA: Corwin, a SAGE company.

Raaper, R., & Brown, C. (2020). The Covid-19 pandemic and the dissolution of the university campus: Implications for student support practice. *Journal of Professional Capital and Community*, 5(3–4), 343–349. doi:10.1108/JPCC-06-2020-0032

Ratten, V. (2020). Coronavirus (Covid-19) and the entrepreneurship education community. *Journal of Enterprising Communities: People and Places in the Global Economy*, 14(5), 753–764.

Sabharwal, M. (n.d.). Education, employability, employment, and entrepreneurship: Meeting the challenge of the 4Es. Retrieved from https://core.ac.uk/download/pdf/81552944.pdf

Sato, S., Kang, T., Daigo, E., Matsuoka, H., & Harada, M. (2021). Graduate employability and higher education's contributions to human resource development in sport business before and after COVID-19. *Journal of Hospitality, Leisure, Sport & Tourism Education*, 28, 100306. Retrieved from https://www.sciencedirect.com/science/article/pii/S1473837621000071

Schneider, S. L., & Council, M. L. (2021). Distance learning in the era of COVID-19. *Archives of Dermatological Research*, 313, 389–390. https://doi.org/10.1007/s00403-020-02088-9

Schwab, K. (2016). The fourth industrial revolution: What it means and how to respond. World Economic Forum. Retrieved from https://www.weforum.org/agenda/2016/01/the-fourth-industrial-revolution-what-it-means-and-how-to-respond/

Sheely, S. (2008). Latour meets the digital natives: What do we really know. In Hello! Where are you in the landscape of educational technology?. *Proceedings ascilite Melbourne 2008*. Retrieved from http://www.ascilite.org.au/conferences/melbourne08/procs/sheely.pdf. Accessed on November 14, 2020.

Shohel, M. M. C., Ashrafuzzaman, M., Ahsan, M. S., Mahmud, A., & Alam, A. T. M. (2021a). Education in emergencies, inequalities, and the digital divide: Strategies for supporting teachers and students in higher education in Bangladesh. In L. Kyei-Blankson, J. Blankson, & E. Ntuli (Eds.), *Handbook of research on inequities in online education during global crises* (pp. 529–553). Hershey: IGI Global.

Shohel, M. M. C., Mahmud, A., Urmee, M. A., Anwar, N., Rahman, M. M., Acharya, D., & Ashrafuzzaman, M. (2021b). Education in emergencies, mental wellbeing and E-learning. In M. M. C. Shohel (Ed.), *E-learning and digital education in the twenty-first century: Challenges and* (pp. 1–22). London: IntechOpen.

Shohel, M. M. C., Sham, S., Ashrafuzzaman, M., Alam, A. T. M., Mamun, A. A., & Kabir, M. M. (2022). Emergency remote teaching and learning: Digital competencies and pedagogical transformation in resource-constrained contexts. In M. Islam, S. Behera, & L. Naibaho (Eds.), *Handbook of Research on Asian Perspectives of the Educational Impact of COVID-19*. Hershey: IGI Global.

Simamora, R. M. (2020). The challenges of online learning during the COVID-19 pandemic: An essay analysis of performing arts education studies. *Studies in Learning and Teaching*, *1*(2), 86–103.

Sykes, D. (2020). Online education during a pandemic: Teaching and learning in home spaces, literacies and language education: Research and practice, 2020 special section: Teaching during a pandemic. English Language Institute, KUIS. Retrieved from https://www.researchgate.net/publication/344013498

Takahashi, T. (2011). Japanese youth and mobile media. In M. Thomas (Ed.), *Deconstructing digital natives*. New York, NY: Routledge. Retrieved from https://www.taylorfrancis.com/chapters/edit/10.4324/9780203818848-11/japanese-youth-mobile-media-toshie-takahashi-harvard-university-usa-rikkyo-university-japan

Tapscott, D. (2009). *Growing up digital: How the net generation is changing your world*. New York, NY: McGraw-Hill.

Uddin, M. (2020). Effects of the pandemic on the education sector in Bangladesh. *The Financial Express*. Retrieved from https://www.thefinancialexpress.com.bd/views/effects-of-the-pandemic-on-the-education-sector-in-bangladesh-1592061447

UN. (2014). Outcome Document – Open Working Group on Sustainable Development Goals. Retrieved from http://sustainabledevelopment.un.org/focussdgs.html

UNESCO. (2020). Education: From disruption to recovery. Retrieved from https://en.unesco.org/covid19/educationresponse

UNICEF. (2020). Students in Bangladesh adjust to remote learning via national TV during COVID-19 lockdown. Retrieved from https://www.unicef.org/bangladesh/en/stories/students-bangladesh-adjust-remote-learning-national-tv-during-covid-19-lockdown

United Nations. (2020). Policy brief: Education during COVID-19 and beyond. Retrieved from https://www.un.org/development/desa/dspd/wp-content/uploads/sites/22/2020/08/sg_policy_brief_covid-19_and_education_august_2020.pdf

University Grants Commission of Bangladesh (UGC). (2020). Retrieved from http://www.ugc-universities.gov.bd/public-universities

Verawardina, U., Asnur, L., Lubis, A. L., Hendriyani, Y., Ramadhani, D., Dewi, I. P., … Sriwahyuni, T. (2020). Reviewing online learning facing the Covid-19 outbreak. *Talent Development and Excellence*, *12*(3s), 385.

Vial, G. (2019). Understanding digital transformation: A review and a research agenda. *The Journal of Strategic Information Systems*, *28*(2), 118–144.

Wadud, P. (2020). COVID-19, the right to education and Bangladesh. Retrieved from https://www.ejiltalk.org/covid-19-the-right-to-education-and-bangladesh/

Walker, L. R., & Shepard, M. (2011). Phenomenological investigation of elementary school teachers who successfully integrated instructional technology into the curriculum. *Journal of Educational Research and Practice*, *1*(1), 23–35.

Wargadinata, W., Maimunah, I., Dewi, E., & Rofiq, Z. (2020). Student's responses on learning in the early COVID-19 pandemic. *Tadris: Jurnal Keguruan dan Ilmu Tarbiyah*, 5(1), 141–153.

World Bank. (2020). *The COVID-19 crisis response: Supporting tertiary education for continuity, adaptation, and innovation.* Washington, DC: World Bank (License: CC BY 3.0 IGO). https://openknowledge.worldbank.org/handle/10986/34571

Younie, S., & Leask, M. (2013). *Teaching with technologies: The essential guide.* Berkshire: Open University Press.

Zaring, O., Gifford, E., & McKelvey, M. (2019). Strategic choices in the design of entrepreneurship education: An explorative study of Swedish higher education institutions. *Studies in Higher Education*, 46(2), 343–358.

CHAPTER 4

THE IMPACT OF ONLINE EDUCATION ON THE LEARNING EXPERIENCES OF TERTIARY STUDENTS DURING THE COVID-19 PANDEMIC: AN INDIAN CASE STUDY

Nandita Mishra

ABSTRACT

COVID-19 has shown its pandemic powers to the whole world. At times when many countries are forced to go for total lockdown of its economic activities, unusual economic crisis is inevitable. Amid all the crisis, the impact on education sector was also massive. In India also COVID-19 has resulted in a country-wide lockdown, which led to closure of schools and colleges. University Grant Commission, an apex educational body has come up with several guidelines for higher education institution. This study is an attempt to understand the perceptions of Indian tertiary students toward online teaching which has become the no-other-choice method of instruction for educational institutes during the pandemic. An online survey was conducted in October 2020, to collect information from the students through Google form about their perceptions and experiences with online learning. A total of 248 students completed the survey. Factor analysis has been applied on the collected data to understand the factors which most impacted the students. Results showed that "less effectiveness," "stress and boredom" and "connectivity challenges" were among the major challenges faced by these students in their online learning experience. This study urges the need for an educational strategy to be set by policy makers to respond to the challenges encoutered during online learning.

Keywords: Online education; learning experiences; tertiary students; challenges; COVID-19; factor analysis; higher education.

INTRODUCTION

The world is facing one of its worst pandemic and economic turmoil. COVID-19 has severely impacted the economic activity. Due to lockdowns imposed in various parts of world, we are witnessing the impact on businesses and households. Because of the widespread of the virus, the World Health Organization (WHO, 2020) declared it as a "pandemic" on March 11, 2020. Most of the governments have been introducing massive inducement programs. The trend shows that the measures which government is applying to curb the spread of COVID-19 is putting a negative impact on the economic position of the country. But other than the impact on the global economy, this has also impacted education sector. Following the government instructions, India went into a total lockdown on March 25, 2020. Academic institutions being the hub of students and social gatherings are at utmost risk and hence stopping on-campus education was an inevitable decision. The government has already given indications that educational institutions will not be allowed to reopen in near future. With total lockdown, educational institutions faced the problem of interrupted studies which they solved by providing online classes. Amid COVID-19, the biggest impact on education institutes was adoption of online learning. It is estimated that because of lockdown more than 600 million students were affected across the world in different countries (Goyal, 2020). In India also different states came up with additional policies and rules in addition to the central government, but educational institutions were closed across all the states. With this shift there was a need to adopt innovative methods of teaching to overcome the challenges of online teaching (Toquero, 2020). This led to more and more dependence of higher education on online teaching, digital books, online exams and telecommunications (Strielkowski, 2020). In India, it was estimated that 320 million students were using an online learning mode for their studies (UNESCO, 2020).

In the given situation, it is very important to understand the challenges and the process of learning amid COVID-19. With this background, the present study is designed to understand the learning status, challenges and methods of online teaching during the lockdown in India. This chapter is a survey-based study about Indian tertiary students' perceptions and experience with online learning.

THEORETICAL BACKGROUND

Higher education is always subjected to changes, universities always try to keep pace with the requirements and expectations of the students and this focuses on innovation. E-learning has always been part of higher education. Universities have always invested a lot into devices and E-learning applications (Popovici & Mironov, 2015). However, it is always challenging for them to integrate the E-learning with teaching process (Fischer, Heise, Heinz, Moebius, & Koehler, 2014).

There have been many studies about online learning and E-learning in the past two decades, the majority of which have focused on student's perceptions and attitudes toward E- learning (Martínez-Argüelles, Castán, & Juan, 2010). Keller and Cernerud (2002) carried out a study to identify the various factors which impact the acceptance of technology. Factors like age, experience with computers, gender and individual style were found of significance in this context. Many studies have highlighted that the E-learning had a positive impact on the students and was well-accepted by them (Bharuthram & Kies, 2013; Martínez-Argüelles et al., 2010; Selim, 2007). Prior to the pandemic, E-learning covered teaching and learning processes and activities that were carried out via information and communication technology (ICT) on campus or remotely. However, during the pandemic and forced by the obligation to physical and social distancing, E-learning had to be restricted to the remote setting only: online education.

The current situation of pandemic poses very different challenges as compared to the recent past where the adoption of technology for online teaching was assumed to be a support in teaching. After declaration of COVID-19 as a pandemic and different countries going for total shut down, online teaching was the only option to continue with the process of teaching (Whittle, Tiwari, Yan, & Williams, 2020). Due to the current pandemic, education, teachers, students and universities have been subjected to a great level of interest from the researchers. Allo (2020) has shown that the students have positive perception toward the online teaching.

Many of the universities have used E-learning before the pandemic, but still they are finding that they are not ready for the complete online teaching. Many challenges were highlighted in studies conducted during this pandemic, like lack of student–teacher interaction and less clarity of language used during the classes (Sun, Tang, & Zuo, 2020). Studies have also highlighted the expectation of students during online teaching. They don't want teachers to simply transfer information in the class as they use to do in traditional teaching but they want teachers to adopt the new ways of teaching.

COVID-19 and the new policies required a new methodology of teaching which was demanding social distancing (Mahaffey, 2020). Sarkar (2020) has also contributed to the study post COVID and has used methodological format for understanding the experience of the pandemic on micro- and macro-level. Few studies have also focused on the activities which were assumed to be impacted the most and which needed physical presence of the students. Like Foster, Lepore-Stevens, Adams, and Lepore (2020) have tried to study the impact of COVID on summer sports camp and the sports activities such as fitness and wellness sessions which also managed to move on virtual mode. Many of the studies around the world have identified that moving to online mode from conventional mode was not a smooth move (Khanom, Hoque, Sharif, Sabuj, & Hossain, 2020; Mishra, Tandon, Tandon, & Gupta, 2020). Thus, it was less about the quality of online teaching and more about the immediate and most effective option which could have been adopted then (Liguori & Winkler, 2020).

When compared to school education, the impact on higher education will have a different view because in higher education, E-learning has already been integrated in the curriculum for many years. Also, the maturity level and the exposure to technology is much higher for tertiary students (Ellis, Ginns, & Piggott, 2009). It was also argued that online teaching has already been used across various courses to ensure more inclusion and reach to a wider audience (Kassean, Vanevenhoven, Liguori, & Winkel, 2015; Neck & Greene, 2011). Nonetheless, KPMG (2020) has also identified that the students who have just completed their basic studies and will be going for higher studies will have more problem as they will have limited options of higher studies and also with delay in entrance exams things are more complicated for them. Few studies have highlighted the difference in adoption of online teaching in different type of subjects. Recent studies have argued that practical courses like mathematics, science, and engineering are more challenging to be delivered online when compared to theoretical subjects (Mishra et al., 2020; Mulenga & Marbán, 2020). Few studies have also highlighted the differences between the condition of developed countries and developing countries because for adoption of online learning the financial stand of education system is also an important factor. Sometimes, despite the high level of investment, the adoption is slow in developing countries because of financial condition of the students and faculty (Bigirwa, Ndawula, & Naluwemba, 2020a, 2020b). Due to the rise of new technology, spread of COVID-19 and importance of education there has been a large number of studies which have focused toward the education technologies (Iyer, Aziz, & Ojcius, 2020; Mulenga & Marbán, 2020; Sintema, 2020; Strielkowski, 2020; Toquero, 2020; Wollina, 2020).

Huang et al. (2020) have identified seven important aspects of online teaching. These are related to managing and developing infrastructure, using user friendly tools, helping student understand, providing good E-resources, using social media to connect with students and using techniques like debate and presentation to make the class interactive.

Amid various studies it is very important to understand the status of online education in India. This study specially focuses on the urban area which is the hub of education in India: the Delhi National Capital Region. This chapter aims to study both undergraduate and postgraduate students' perceptions, experiences and attitudes toward online learning. The chapter will also generate understandings about students' most preferred mode of online teaching.

RESEARCH METHODOLOGY

To achieve the chapter's aim and informed by the literature review, a questionnaire-based survey was conducted to understand tertiary students' perceptions, experiences and attitudes toward online learning in India. The questionnaire was designed on Google form and was circulated via email. A follow up email was sent after 15 days. A total of 400 email invitations were sent, where 248 students fully completed the questionnaire generating a rich source of data.

Questionnaire Design, Pilot Testing and Reliability Test

Pilot testing of the questionnaire was done with 10 respondents. This was done to get an understanding of questions and based on the comments and review given by the respondents the questionnaire was modified.

Questionnaire was constructed on the base of literature review and was divided into three parts. Each question is framed on the 5-Likert scale, with 1 taken as "strongly agree" and 5 taken as "strongly disagree." Section A dealt with the demographic study. Section B had questions related to the challenges faced by the students in online teaching. Section C dealt with the mode of E-learning and their challenges.

Goforth (2015) suggested that reliability analysis should always be done to determine the internal consistency of the scale. Cronbach's alpha is used in the study to test the reliability.

Research has suggested that factor analysis is a method that can always be used by the researchers to organize, identify and the concise big number of variables affecting the study (Boyd, 2013; Keith, 2019). Kaiser-Meyer-Olkin (KMO) test is done to identify whether the data are suitable for factor analysis or not.

DISCUSSION OF THE RESULT

The result has been discussed in this section, in which first the response rate is discussed. The response rate is 62%. The response rate is considered to be fairly good and it was majorly because of continuous follow ups with the respondents. Section A of the questionnaire dealt with the demographic study of the respondents and the result is shown in Table 1.

From Table 1 it is clear that majority of the students are female and postgraduate students. Students belong to both urban and rural areas, but the urban living students are more. On the basis of literature review, respondents were asked if they had previous exposure to E-learning. Majority of the students (92.7%) had prior exposure to E-learning. When the respondents were asked about the gadgets they use for their classes, 59.3% of the respondents say that they attend classes in their computer. But still a large number of students attend class through their mobiles.

Table 2 shows the value of alpha. As suggested by Goforth (2015), any value above 0.6 is considered satisfactory and the statement can be run through factor analysis to understand the major factors.

All the 23 statements show acceptable alpha score and therefore the correlation was calculated among various statements. Fig. 1 shows the result of correlation.

Table 1. Demographics of Respondents.

	Response in Numbers	Response in %
(a) *Gender*		
Female	163	65.72
Male	85	34.27
Prefer not to say	0	0.0
Total	248	100
(b) *Education*		
Graduate	103	41.54
Postgraduate	145	58.46
Total	248	100
(c) *Residential area*		
Urban but not metro city	109	43.9
Rural	52	21.1
Metro	87	35
Others	00	00.0
Total	248	100
(d) *Exposure to E-learning*		
Yes	230	92.7
No	18	7.3
Total	248	100
(e) *Gadgets used for online class*		
Mobile	147	59.3
Computer	101	40.7
Total	248	100

Source: Author's calculation.

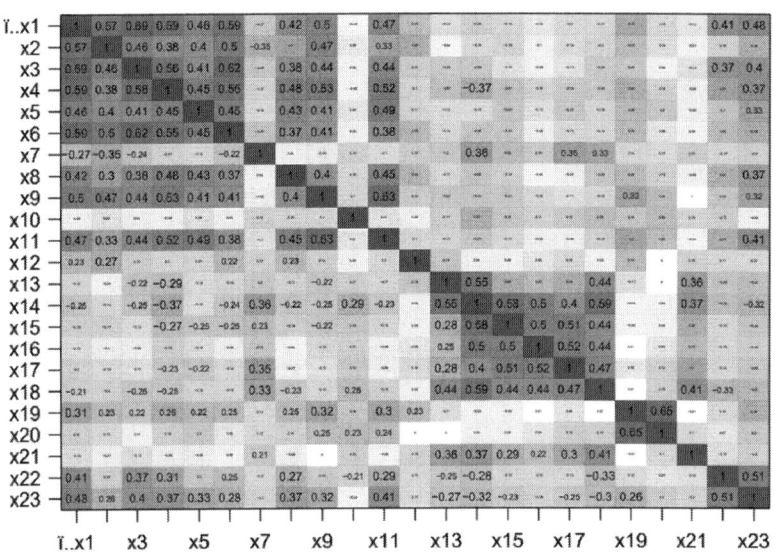

Fig. 1. Correlation Matrix. *Source*: Author's calculation.

Table 2. Cronbach's Alpha Results.

Alpha reliability = 0.7539
Standardized alpha = 0.7518
Reliability deleting each item in turn:

	Alpha	Std. Alpha	r(item, total)
×1	0.7299	0.7288	0.5194
×2	0.7375	0.7372	0.4071
×3	0.7337	0.7330	0.4616
×4	0.7380	0.7367	0.4002
×5	0.7378	0.7361	0.4146
×6	0.7333	0.7329	0.4609
×7	0.7586	0.7585	0.0579
×8	0.7361	0.7341	0.4337
×9	0.7328	0.7321	0.4630
×10	0.7498	0.7463	0.2440
×11	0.7325	0.7306	0.4874
×12	0.7429	0.7407	0.3330
×13	0.7637	0.7590	0.0506
×14	0.7585	0.7553	0.1031
×15	0.7596	0.7562	0.0862
×16	0.7525	0.7507	0.1793
×17	0.7534	0.7508	0.1690
×18	0.7562	0.7542	0.1235
×19	0.7378	0.7329	0.4405
×20	0.7417	0.7378	0.3620
×21	0.7519	0.7499	0.1969
×22	0.7531	0.7518	0.1708
×23	0.7471	0.7453	0.2714

Source: Author's calculation.

The result shows that many of the statements have high correlation between them. The negative values are shown in red and positive values are shaded in blue, and the greater the absolute value of the correlation, the deeper the color. For fulfilling the objective of finding out the factors that impact the satisfaction level of the students toward online teaching post COVID, responses were collected by questionnaire with multiple questions. As we know there are too many factors or variables in a study, factor analysis is the best tool which can be used to analyze data exploration and represent it by extracting a small number of independent factors (Boyd, 2013; Moore & Benbasat, 1991).

After identifying the method of analysis the extraction step was performed to determine the minimum number of common factors that would satisfactorily produce the correlations among the observed variables (Emerson, 2017). Fig. 2 presents the Eigenvalues graphically. Three factors have been extracted by using the Eigenvalues. After identifying the number of factors, the data rotation technique was used. The main aim of the factor rotation is to simplify the data and to get a better interpretation of the variables. The Varimax rotation method gives a more precise result, which can be easily interpreted. In this study, the Varimax rotation method is used.

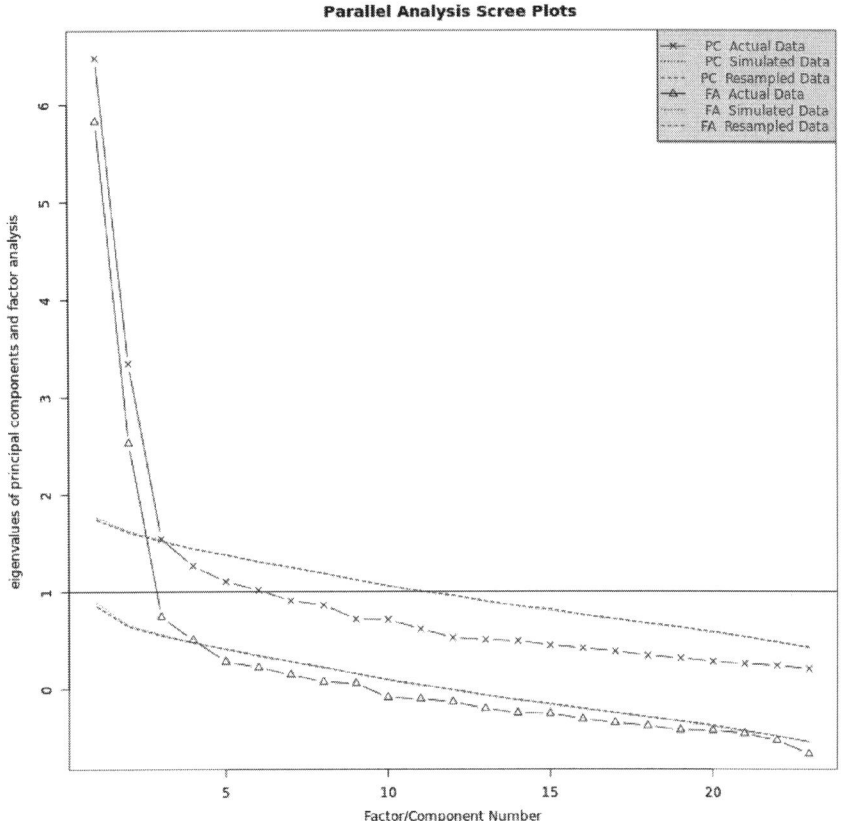

Fig. 2. Screen Plot of Eigenvalues. *Source*: Author's calculation.

Table 3 shows the loading value of the three factors identified after the Varimax rotation and then according to the loading the three factors are identified and renamed according to the questions categorized under the factor.

On analyzing different questions it was found that the three factors which emerged as relevant challenges for online education were named as "less effiectiveness," "stress and boredom" and "connectivity challenges." It was found that 11 questions which were about challenges like less effective online classes, less attendance, less attention, less control over class and less understanding of the subject has been categoried under the first factor and therefore the factor was named as "less effectiveness." It basically highlights that online classes are less effective when compared to face to face classes. Respondents also agreed to the questions where they were asked about the attendance in their online classes is lesser than the face to face classes. Respondents show positive response to the questions like faculty have lesser control over the class as compared to face to face class and therefore students also pay less attention to the class. All these factors lead to the less effectiveness of online classes.

Table 3. Factor Loading.

	MR1	MR2	MR3	Communality	Uniqueness	Complexity
×1	0.82	−0.14	0.03	0.68	0.32	1.06
×2	0.64	−0.06	−0.02	0.42	0.58	1.02
×3	0.76	−0.12	−0.05	0.6	0.4	1.06
×4	0.68	−0.24	0.13	0.54	0.46	1.33
×5	0.58	−0.12	0.15	0.37	0.63	1.22
×6	0.73	−0.06	−0.04	0.54	0.46	1.02
×7	−0.22	0.38	0.26	0.26	0.74	2.47
×8	0.55	−0.1	0.21	0.35	0.65	1.35
×9	0.62	−0.12	0.27	0.47	0.53	1.47
×10	0.07	0.34	0.23	0.17	0.83	1.85
×11	0.61	−0.12	0.28	0.47	0.53	1.49
×12	0.3	0.21	0.04	0.13	0.87	1.81
×13	−0.13	0.56	−0.11	0.35	0.65	1.2
×14	−0.2	0.79	−0.03	0.66	0.34	1.13
×15	−0.17	0.63	−0.01	0.43	0.57	1.14
×16	−0.05	0.61	0	0.37	0.63	1.02
×17	−0.13	0.62	0.13	0.42	0.58	1.18
×18	−0.19	0.71	0.08	0.55	0.45	1.17
×19	0.31	0.05	0.69	0.58	0.42	1.39
×20	0.15	0.12	0.74	0.59	0.41	1.14
×21	0	0.5	0.02	0.25	0.75	1
×22	0.38	−0.28	0.04	0.22	0.78	1.86
×23	0.47	−0.32	0.2	0.37	0.63	2.19

Source: Author's calculation.

Second factor consist of nine questions which were mainly about the interest created in online classes: do students feel bored in online classes, do faculty use innovative mehod of teaching, do long hours of online classes act as hindarance in the learning process and do the online classes create stress. Because generally the questions categoried under it deal with the stress level of students and innovativeness of the online class, therefore this factor has been named as "stress and boredom." Maximum respondents agree to the statement that the online classes create lot of stress and long teaching hours through online mode create boredom. Respondents also gave affirmative answer to the question that they open other windows also while their classes are going on.

Third factor had only two questions categorized under it but the weights of these questions were very high and therefore categorized as third factor. The factor was named as "connectivity challenge" as most of the respondents agree to the questions like do you face connectivity issue while attending classes and do lack of connectivity act as a challenge in the online teaching. Respondents agreed to the questions like many times classes are stopped or interrupted because of connectivity issue.

The question which was asked but not used for factor analysis was analyzed through pie chart. The respondents were asked which mode or software was used

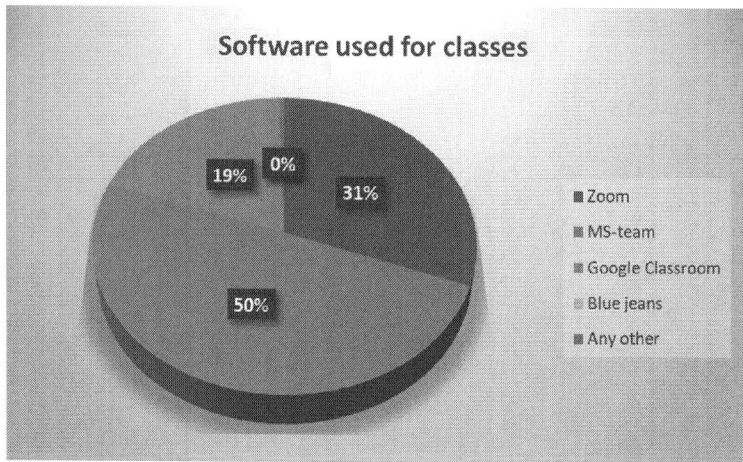

Fig. 3. Most Prefered Software. *Source*: Author's calculation.

for their classes and which is most prefered software according to them. The result is shown in Fig. 3, which clearly reflect that most of the respondents prefer MS-team.

The result shows that around 50% of the respondents use and prefer MS-team, Zoom has 31% of the share. Many of the colleges and universities have put a ban on use of Zoom, may be because of this the use of Zoom is less in India as compared to other countries.

CONCLUSION

The outbreak of COVID-19 which was followed by lockdowns in various countries created a big commotion in the academic world. Many universities, colleges and schools were temporarily shut down and to continue the learning process was a challenge for the government and the educational institutions. This study is an attempt to understand the learning challenges of undergraduate and postgraduate students who are undergoing online classes in their respective colleges and institutes. The study shows that although the majority of the respondents had experienced E-learning before and hence are familiar with the digital platforms for online classes and ICTs, but still they feel that the online classes are less effective when compared to face to face classes. It was also found that a considerable number of the respondents attend their classes from their computers but still the majority considerable number joins their online classes through mobile phones. On analyzing the result, three factors came as most important factor/challenges reported by the students, which were: "less effectiveness," "stress and boredom" and "connectivity challenges." These are the major challenges in online classes. Students feel bored with long online sessions and also connectivity play an important role in decreasing the effectiveness of online classes. Identifying these challenges is important to inform a strategic plan for online education.

The study argues that policy makers should adopt a standardized education plan to improve online teaching and learning amid and post COVID-19. Adequate funding and training to faculty members are inevitable to ensure a more interactive, connected and effective online learning experience for the students.

REFERENCES

Allo, M. D. G. (2020). Is the online learning good in the midst of Covid-19 pandemic? The case of EFL learners. *Jurnal Sinestesia, 10,* 1–10.

Bharuthram, S., & Kies, C. (2013). Introducing e-learning in a South African higher education institution: Challenges arising from an intervention and possible responses. *British Journal of Educational Technology, 44*(3), 410–420. https://doi.org/10.1111/j.1467-8535.2012.01307.x

Bigirwa, J. P., Ndawula, S., & Naluwemba, E. F. (2020a). Does the school financing role matter in E-learning adoption? An explanatory sequential study in midwifery schools in Uganda. *Contemporary Educational Technology, 12*(1), ep264. https://doi.org/10.30935/cedtech/7630

Bigirwa, J. P., Ndawula, S., & Naluwemba, E. F. (2020b). E-learning adoption: Does the instructional design model matter? An explanatory sequential study on midwifery schools in Uganda. *E-Learning and Digital Media, 17*(6), 460–481. https://doi.org/10.1177/2042753020946286

Boyd, K. C. (2013). Factor analysis. In *The Routledge handbook of research methods in the study of religion*. New York, NY: Routledge. https://doi.org/10.4324/9780203154281-22

Ellis, R. A., Ginns, P., & Piggott, L. (2009). E-learning in higher education: Some key aspects and their relationship to approaches to study. *Higher Education Research and Development, 28*(3), 303–318. https://doi.org/10.1080/07294360902839909

Emerson, R. W. (2017). Exploratory factor analysis. *Journal of Visual Impairment and Blindness, 111*(3), 301–302. https://doi.org/10.1177/0145482x1711100313

Fischer, H., Heise, L., Heinz, M., Moebius, K., & Koehler, T. E. (2014). Learning trends and hypes in academic teaching. Methodology and findings of a trend study. In *Proceedings of the International Association for Development of the Information Society (IADIS) international conference on cognition and exploratory learning in the digital age* (CELDA), Porto, Portugal, 25–27 October 2014, pp. 63–69.

Foster, E. A., Lepore-Stevens, M., Adams, D., & Lepore, M. (2020). The sports camp experience continued during COVID pandemic for children with visual impairments. *Palaestra, 34*(3), 8–10.

Goforth, C. (2015). *Using and interpreting Cronbach's alpha*. Charlottesville, VA: University of Virginia Library.

Goyal, S. (2020). Impact of Coronavirus on education in India. Retrieved from https://www.jagranjosh.com/general-knowledge/impact-of-coronavirus-on-education-in-india-1587642880-1

Huang, R., Tlili, A., Yang, J., Chang, T.-W., Wang, H., Zhuang, R., Liu, D. (2020). *Handbook on facilitating flexible learning during educational disruption: The Chinese experience in maintaining undisrupted learning in COVID-19 outbreak*. Beijing: Smart Learning Institute of Beijing Normal University.

Iyer, P., Aziz, K., & Ojcius, D. M. (2020). Impact of COVID-19 on dental education in the United States. *Journal of Dental Education, 84*(6), 718–722. https://doi.org/10.1002/jdd.12163

Kassean, H., Vanevenhoven, J., Liguori, E., & Winkel, D. E. (2015). Entrepreneurship education: A need for reflection, real-world experience and action. *International Journal of Entrepreneurial Behaviour and Research, 21*(5), 690–708. https://doi.org/10.1108/IJEBR-07-2014-0123

Keith, T. Z. (2019). *Multiple regression and beyond: An introduction to multiple regression and structural equation modeling*. New York, NY: Routledge. https://doi.org/10.4324/9781315162348

Keller, C., & Cernerud, L. (2002). Students' perceptions of E-learning in university education. *Journal of Educational Media, 27*(1–2), 55–67. https://doi.org/10.1080/0305498032000045458

Khanom, M., Hoque, A., Sharif, P. I., Sabuj, M. U., & Hossain, M. A. (2020). How were the online classes in undergraduate medical teaching during COVID pandemic? Students' views of a non-government medical college in Bangladesh. *Bangladesh Journal of Medical Education, 11*(02), 3–13. https://doi.org/10.3329/bjme.v11i2.49244

KPMG. (2020, April). Higher education in India and GATS: An opportunity. Retrieved from http://commerce.nic.in/trade/Consultation_paper_on_Education_GATS.pdf

Liguori, E., & Winkler, C. (2020). From offline to online: Challenges and opportunities for entrepreneurship education following the COVID-19 pandemic. *Entrepreneurship Education and Pedagogy, 3*(4), 346–351. https://doi.org/10.1177/2515127420916738

Mahaffey, A. L. (2020). Chemistry in a cup of coffee: Adapting an online lab module for teaching specific heat capacity of beverages to health sciences students during the COVID pandemic. *Biochemistry and Molecular Biology Education, 48*(5), 528–531. https://doi.org/10.1002/bmb.21439

Martínez-Argüelles, M., Castán, J., & Juan, A. (2010). How do students measure service quality in e-learning? A case study regarding an internet-based university. Electronic *Journal of e-Learning, 8*(2), 151–160.

Mishra, N., Tandon, D., Tandon, N., & Gupta, I. (2020). Online teaching perceptions amidst Covid-19. *The Journal of Indian Management and Strategies, 25*(September), 46–54. https://doi.org/10.5958/0973-9343.2020.00023.X

Moore, G. C., & Benbasat, I. (1991). Development of an instrument to measure the perceptions of adopting an information technology innovation. *Information Systems Research, 2*(3), 192–222. https://doi.org/10.1287/isre.2.3.192

Mulenga, E. M., & Marbán, J. M. (2020). Prospective teachers' online learning mathematics activities in the age of COVID-19: A cluster analysis approach. *Eurasia Journal of Mathematics, Science and Technology Education, 16*(9), em1872. https://doi.org/10.29333/EJMSTE/8345

Neck, H. M., & Greene, P. G. (2011). Entrepreneurship education: Known worlds and new frontiers. *Journal of Small Business Management, 49*(1), 55–70. https://doi.org/10.1111/j.1540-627X.2010.00314.x

Popovici, A., & Mironov, C. (2015). Students' perception on using eLearning technologies. *Procedia – Social and Behavioral Sciences, 180*, 1514–1519. https://doi.org/10.1016/j.sbspro.2015.02.300

Sarkar, S. (2020). Of late alarms, long queues, and online attendances: My experiences of COVID time. *Qualitative Inquiry*, 1–14. https://doi.org/10.1177/1077800420960157

Selim, H. M. (2007). Critical success factors for e-learning acceptance: Confirmatory factor models. *Computers and Education, 49*(2), 396–413. https://doi.org/10.1016/j.compedu.2005.09.004

Sintema, E. J. (2020). Effect of COVID-19 on the performance of grade 12 students: Implications for STEM education. *Eurasia Journal of Mathematics, Science and Technology Education, 16*(7), 1–6. https://doi.org/10.29333/EJMSTE/7893

Strielkowski, W. (2020). COVID-19 pandemic and the digital revolution in academia and higher education. *Preprints*, 2020040290. https://doi.org/10.20944/preprints202004.0290.v1

Sun, L., Tang, Y., & Zuo, W. (2020). Coronavirus pushes education online. *Nature Materials, 19*, 687.

Toquero, C. M. (2020). Challenges and opportunities for higher education amid the COVID-19 pandemic: The Philippine context. *Pedagogical Research, 5*(4), em0063. https://doi.org/10.29333/pr/7947

UNESCO. (2020). *Education: From disruption to recovery*. UNESCO Institute for Statistics Data. Retrieved from https://en.unesco.org/covid19/educationresponse

Whittle, C., Tiwari, S., Yan, S., & Williams, J. (2020). Emergency remote teaching environment: A conceptual framework for responsive online teaching in crises. *Information and Learning Science, 121*(5–6), 311–319. https://doi.org/10.1108/ILS-04-2020-0099

WHO. (2020). Timeline of WHO's response to COVID-19. Retrieved from https://www.who.int/emergencies/diseases/novel-coronavirus-2019/interactive-timeline?gclid=CjwKCAjw5p_8BRBUEiwAPpJO67v7rV7cQXnOGBygTJBM_D-dZuoFHKDeQfCaoBdmdjFwpmGJbS6-lxoC9K8QAvD_BwE#event-115

Wollina, U. (2020). Challenges of COVID-19 pandemic for dermatology. *Dermatologic Therapy, 33*(5), e13430. https://doi.org/10.1111/dth.13430

CHAPTER 5

UNCERTAINTY IN AN UNCERTAIN LAND – BATTLING OF COVID-19 IN AFGHAN EDUCATIONAL SYSTEM

Enakshi Sengupta, Mohammed Gul Sahibbzada, Madina Ibrahimi, Nelab Haidari and Elaha Yousufi

ABSTRACT

The battle to fight and resist the COVID-19 virus continues worldwide and even the vaccination drive is failing to control the new strains of viruses which are resulting in death and disruption of a normal life. The higher education sector, like others, has been affected by billions of students unable to return to their campus life. Universities have been forced to scale up their online learning ability, try out new and effective learning management systems and train their faculty and staff members to teach and operate remotely. This has led to a financial strain on the higher education institution with dwindling enrollment and student mobility. Afghanistan's vulnerable and fragile higher education system, fraught with war and internal strife, has suffered a huge setback. Electricity and access to the internet is a perilous problem and with the additional burden of students studying online, both providers of utility services and educational institutions are finding it increasingly difficult to face the unprecedented demand. This chapter aims to highlight such issues that are plaguing the already uncertain future of this country – even when the presence of the COVID-19 virus was unheard of. Qualitative interview method was used to gather data from the officials from the Ministry of Higher Education, faculty members from different universities and students from various provinces who voiced their opinion and hardships that they are facing in the current pandemic situation. The data were analyzed to suggest possible outcomes and recommendations were based on the data collected.

Keywords: Higher education; pandemic; COVID-19; enrollment; campus life; financial strain; universities; online teaching; internet; accessibility; Afghanistan

INTRODUCTION

The world has witnessed several unprecedented events, which included mass destruction and renewal of life post trauma. These incidents took place in some parts of the world while others enjoyed an almost perfect state of being, untouched or unharmed from those devastating, life-shattering events. However, never has it witnessed the closure of the world and everyone getting affected at the same time before COVID-19. If the world united this time, it united to face a deadly virus that was not sparing any particular nation or strata of people. Institutions declared themselves close, modes of transportation came to a halt and even the economy came to a grinding stop. Education both school level and higher education faced the same predicament. Classes were declared closed and classrooms moved from the school building to the living rooms of an individual. Around 1.6 billion learners in more than 190 countries and all continents were left in limbo with closures of educational institutions and other learning spaces which impacted 94 percent of the world's student population, up to 99 percent in low and lower-middle-income countries (United Nations, 2020). While an attempt was made to get back to the online mode of education, it exposed the vulnerability of educational institutions to adapt to technology with no turnaround time and worsened the predicament of those that are from the vulnerable and economically poor section of society. Internet and electricity were a rare and scarce resource in remote villages that barely supported education through chalk and writing board, laptop and other hand-held devices an unthinkable luxury.

The disruption in education has implications that are far beyond attaining of degree, substantial effects can be felt in other sectors as well. The higher education sector has felt an acute shortage of funds with more students, mainly international students who have restricted their travel and hence there has been a reduction in the enrollment numbers. Government and other funding bodies have restricted the flow of funds to these institutions, exacerbating a huge funding gap. Low-income countries and lower-middle-income countries have been feeling the brunt for some time, and the gap had reached a staggering $148 billion annually and it could now increase by up to one-third (United Nations, 2020). Yet, the picture is not always morbid. We are witnessing a myriad of innovative approaches from free software, use of radio and television and social media to keep the flow of education and ensuring that the students do not suffer a setback in achieving their degrees. The changes have highlighted the promising future of education and that education and its delivery will carry on irrespective of the situation.

Faculty members are trying to cope with these new methods and help is coming from all quarters with educational videos and training modules to better equip them with their online teaching and learning methods.

Afghanistan was suddenly catapulted into the online learning community despite having limited infrastructure as far as digital learning is concerned. In this war-torn community access to the internet and uninterrupted power supply to support digital education is rare. Television, laptop and smartphones are not available to all members of the family and is often a shared resource and the accessibility grows thinner with geography and location of an individual. Parity is often noted among economically weaker sections and even in the gender distribution of such facilities (Baiza, 2020). Families with high digital literacy and those in the city are found to have been faring well although they are trying to match with the cultural shock of not being physically present on campus but learning and getting graded while being at home. The government has beefed up its efforts of offering hundreds of hours of audio and video content for general education. Universities are offering free data packages to its students to continue with their education, yet the struggle and desire to return to the once normal life remains equally among students as well as facilitators of higher education.

CONTEXT OF AFGHANISTAN AND ITS HIGHER EDUCATION

It is a well-known fact that Afghanistan has been one of the most volatile countries since 1979 when the ex-USSR invaded it. The impact of the ravages of war can be felt in the major state pillars of the country including education, economy and defense. The country was profoundly affected when schools, universities and training institutions were destroyed and students were banned from attending classes for years (during Mujahideen Government – 1990–1995, and the Taliban reign – 1995–2001). The younger generation of Afghanistan was deprived of education this entire decade, which left the country struggling to keep the state institutions running. The US invasion post 9/11 did nothing to change the fate of the country but pushed it further to destruction and devastation of its economy. International communities and the United States and regional friendly countries such as India sanctioned billions of dollars into Afghanistan to address an acute shortage of resources and helped build thousands of schools and clinics. Skilled and educated immigrant workers, which included teachers and faculty members, were invited to become a part of the education system with the rebuilding effort of Afghanistan. Since 2002, millions of Afghan boys and girls have started attending classes in schools and universities. Professional training courses are initiated to train skilled laborers, resulting in an entirely new generation of educated Afghan youths with Bachelor and Masters' degrees working in tandem with the government and aid agencies to assist in the process of rebuilding their country's institutions. Countries have come forward extending their helping hand in the form of offering scholarships to Afghan students for the last two decades, thus providing a boost to the fragile health of education. Turkey, Iran, European countries and the United States have also accepted thousands of Afghan students to impart higher education which included technical training.

MINISTRY AND ITS READINESS TO COMBAT COVID IN AFGHANISTAN

The COVID-19 pandemic took its toll on Afghanistan as well and started spreading rapidly with refugees returning from the Islamic Republic of Iran and saw a sporadic growth of the infected in the Western part of the country mainly in the provinces of Herat, Farah and even stretched to Kandahar, Kabul and central Afghanistan. The ring-road that connects Afghanistan with Iran and Turkmenistan and runs through these provinces saw fresh cases of COVID-19 with an ongoing exchange of goods and traffic. Soon the Afghan government realized the highly contagious nature of the virus and Afghanistan imposed lockdown across the country for three consecutive months, shutting down businesses, universities, schools and large public and social gatherings. With the onset of summer, it was assumed that the destructive tides of the COVID-19 may decrease, which paved the way for phased relaxation of the lockdown. Universities, schools and other educational institutions had to ensure implementing mitigating measures against the spread of COVID-19. As the fatality rate was rising, universities, other educational institutions, schools and training centers were struggling to keep up with imparting education to students. While the fatalities reached a plateau, the graph of those infected started to plummet, the Afghanistan Ministry of Higher Education (MoHE) and the Ministry of Education (MoE) took stock of the situation and decided to initiate virtual teaching in most of the universities and schools, and also allowed some of these institutions to attend classes physically, but under stringent COVID-19 related rules and regulations.

Barakzai, Deputy Minister of MoHE, issued mandates to universities across the country laying out methods and ways for educational institutions to conduct classes virtually and/or attending classes physically. These rules include virtual teaching using various software. For universities that were allowed to conduct classes physically, measures such as an emphasis on keeping distance, wearing masks and sanitary gloves, distribution of sanitization items among students, administrative staff and teachers were initiated. Ban was imposed on large gatherings such as seminars, educational functions and other social gatherings, breaking of classes into two or three smaller units with each team attending classes in different times were also advised to educational institutions. Three membered medical committees comprising pharmacist, nurse and a medical doctor were deployed whose job was to visit classes and disseminate COVID-19 related safety information. Rooms were designated in the student dormitory to quarantine students exhibiting COVID-19 symptoms. Zubair Hashimi, a lecturer at Kabul University voiced enthusiastically that these measures had been so effective that not one life – including students, professors or administrative personnel – were lost to COVID-19 during the entire 2020 year when the COVID-19 virus was at its peak. He further added that universities did face some number of challenges as students at times failed to take heed of safety regulations and follow other measures to mitigate COVID-19. Some other challenges included managing a large number of students (Kabul University has 26,000 students), and monitoring the vast area of the university. Barakzai, Deputy Minister at MoHE added that the ministry would continue to implement the COVID related measures all over the country for a foreseeable time, and if challenges occur, they will refer to lessons learned improving the measures to mitigate the spread of virus among students, faculty and administrative staff (Face-to-face interviews conducted by the authors).

Nabila Nazari, a Senior Official at MoHE further added that with the assistance of World Bank, the Ministry have established 12 information and communication technology centers in various provinces in Afghanistan, including Faryab, Khost, Ghazni, Takhar, Kunar, Bamyan and Baghlan, in Kabul University and Kabul Polytechnic to initiate training for teachers in the online mode of teaching. Computer labs in these centers are dedicated to facilitating e-learning for teachers in the lockdown period. In normal times, these centers are open for the students to use while during lockdown, only teachers have the accessibility to these centers to conduct classes virtually.

A senior official from Kardan University in Kabul shared a document that outlined rules and regulations for students, faculty and administrative staff which would help guide them to follow the directives laid down for COVID related continuation of education. Some of these rules included: (1) COVID-19 awareness program where the university would print posters and spread messages about mitigation of COVID-19 spread; (2) observation of body temperature of individuals by assigned staff at the entry control point of the university; (3) obligatory use of mask; (4) obligatory hand wash; (5) ban on large gatherings in close structures, instead of conducting such gatherings in the open area outside buildings; (6) sanitizing classes, eating areas, tables, chairs, offices and all classes; (7) the university would continue to connect senior and graduate students with employment agencies, companies and government agencies for employment opportunities, despite COVID-19 pandemic.

MoE of Afghanistan, responsible for all educational institutions in the country, had issued its own set of guidelines concerning COVID-19. At the very outset of the pandemic, MoE issued administrative directives under which all educational institutions would remain closed for physical attendance until instructed otherwise and was asked to conduct virtual classes. Ninety percent of the schools in Afghanistan are government funded, and with resources in the MoE running dry, it was not possible to set up a virtual learning system in the entire country. Hence, government-funded institutions were shut down for almost the entire year, with the only exception for grades 11 and 12 which were opened for physical attendance of classes in the last quarter of the 2020 educational year. Private institutions resorted to conducting virtual classes having resources at their disposal yet adaptability and inadequacy of technical knowledge did not allow these private institutions to establish virtual classes for students apart from using basic means such as WhatsApp application. These schools prepared monthly teaching materials and started sending copies of these materials to every students' and issued instructions to students via WhatsApp group. The class teachers would form WhatsApp groups for students and continued teaching through this App.

The most debilitating effects of COVID-19 was the economic hardship which crippled the abilities of families to pay for their children's school fees and non-payment of fees in turn, depleted schools' resources to keep up with the virtual classes as fees were received only from a small number of students who could pay which event impacted the payment of teachers' salaries. International funds from donor agencies were used by the Afghan government to pay teachers' salaries, support private schools and upgrade government-funded schools.

At present, almost all universities and schools are open for physical attendance of students under' instructions issued by MoHE and MoE, yet some universities are still not open for physical attendance of classes under the discretionary rights of these educational organizations. Having conducted some qualitative interviews with students, families and teachers it was found that these affected families collectively requested to support the education system. Government should design assistance packages for school children so that the COVID-19 pandemic economic effects that down spiraled the entire family's purchasing power could recover. In a country that is already ravaged with devastating insurgency for more than four decades and devastating economic problems, the virus worsened both the education and economic scenario.

VOICE OF THE STAKEHOLDERS

Economy and education paid the highest price during COVID-19 and is still a raging battle with few and meager attempts to control it. Afghanistan's education system which was already ailing suffered a setback right from the onset of the pandemic. On an average basis, university classes in Afghanistan consist of more than 30 students which makes it hard to operate in a virus contagious situation; thus, it was the very first sector that went under lockdown on March 15, 2020. Since then, 169 education institutions across the country were closed down as many rural provinces do not have a suitable environment for online education in Afghanistan (Center for Strategic & Regional Studies, 2020). In the first phase of adjusting to off-campus classes, universities did not have online systems and portals in place and students were not familiar with using web-based applications. Therefore, the only way that universities could operate was to have teachers record lectures ahead of time and deliver them along with other study materials to students via USB devices. Another alternative way of sharing the teaching material was to use easy to access platforms such as WhatsApp and Telegram (interview: Abdul Hamid Bakhtyar, 2021) that could work with less internet bandwidth and reach out to a greater number of students.

As the pandemic continued, universities realized that recorded videos were no longer adequate as they lacked interactions and Q&A sessions; therefore, making the learning process unproductive. Consequently, many universities adopted free of charge and existing online applications (i.e., Zoom, Google Meet, Skype, etc.) as their teaching methods. Some universities – mostly in the capital of

Afghanistan (Kabul) – made further effort and high-quality teaching portals, customized to their students' needs.

Eventually, during the second lockdown, the MoHE was able to design software named HELMS (Higher Education Learning Management System) that made a huge breakthrough in Afghanistan's academic sphere, making online classes effective and feasible. Currently, the system is being used in 38 governmental universities, 11 private universities as a result of which 140,000 students got access to online learning across the country (Ministry of Higher Education, 2020).

To closely evaluate this situation from the students' perspective, a research survey was conducted among 190 students from 33 universities in 10 provinces of Afghanistan. About 63% of the students reported that online classes were ineffective, especially in undeveloped provinces such as Jawzjan, Khost and Daikundi. Students further explained that the reasons for ineffective online classes were power outages, weak internet connectivity, lack of face-to-face interactions and unfamiliarity with online teaching methods and technologies.

Fig. 1 shows the statistics of the research in further details:

As the above bar chart illustrates, 32.6% of the students were not happy with online classes as it was expensive for them in terms of excessive charges spent in topping their internet cards. This is also linked to students' accessibility to online teaching supplies namely laptops and smartphones. For students in a country with 54.5% of the population living under the poverty line (the rate is expected by the World Bank to increase to 72% during the pandemic), it is hard to pay such extra expenditures. This is also true that some universities paid for the top-up card of their students and others provided their students with discounts during the online class. However, such universities are not salient in number, because private universities themselves were under the financial crisis at the time of the pandemic.

For students in the last semester, the COVID-19 lockdown was another misery as was mentioned by a professor from a local university. They complain about the lack of online resources for their thesis research. Senior students needed to pay even higher costs to access the paid books in lieu of their closed university library. Not only this, but lockdown and the restriction on movements also made it difficult for these students to conduct field research that required interviewing and surveying their target groups.

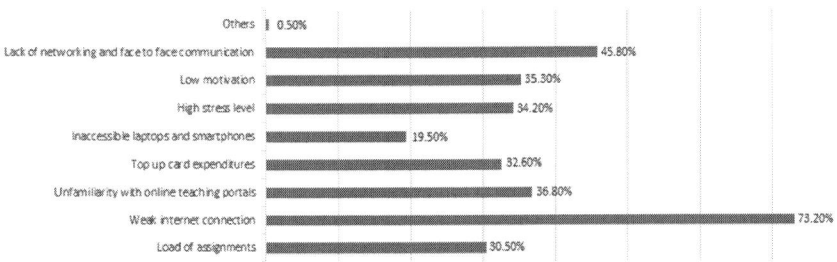

Fig. 1. Student Challenges.

According to the interviews with a number of students in Kabul and the provinces, it was discovered that universities in Kabul were more effective in e-learning compared to those in provinces as more facilities were available in the center of the country. "At the first weeks of the pandemic-time classes, we were only taught through pre-recorded videos of professors which were delivered to us through USB devices. The uncertainty and quality of education were stressful as we had no live interactions with professors and classmates," says Zeba Karimi an LLM student of Nangarhar Public University. Zeba adds "Although now classes are conducted online, we still cannot complete the curriculum, and this is mainly because we are faced with low internet connection issues." In contrast, Leeda Hamrah, a Business student from Kardan University in Kabul, discusses a different experience with her online classes: "In a world moving to online and internet-based activities, online learning was an opportunity for me to master new technology and think outside the box."

Despite all the drawbacks of online learning systems, 21% of students in the pre-mentioned students' research survey agreed that online classes were productive for it provided them with benefits such as learning new technologies and discovering new sources of distance learning. The survey also showed that students preferred online classes because it was time-efficient, cost-saving and comfortable in terms of transportation. In the meantime, given the tense security situation in Afghanistan because of the Afghan Peace Negotiation with the Taliban, students better liked online classes in some insecure areas of the country.

Fig. 2 illustrates students' response to a question related to the advantages of off-campus learning during the pandemic.

Data gathered from the perspective of the faculty members show that their challenges throughout the pandemic courses were no different than student's experiences. Online education for universities in Afghanistan was completely unprecedented and a whole new system.

The teacher's challenges were onboarding their students to the e-courses. Students related issues remained as the biggest challenge to teachers and the very reason for delaying education processes. This was evident after interviewing 22 university teachers, in 11 universities from the 5 provinces of Afghanistan. As Rahmat Bahar, Assistant Professor at Kunar University said that professors had

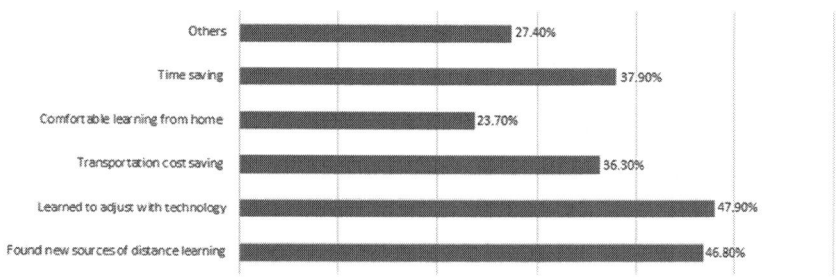

Fig. 2. Benefits of e-Education.

to redo classes on many occasions because the required number of students were not able to attend the online classes; and so, a chapter that was supposed to be completed in two days, would have taken a week to be delivered to all students.

Additionally, a few university professors explained that the quality of their teaching in the pre-recorded system was diminished because of the lack of interaction. Abdul Hamid Bakhtyar, who is an Economics Professor in two different universities in Jawzjan province, compares his teaching experience in both universities:

> Teaching in the university with the HELMS system in place has been more productive because we have live interaction with our students via this system. Conversely, teaching via pre-recorded videos in the second university has not yielded good results as in this system teachers lack the interest in teaching, and students lack learning motivation.

As digital learning in Afghanistan is at its nascent stage, the method of assessing and evaluating the students does not allow teachers to conduct a transparent evaluation of their students, especially in universities with no such system in place. Examinations via online methods were therefore not very responsive and realistic. That is why many universities provided online learning but kept examinations on hold till physical classes can resume after the pandemic. It resulted in an increased burden on both students and teachers as they would need another round of preparation for physical examination, and needless to mention it did increase the uncertainty and anxiety level of the students.

Despite these issues, academics highlighted a positive impact of the COVID-19 lockdown in the higher education of Afghanistan and they called it "the online education revolution in Afghanistan." The pandemic provided a good opportunity for Afghanistan's higher education community to step into distance learning and exploit their technology advantages. It forced universities to build systems and online archives for their teaching materials and even lectures. Fawad Zalmai, Assistant Professor at the Administrative and Accounting Institute of Nangahar, shares his experience in this regard that

> for the first time in Afghanistan, 100s of lecture videos in the Pashto language (one of the national languages of Afghanistan) were recorded and shared on YouTube for use of students. If it were not for the COVID-19 lockdown, such initiatives would have never taken place. All these systems built-in today will be of immense use for tomorrow if universities resume following technology advancements after the pandemic.

The community of higher education in Afghanistan considers the COVID-19 pandemic as a disruption in the educational system. It was a lesson learned for teachers, universities' management and government to be better prepared and have pre-established systems for future crises. The occurrences and challenges temporarily solved today shall remain as an example for a continuous effort to resume and establish beneficial and fundamental systems for a modern and developed tomorrow of Afghanistan.

The University of Tabish in Kabul can be a good example in this regard. The university has structured an e-learning committee in their university that focuses only on improving the quality of e-education. "E-learning committee is not subjected to COVID-19 time only. It will resume its operations to keep staff and students mentally and practically ready for distance learning" states Abdullah Tawafi, Assistant Professor of Journalism in this university. Another Professor at Tabish University further explained that the university already had its website; although it was not very robust and active. However, with the current pandemic situation, the university decided to include other options such as online teaching portals, student assignment submission portals, to make online learning a worthwhile and effective experience for its students.

Students continue to work and familiarize themselves with up-to-date technology as a part of their education journey. The survey of students shows that from 190 students, 77 has agreed that a major way of overcoming such issues in the future is to stay connected with technology and constantly explore new sources of e-learning.

The government has also played a key role in the planning and preparation of these emergency pandemics in the future. Universities and students expect the MoHE, the Ministry of Communication and Information Technology and the Afghanistan Telecommunication Regulatory Authority to work closely in supporting them with developing management systems and offering quality and affordable internet services in the future. Providing sufficient electricity to the residence of the country is also one of the infrastructural developments that the government, Da Afghanistan Breshna Sherkat in particular, may work to support e-learning in Afghanistan.

SHIFTING SCENARIOS

The shift from higher educational institutions to distance learning was sudden and difficult and it is presumed that moving back to school may even pose some challenges, apart from the ongoing battle with the pandemic or other strains of viruses. The role of digital literacy and digital technology cannot be denied in transforming the changing face of the economy and social divide. The accessibility of education to all economic strata can be mitigated with governmental aid and digitization of education. However, it is yet to be seen that if grading and performance level of students will fall below expectations when students return to offline classes and evaluated by using face-to-face examinations.

Research-based institutions are also facing huge challenges due to reduction in funds and manpower to conduct fieldwork. The career path of many research assistants and post-doctoral students remains uncertain with constraints in funding and reduction in recruitment opportunities. Scholarships and study abroad programs had to be kept on hold yielding an impact on the career and future planning of these scholars. Universities requiring physical laboratories had to rethink their entire curriculum which affected their teaching standards and the knowledge imparted to the students. Scientists cannot be trained if they are barred from entering universities and their designated laboratories to conduct experiments. Training models and social distancing protocols had to be relooked with new policies and procedures in place.

CONCLUSION

The pandemic was sudden and there were no benchmarking reports or established protocols that one could follow. Every university was trying to do its best as a work in progress mode. Still, there is no "one size fit all" model that can be followed although every educational institution is trying to engage in research-based activities that might yield some kind of guidelines and policies that can be shared among all as best practices while facing similar situations, now and in the future. Higher educational institutions continue their strife to excel and not to compromise the quality of education delivered to their students. Stakeholder engagement is required to create an additional body of knowledge based on experiences gathered during the pandemic and how they can be best suited to the vision and mission of the educational institutions. The hope of being better equipped next time continues and to steer the nation toward betterment despite the challenges ahead.

REFERENCES

Baiza, Y. (2020). *Coronavirus and education in Afghanistan: Responses, challenges, and the threats of educational divide*. Institute of Ismaili Studies. Retrieved from https://www.researchgate.net/publication/341900712_Coronavirus_and_Education_in_Afghanistan_Responses_Challenges_and_the_Threats_of_Educational_Divide

Ministry of Higher Education. (2020, May 06). سیستم مدیریت آموزش تحصیلات عالی (HELMS) امروز رسما سوی جلالتمآب ریس جمهور کشور افتتاح شد. Retrieved from https://mohe.gov.af/index.php/dr

PART II

MENA REGION, AFRICA AND EUROPE

CHAPTER 6

UNIVERSITY PREPAREDNESS FOR ONLINE TEACHING AND LEARNING AMID COVID-19 IN KENYA

Stanislaus Agava, Sahaya G. Selvam and Judith Pete

ABSTRACT

Globally, the COVID-19 pandemic took institutions of learning and the workplaces by surprise. Offering online learning was an alternative for institutions of higher learning. Were the Kenyan institutions adequately prepared for this? The present study had three specific objectives: (a) to establish the status of policy preparedness of online teaching and learning in Kenyan universities; (b) to explore the infrastructural preparedness of the universities; and (c) to find out the level of competency preparedness of lecturers and students in embracing the facilities for online teaching and learning. The study had an embedded mixed method research design. Data were gathered using an online questionnaire, from 112 lecturers and 372 students, who were conveniently sampled, representing 34 universities and university colleges. Findings suggest that almost all represented institutions have a policy on online teaching and learning, though 50% of participants' report that the policy did not exist prior to the onset of COVID-19. On the level of infrastructural preparedness, the personal ownership of digital devices among participants is very impressive, though 50% of institutions do not provide any device. Thirdly, the level of competency in the use of the three sets of online platforms for teaching and learning is far below the expected average, but this is improving since the onset of

COVID-19. Lecturers have statistically more perceived competence than students ($p<0.01$). The implication of these results is discussed. And we conclude that the period of forced online teaching and learning need not be considered as a stop-gap measure during COVID-19, but as a way forward for improved self-learning and lifelong learning.

Keywords: COVID-19 pandemic; online teaching; online learning; Kenyan universities; digital learning preparedness; learning management system

INTRODUCTION

The first case of COVID-19 infection was reported in Kenya on March 13, 2020. To curb the spread of the disease, stringent measures, which included lockdowns and social distancing, were to be implemented. An order was also issued by the government to shut down all learning institutions. Kenya's leaners became part of the 1.6 billion learners in more than 190 countries whose academic calendar was disrupted by the pandemic (De Giusti, 2020). For most institutions of higher learning in Kenya, this was well into the second semester of the academic year. Institutions had to strategize on how to conclude the remaining part of the semester, and to continue with teaching and learning in the subsequent semesters. The continuation of operations also had crucial impact on the financial and human resources stability of the institutions.

Offering online learning was the alternative mode for the universities to keep the operations going. As Martinez (2020) observes, the rapid spread of the virus left institutions of higher learning with no option but to adopt new methodologies in teaching and learning. In this case online teaching was the only option. In Kenya, some universities that offered online or blended courses handled the transition better. There were other universities, mostly private ones, that had already integrated learning management systems (LMS) to their normal teaching and learning, to offer an experience of a flipped classroom (Gilboy, Heinerichs, & Pazzaglia, 2015) to their learners. These might have handled the transition with even more ease. What was the general situation across Kenyan educational institutions?

In order to ensure minimal interruption to learning, the Government of Kenya (2020) developed and implemented the "Kenya Basic Education COVID-19 Emergency Response Plan." The plan targeted school-level learning. It encouraged institutions to provide online learning material, and to offer professional development and psychosocial support to teachers and learner. However, as Moyi (2020) points out, this plan received very skeptical response from stakeholders in the education sector. Was the skeptical response on account of the lack of previous preparedness of educational institutions for such a task? This situation refers to primary and secondary schools, but what about tertiary level institutions?

The Commission for University Education in Kenya elicited a report from public and private universities describing the specific steps that they had taken to enable continuity of learning. In the report, the universities were required to provide details of courses that were being offered, the platforms that were being used to deliver the courses, and the level of accessibility of students, among other elements. It is likely that there was a smooth transition and continuation of remote teaching and learning for institutions which had systems in place either before the onset of COVID-19, or at least during it. But this may not have been the case for some of the universities. Generally, amid the online teaching and learning option, universities were left to deal with challenges such as absence of policy on online teaching and learning, inadequate information and communications technology (ICT) infrastructure, and lack of competency preparedness of faculty and students in the use of online platforms. Economic disparity and lack of digital literacy among students and faculty compounded the imminent challenges. The manifestation of these challenges has raised the question of the overall preparedness of Kenyan universities in the integration of online facilities for remote or blended learning. The study being reported here was carried out to assess the preparedness of universities and university colleges in Kenya in delivering online teaching and learning amid COVID-19.

According to the World Bank, as of 2019, 22.6% of the population of Kenya had access to the internet. However, as of January 2021, this number has risen to 40% (Kemp, 2021). Corresponding to the national uptake, the institutions of higher education have been investing on digital infrastructural development since the early 2000s (Macharia & Nyakwende, 2009). This may not be proportionately reflected in the development of competency and the actual use of internet for education among lecturers and students. Previous studies (Kamonde, 2003; Waithaka, 2013) suggest that university students in Kenya generally have a good level of competency in the basic use of computer and internet. However, they tend to use them more for entertainment and social interaction as compared to research and self-learning because they lack advanced skills. This could be attributed to the lack of training in digital information skills to both lecturers and students. Have the disruptions caused by COVID-19 in face-to-face teaching and learning made any difference in the use of internet for higher education? That is the subject of our study.

For purposes of this study, we define "online teaching and learning" as a process in which lecturers and students interact with the course content and communicate with each other using internet-based online technologies (Curran, 2008). Generally, if over 80% of the course content is offered via internet, then the course is considered to be online (Simonson, Zvacek, & Smaldino, 2019). We consistently focus on "teaching and learning" as two distinct but not always as separate entities. Learning can take place independent of teaching. In fact, teaching should be seen only as a tentative scaffolding process (Vygotsky, 1987). However, as long as someone is registered as a student in an educational institution, it is only relevant to talk about "teaching and learning" as co-existing. Within this context, with the advent of LMS independent learning has been highly facilitated.

On another plane, some studies have pointed out the difficulty in breaking down variables related to integration of ICT in education (Tondeur, Van Keer, Van Braak, & Valcke, 2008). However, based on literature, in this study, we operationalized "the preparedness of universities for online teaching and learning" in terms of three examinable dimensions as listed below.

(a) Presence of online teaching and learning policy at the institution, and the level of awareness of the same among lecturers and students. We were particularly interested in knowing if the policy existed before COVID-19 and if the educative community, which, for the purposes of this study includes lecturers and students, was aware of the existence of the policy and its dimensions. According to Kennewell, Parkinson, and Tanner (2002), presence of policies at the school level could, to a large extent, reflect the dynamics in the actual teaching and learning. If the teachers are able to share the values captured in the policy, then it is likely that they are making an effort to practice it (see also Tondeur et al., 2008).

Based on literature (Holt & Challis, 2007; Wallace, 2007; Waterhouse, 2004), we focused on the following components of online teaching and learning policy: modes of instruction, curricular control, intellectual property, enrollment and attendance, academic integrity, evaluations and assessments, faculty support, and student support.

(b) The presence of ICT infrastructure and the level of accessibility of the same to lecturers and students could be another indicator of the preparedness for online teaching and learning.

We operationalized general variable of "the presence of ICT infrastructure," in terms of the following elements: the device that lecturers and students own, the device that they most use, the device that lecturers and students are offered to use or to own from their institution of teaching and learning, and the accessibility to internet.

(c) Finally, "the computer experience" (Williams, Coles, Wilson, Richardson, & Tuson, 2000) in terms of the conversancy in the use of the standard platforms for online teaching and learning among lecturers and learners could be another indicator of preparedness for online teaching and learning. Again here, we intended to know how much of familiarity was gathered during COVID-19. Furthermore, for purposes of the present study, online teaching and learning platforms are grouped into three categories:

   (i) *LMS*: These include those software platforms that facilitate communication between the lecturer and the learners in sharing learning resources, posting, and submission of announcements and assessments, grading, and plagiarism check, among other related functions. In this category fall online platforms such as Moodle, Google Classroom, BlackBoard, Canvas, and M-Elimu – which is a local platform.

   (ii) *Participation facilitation technology*: These are online tools that facilitate participatory teaching and learning. These web-based tools comprise those used to elicit participation of learners during face-to-face or online sessions. These include Menti, Socrative, Kahoot.it, PollEveryWhere, NearPod, and the like.

   (iii) *Remote video conferencing*: These refer to online facilities that provide possibility for videotelephony and chat services. Under this category fall services such as Zoom, Google Meet, Microsoft Teams, Cisco Webex, etc.

Against the above parameters, the present study aimed to examine the level of preparedness of Kenyan universities in offering online education during restrictions necessitated by COVID-19. More specifically, the study focused on the following research objectives:

1. To establish the status of policy preparedness of online teaching and learning in Kenyan universities.
2. To explore the infrastructural preparedness in Kenyan universities in order to adopt online teaching and learning.
3. To find out the level of competency preparedness of lecturers and students in Kenyan universities in embracing the facilities for online teaching and learning.

METHOD OF STUDY

Study design

The study had an embedded mixed method research design, largely using quantitative data and a little qualitative data. On the one hand, the qualitative data were used to provide a supportive but secondary role to the quantitative data (Creswell & Clark, 2017). The quantitative design played an important role because the study was meant to be a survey of the situation involving a relatively large sample. The quantitative data helped in arriving at some significant conclusions, and to test interaction between different variables. On the other hand, qualitative data helped in describing the interaction of the numbers. It gave voice to the perception and experience of the participants (Selvam, 2017) in handling the transition in teaching and learning during COVID-19.

Participants of the Study

There are 74 accredited universities and university colleges in Kenya, of these 38 of them are public (51.5%) and 36 are private (48.5%). At least 34 universities and university colleges were represented in the data of the study being reported here, amounting to about 46% of the total number of approved universities and university colleges. The data were not collected from certificate and diploma colleges. As for the sampling of lecturers and students from within these institutions, convenience sampling had to be used due to the pressure of time and the restriction of movements during COVID-19. In the present data gathered from a total 484 participants, 23% were lecturers and 77% were students, as shown in Table 1. Of this, 22% of the participants claimed to be hailing from public universities or campuses, about 77% claimed to be at a private university or college, others were not sure of the ownership of their institution. A higher number of participants in the study came from private universities probably because the public universities were less accessible to the online questionnaire.

As regards the gender of the participants, including lecturers and students, nearly 60% were female. The mean age of the lecturers was 43.49 (SD=11.16), and mean age of students was 34.55 (SD=10.18). In the whole sample, the youngest participant was 18, and the oldest person was 67 years old. The average age of students being higher than expected could indicate that a lot of older people

Table 1. Description of Participants.

	Ownership of Institution[a]		Gender[a]		Total
	Private	Public	Male	Female	
Lecturers	73	39	57	54	112 (23%)
Students	300	63	133	235	372 (77%)
Total	373	102	190	289	**484** (100%)

[a]Total in the categories does not tally, because nine participants were not sure of the ownership of their institution, and five participants did not declare their gender.

are returning to higher education in Kenya, and since our survey was conducted online older students might have had better access to devices and internet. As for their educational level, as it could be assumed in the Kenyan context, 50% of lecturers had completed master's degrees and others were PhD holders; however, among student participants, majority of them (74%) were undergraduates.

Data Collection

The quantitative data were collected using an online questionnaire. There were two different versions of the questionnaire for lecturers and students. The two versions examined the same variables, with the difference only in the phrasing of the items. Hence, the data from the two versions could be comparable, and at times totaled up, for analysis. The questionnaire had four sections. The first section focused on some demographic details about the participants and their institutions. The second section pertained to the presence and awareness of the institutional policy on online teaching and learning. The third section had items regarding the situation of ICT infrastructure in the learning institutions. And finally, the fourth part explored the experience and competencies of the lecturers and students in their use of the three categories of online teaching and learning platforms. We also included an open-ended question for the participants to express anything not foreseen in the questionnaire. This was the only item eliciting qualitative data. The question itself was phrased thus: "Add any other comment about how COVID-19 has affected your teaching and/or learning."

Data Analysis

Quantitative data were analyzed using descriptive and inferential statistics. While descriptive statistics was used to present summaries of data collected, inferential statistics was used to establish if the interaction between variables was statistically significant, particularly examining the difference between lecturers and students in their quantified perception and experience of the dimensions of preparedness of universities for online teaching and learning. The data collected from the qualitative item amounted to nearly 8,000 words (16 pages). Content analysis was carried out to pick up the patterns in qualitative data emerging from the single open-ended item. They were grouped according to their relevance to the three objectives of the study and reported accordingly.

Ethical Considerations

As per standard practices in Kenya, the research project was first approved by the Research Committee of the affiliate institution of the authors, and then it was officially approved by one of the accredited Institutional Ethics Review Committees in Kenya, and finally the permit to collect data was obtained from the National Commission for Science, Technology, and Innovation. Data were collected from those who had completed 18 years of age. And the participants were required to tick an item expressing their informed consent before the online platform opened up the rest of the questionnaire for them to respond to. The participation in the study was voluntary. No individual details of students, lecturers, or universities are mentioned in the report, all conclusions of the study are based on the summary of the data.

FINDINGS

The findings of the study are reported here in three sections corresponding to the three specific objectives of the study. For each section, we present the findings emerging from the quantitative data and add a few additional expressions from participants' reply to the single open-ended question, if the replies add support and further explanation to the quantitative data (Creswell & Clark, 2017).

Policy Preparedness for Online Teaching and Learning

The existence of an institutional online teaching and learning policy is seen as one of the indicators of the preparedness of the institution (Kennewell et al., 2002). Moreover, the awareness of members of the institution about its existence and contents could be an additional indication. Therefore, one of the items in the questionnaire asked participants if in their knowledge a policy existed in their respective institution. An overwhelming 88.8% of all lecturers and students in the study answered it in the affirmative (Table 2). However, when asked if the policy existed before the onset of COVID-19, only 41.5% offer an affirmative answer, and over 15% of them are not sure. The difference the perceived existence of the policy before and after COVID-19 was confirmed to be statistically significant by the results emerging from McNemar–Boker test, $\chi^2 = 224.831$, $p<0.001$. This suggests one of two possible scenarios: (a) that institutions had to work on an online teaching and learning policy in response to the need necessitated by COVID-19, or (b) that the lecturers and students were just not aware of its existence prior to COVID-19. In any case, 65.5% of the participants of the study claim that they have been trained in the contents of the policy. It could be assumed that this took place in the context of COVID-19 given the difference in the awareness of the existence of the policy before and after COVID-19.

Comparing private and public universities in their policy preparedness, there was no significant difference between them in terms of policy existence, $F(1)=2.566$, $p=0.078$, and in terms of policy training, $F(1)=1.771$, $p=0.171$.

Table 2. Difference between Opinion of Lecturers and Students on Policy.[a]

		Lecturer (%) (n1 = 112)	Students (%) (n2 = 372)	χ^2 (df = 2), p
Policy existence	Yes	92.0	87.9	1.480, $p = 0.477$
	No	4.5	7.3	
	Not Sure	3.6	4.8	
Policy before COVID-19	Yes	47.3	39.8	2.394, $p = 0.302$
	No	36.6	44.4	
	Not Sure	16.1	15.9	
Training on policy	Yes	75.0	62.6	11.968, $p = 0.003$
	No	17.9	33.9	
	Not Sure	7.1	3.5	

[a] % within category of lecturers and students separately considered.

Comparing the opinion of lecturers and students on policy on online teaching and learning, as Table 2 suggests, teachers seem to be better informed about the existence of the policy and better trained on it. Going by the descriptive data, across three elements, the lecturers offer a more optimistic answer as compared to the students. However, this difference is statistically significant only in the training dimension as confirmed by a chi-square test, $\chi^2(2) = 11.968$, $p=0.003$. More lecturers as compared to the students acknowledge that they have been trained on the policy.

As regards the contents of the policy (Fig. 1), the most remembered element by lecturers and students is the dimension of evaluations and assessments. This is followed by enrollment and attendance, and modes of instruction. Issues regarding curricular control and intellectual property are the least scored. On the part of the students, the most recalled element is enrollment and attendance. This could be due to selective memory of the participants according to relevance of the elements for them. These elements also show that the participants are more focused on the practical dimensions of the policy than the theoretical dimension. The qualitative data add further support of this finding. Most students voiced the difficulty they encountered in end-of-term assessments that were held online. Since this was their first experience of writing exams online, they became overly anxious. And because the policy had not overseen all the possible snags that could occur such as inconsistent access to internet connectivity and collapsed server systems, the students felt that the "educational institutions were making the path as they walked."

Finally, one item in the questionnaire assessed the level of satisfaction on the online teaching and learning policy. The item was scored on a 5-point Likert scale with scores ranging from 0 to 4. Table 3 presents the findings from this item, comparing the results of lecturers and students with the test for statistical significance using an independent samples Mann Whitney U test. The mean scores show that lecturers are more satisfied with the policy as compared to the students, this difference is statistically significant, $U = 17,089.50$, $p = 0.003$.

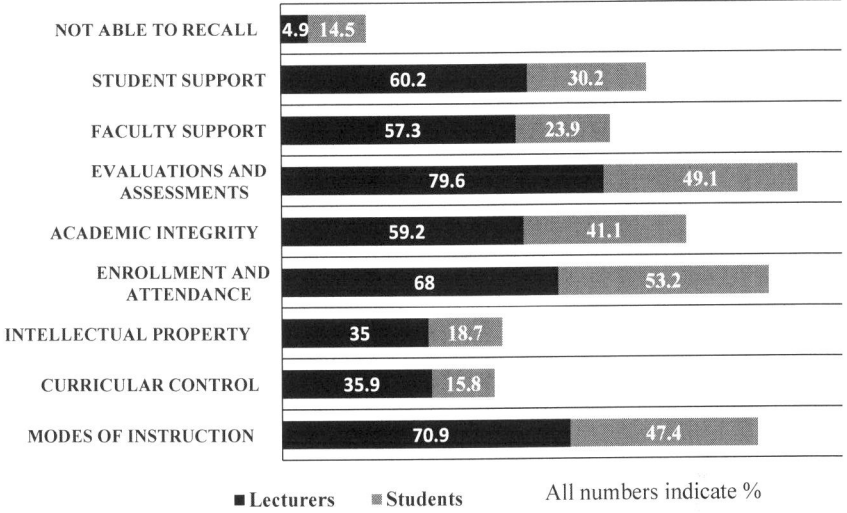

Fig. 1. Contents of Policy.

Infrastructural Preparedness in Adopting Online Teaching and Learning

The second objective of the study aimed at exploring the infrastructural preparedness in Kenyan universities in order to adopt online teaching and learning amid COVID-19. As said earlier, ICT preparedness was broken down in terms of the following variables: the device that lecturers and students own, the device that they most use, the device that lecturers and students are offered to use or to own from their institution of teaching and learning, and the accessibility to internet.

Regarding ownership of devices, as shown in Fig. 2, consistently lecturers own more devices than the students. This is not a surprise as lecturers have more access to resources. The most owned device is the laptop, and this is followed by smart phones. Only about 1% of the students do not own any of the devices, they might access a desktop provided by the institution of learning or might be sharing devices with someone else. Taken together, almost every participant in the study has access to at least one of the devices. However, a caveat is in place here: since the questionnaire for the study was online it is possible that those who do not own any device got naturally eliminated from the study. Therefore, these data only offer us an indicative trend and cannot be used to generalize for the whole country.

Table 3. Level of Satisfaction Regarding Policy and Internet Accessibility.

	Lecturers (Mean, SD)	Students (Mean, SD)	U, p
Satisfaction on online teaching and learning policy	2.73 (1.04)	2.34 (1.15)	$U = 17,089.50, p = 0.003$
Satisfaction on internet accessibility	3.53 (1.23)	3.11 (1.10)	$U = 16,386.50, p < 0.001$

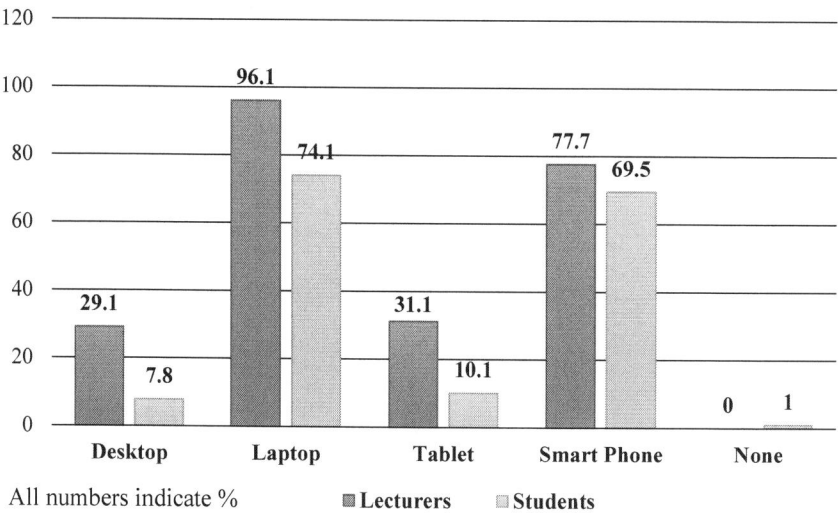

Fig. 2. Ownership of Devices.

Going beyond ownership to the *use* of the devices, there were some interesting findings. Among the use of the top two owned devices, students tend to use smart phones (65.5%) more than the laptops (60.1%), whereas lecturers tend to use laptops (84.5%) more than smart phones (63.1%). Across the categories of participants, the Tablet (such as I-Pad or Samsung Tab) is the least used device.

What devices are provided by the institution for use of the lecturers and students? The most accessible device is desktop and the least provided for use is smart phone (see Fig. 3). Again here, lecturers are better privileged than students. About 8.5% students and 3.5% of lecturers also claim that the device that they possess was given by the institution at a subsidized cost or purely as a gift. In this case, the students seem to be better privileged than the lecturers. The most surprising finding here, suggesting a low level of infrastructural preparedness for online teaching and learning, is that almost 50% of the participants (both lecturers and students) claim that the institution provides no device at all.

Finally, one item in the questionnaire assessed the level of satisfaction about internet accessibility in the campus. The item was scored on a 5-point Likert scale with scores ranging from 1 to 5, where 1 indicated "very low-quality connectivity" and 5 indicated "very high-quality connectivity." Table 3 presents the findings from this item, comparing the results of lecturers and students with the test for statistical significance using an independent samples Mann Whitney U test. The mean scores show that lecturers are more satisfied with internet connectivity as compared to the students, this difference is again statistically significant, $U=16,386.50$, $p<0.001$. This situation was further explained by the qualitative data. Over 80% of the students profusely complained about the lack

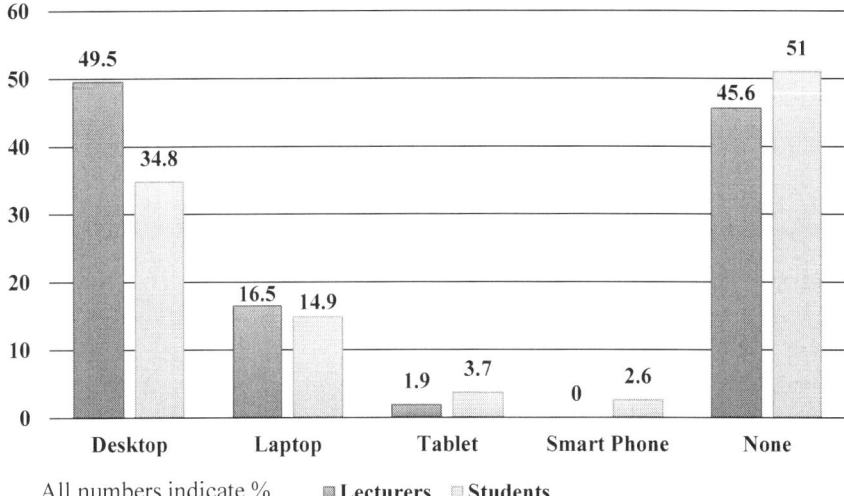

Fig. 3. Devices Provided for Use by the Learning Institutions.

of consistent internet accessibility particularly in rural Kenya. The cost of buying internet data bundles was also not budgeted for many students. This made them not only miss classes or assessments, but also increased their anxiety levels challenging their learning process.

Level of Competency Preparedness of Lecturers and Students

The third objective of the study sought to explore levels of competency preparedness of lecturers and students in Kenyan universities in embracing online teaching and learning. More precisely, we examined their level of competency across three groups of online facilities: LMS, participation facilitation technology, and teleconferencing platforms.

Two aspects stand out when all participants' (lecturers and students) perceived level of competency preparedness was examined (Table 4). One, their level of mean scores before COVID-19 fall below the expected mean of 2.5. Two, there is a statistically significant improvement in the scores of perceived competencies across the three groupings of online platforms during COVID-19. This improvement could have happened as a result of just jumping into the task and learning by doing, or they underwent some form of training. When statistical significance was established by carrying out a paired-samples t-test, comparing the scores of before and during COVID-19, only in familiarity in the use of teleconferencing platforms their perceived competency had gone above the expected mean score. This is also the grouping that included the use of Zoom, or Google Meet, or Microsoft Teams that received highest scores. This is understandable given that the teleconferencing platform became indispensable

Table 4. Level of Competency in the Use of Online Platforms for All.

	Before COVID-19 Mean (SD)	During COVID-19 Mean (SD)	$t(df), p$
Familiarity with use of LMS	1.73 (1.53)	2.09 (1.64)	$t(410) = -6.452, p<0.001$
Familiarity with use of facilitation technology	0.79 (1.24)	0.98 (1.35)	$t(379) = -4.212, p<0.001$
Familiarity with use of teleconferencing	2.31 (1.60)	2.82 (1.54)	$t(427) = -8.007, p<0.001$

Range of scoring: 0–5 and expected mean = 2.5.

for online teaching and learning, while the other two groups were important but not necessary platforms.

We compared the perceived competency levels of lecturers against that of the students, before and during COVID-19. As Table 5 indicates, lecturers scored more optimistic levels across the three groupings of technologies both before and during COVID-19. However, in the qualitative data, we found a number of students complaining about the lack of competency among lecturers that often disrupted or at times terminated particular sessions of online teaching.

We further explored if there would be any gender difference on their level of competency, and any correlation between age and competency preparedness for online teaching and learning. We assumed that younger participants may be more conversant with the online platforms. That is, there could be a negative correlation between age and level of competency preparedness in the use of LMS, participation facilitation technology, and teleconferencing platforms, before or during COVID-19. Pearson's test for correlation showed no significant level of correlation between any pair of variables against age. On the contrary, when we ran a one-way ANOVA using gender as the factor variable and the three groups of online platforms as dependent variables, some significant differences were noticed (see Table 6). Going by the mean scores alone female participants consistently scored lower than the other two gender groupings, except in the score

Table 5. Level of Competency – Comparison of Lecturers and Students.

	Lecturers (Mean, SD)	Students (Mean, SD)	$t(df), p$
Familiarity with LMS before COVID-19	2.24 (1.67)	1.53 (1.42)	$t(434) = 4.301, p<0.001$
Familiarity with facilitation technology before COVID-19	1.03 (1.42)	0.68 (1.14)	$t(400) = 2.468, p = 0.014$
Familiarity with teleconferencing before COVID-19	2.75 (1.65)	2.11 (1.56)	$t(450) = 3.750, p<0.001$
Familiarity with LMS during COVID-19	2.80 (1.71)	1.86 (1.57)	$t(419) = 5.161, p<0.001$
Familiarity with facilitation technology during COVID-19	1.39 (1.57)	0.86 (1.24)	$t(384) = 3.364, p = 0.001$
Familiarity with teleconferencing during COVID-19	3.60 (1.57)	2.60 (1.54)	$t(439) = 5.832, p<0.001$

Table 6. Gender Difference on Competency Preparedness.

	Male Mean (SD)	Female Mean (SD)	Gender N/A Mean (SD)	F(df), p
Familiarity with LMS before COVID-19	1.93 (1.46)	1.56 (1.53)	2.00 (1.00)	$F(2) = 3.251, p = 0.040$
Familiarity with facilitation technology before COVID-19	0.68 (1.07)	0.81 (1.31)	1.67 (1.53)	$F(2) = 1.355, p = 0.259$
Familiarity with teleconferencing platforms before COVID-19	2.49 (1.66)	2.10 (1.55)	2.60 (1.53)	$F(2) = 3.278, p = 0.039$
Familiarity with LMS after COVID-19	2.29 (1.67)	1.91 (1.60)	3.67 (1.53)	$F(2) = 4.099, p = 0.017$
Familiarity with facilitation technology before COVID-19	1.02 (1.38)	0.94 (1.30)	2.33 (2.52)	$F(2) = 1.681, p = 0.187$
Familiarity with teleconferencing platforms before COVID-19	2.91 (1.59)	2.76 (1.54)	3.40 (1.82)	$F(2) = 0.870, p = 0.420$

Range of scoring: 0–5 and expected mean = 2.5.

of familiarity with facilitation technology prior to COVID-19. The gender differences were statistically significant in the use of LMS before and during COVID-19, and familiarity with teleconferencing before COVID-19.

DISCUSSION

The present study set out with three objectives. In this section, we state each of these objectives and present the salient results emerging from the data and discuss the findings in the light of literature.

The first objective was to establish the status of policy preparedness of online teaching and learning in Kenyan universities. Almost all participants claim that a policy on online teaching and learning does exist in their institution. However, less than half of the participants, including lecturers and students, report that the policy did not exist prior to the onset of COVID-19. Thirdly, comparing the opinion of lecturers and students on online teaching and learning policy, as Table 2 suggests, teachers seem to be consistently optimistic and better informed about the existence of the policy and its components. The lecturers also claim to be better trained on the policy, and this difference is statistically significant. The level of satisfaction (Table 3) among participants as regards the online teaching and learning policy is above average, though again teachers are better satisfied than the students at statistically significant levels. As regards the components of the policy, we noted that the participants in the present study focus on the practical aspects of the policy. Wallace (2007) points out that there should be equal focus on issues around academic integrity, code of conduct, intellectual property, privacy issues, and lecturers' responsibilities. Another aspect that should feature in the policy is instructional strategies, because those learning activities and strategies that are used in face-to-face teaching cannot be used online. Online teaching requires another set of activities and strategies. This again calls for professional development of lecturers and student trainings on the specific components of policy (Kebritchi, Lipschuetz, & Santiague, 2017).

The second objective was to explore the infrastructural preparedness in Kenyan universities in order to adopt online teaching and learning. The ownership of digital devices among lecturers and students is very impressive, since only a very negligible number (1% of students) do not own any of the digital devices. However, almost 50% of the participants claim that their institutions do not provide access to any digital device. The level of satisfaction (Table 3) among participants as regards access to internet is very high, though the teachers are better satisfied than the students at statistically significant levels.

In the qualitative data, most of the students have expressed practical difficulties in logging on to the online sessions due to inconsistent internet connection, power-outage, remoteness of location, and the cost of buying internet bundles. Similar findings have been reported by Dube (2020) in the South African context, namely, online teaching excludes many rural learners due to lack of resources to connect to internet. Dube (2020) goes on to argue that the rural learners are critical stakeholders even in the fight against COVID-19 in the rural areas, and they should not be left behind.

The third objective was to find out the level of competency preparedness of lecturers and students in Kenyan universities in embracing the facilities for online teaching and learning. Generally, the level of competency in the use of the three sets of online platforms for teaching and learning is far below the expected average. However, across all these three categories there is statistically significant growth in the perceived level of competency between the situation before and after the onset of COVID-19 (Table 3). Particularly in the use of teleconferencing technology, the competency levels went up beyond the expected average.

Given this improving situation in Kenya, we acclaim with Kamal et al. (2020) who state in reference to the situation of Malaysia, that online learning need not be a hindrance, but a blessing toward improved self-learning and lifelong learning even beyond COVID-19. As one female lecturer put it in our qualitative data, "Notwithstanding the negative effects of COVID-19, I have definitely become better at online searching, learning and teaching." Another postgraduate's student states,

> It has broadened my knowledge on how vast and rich the internet is and how when utilized properly can change one's life. Everything is condensed together. Online study is possible.

On the flip side, many of the participants expressed difficulties in carrying out practicum, for instance, in counseling, and the lack of access to laboratory for science subjects. This surely needs some face-to-face contact hours. Also, most participants miss the physical, social interactions that is part of face-to-face classroom sessions. In this light, blended learning is likely to be the new normal, rather than 100% online learning. The mixed sentiments expressed by the participants in the present study are similar to those voiced in studies from elsewhere in the world. For instance, a study from the Sultanate of Oman (Slimi, 2020) points out that majority of the participants in that study claimed to have developed independent learning skills, problem solving skills, and competency in ICT-based communication as a result of online teaching and learning during COVID-19 restrictions. It is also consoling to note that even in countries such as Oman there were challenges related to internet connectivity.

Another finding related to the third objective was the gender parity in competency preparedness. This is a great surprise emerging out of the present study. This situation raises several questions: is this on account of the lack of opportunities for the female lecturers and students, or is it their lack of interest and "aggressiveness" to make use of the opportunities, or is it their other commitments in the household especially if they carryout online learning and teaching from within the home, or is it something else? There is ample literature that discusses the gender dynamics in online learning (for instance, Anderson & Haddad, 2005; Kramarae, 2001; Latchem, 2014; Latchem, 2014). Literature presents a mixed picture of the situation of women in online teaching and learning. On the one hand, women especially from traditional societies find the online learning environment less intimating due to reduced social, gender-based competition, hence they often perform better than men in online learning (Gunn, McSporran, Macleod, & French, 2003). On the other hand, different domestic arrangements of space and time in being available online could influence their access to learning (Burke, 2001). A report by World Bank (2011) also confirmed that many women are not able to benefit from online opportunities because of lack of resources and basic technical skills that will enable their access to internet. Hence, they are also not able to participate equally in knowledge economy. This calls for an affirmative action on the part of educational institutions in collaboration with governments in engendering online teaching and learning.

CONCLUSION

In conclusion, in line with the findings of the study we provide some recommendation to educational institutions, government of Kenya, and to lecturers and students. We also offer a brief proposal for future research. Though these recommendations are within the context of Kenya, they are generalizable to any similar situation. Finally, while acknowledging some of the limitations of the study we also recognize the valuable contribution of this study.

Some clearly emerging conclusions from the present study include lack of sufficient effort on the part of the institutions of higher learning to provide the infrastructural support to the lecturers and students. Almost 50% of the participants claim that the institutions do not provide access to any digital device. Similarly, competency preparedness across the three sets of online platforms falls below the expected average. These situations throw a challenge to the institutions to be proactive in investing on infrastructure and training. Online teaching and learning are not just a stop-gap measure to deal with the restrictions arising from COVID-19, blended learning is the future of education (Bonk, Kim, & Zeng, 2005).

No one was prepared for the enormity of the COVID-19 pandemic in every detail, nor were the institutions of higher learning. The restrictions necessitated by the pandemic put enormous budgetary pressure on the institutions. While the

Government of Kenya, as most governments, pumped in extra-financial resources to save the jobs and to keep the economy going, only a little resource were offered to schools and public universities. Private institutions had to bear the brunt on their own. Therefore, it is not fair to expect them to put all the required measures in place to offer online teaching and learning. Given that online learning will be the norm of the future, the government should have played a greater role. At the least, Government of Kenya and governments elsewhere need to invest heavily on providing universal internet connectivity. After all, as UN (2020) recommends right to education today includes right to internet connectivity.

In the qualitative data, several lectures and students expressed the positive outcomes of the experience of the teaching and learning during COVID-19. Individual lecturers and students need to continue their optimistic perception of the possibilities that online teaching and learning offers. They need to familiarize themselves with the new environment. Even self-training is possible using the online resources on instructional strategies and the adaptation of curriculum contents as appropriate for online teaching.

The study being reported here focused on preparedness for online teaching and learning. More studies are needed in order to examine the experience of lectures and students during COVID-19 (see, for instance, Kathula, 2020). Future studies in this area could center more on developed competencies of lectures and students. In any case, more systematic studies are needed in taking stock of the outcome of the online teaching and learning, and their impact for the new normal.

One of the blatant limitations of the study is the sample size. Given that there are 74 accredited universities and university colleges in Kenya, and the student population of these institutions of higher learning is estimated to be about 500,000 (Statistica, 2020). Data gathered from mere 372 students are not meant to be a representative sample. The findings provide an indication of the situation of preparedness in offering online teaching and learning in the institutions of higher learning. The second limitation is that the data for this study were drawn from self-reported questionnaire that was circulated online. Being an online questionnaire, there is a great possibility for self-selection and bias in the selection of those who have online access already. Being a self-reported questionnaire, the competency preparedness of the participants was from their own self-perception, hence individuals could be more optimistic. This has been consistently acknowledged throughout the research report. Given the urgency of this study and the current restrictions of movement arising from the COVID-19, an online self-reported questionnaire was the most suitable means of gathering data.

Despite these limitations, the present study sheds some valuable light on the preparedness for online teaching and learning in the Kenyan institutions of higher learning. Since it is likely that online teaching and learning will become an aspect of the new-norm even after the end of COVID-19, the findings of this study have provided some valuable points on the way forward in improving the ICT situation in Kenyan educational institutions. What Kohnstamm (2020) says of work could be applied to teaching and learning too, that it goes without saying that the pandemic has upset study life in 2020. But rather than seeing this period of forced online teaching and learning as a one-off by-product of COVID-19, it can be understood as an inflection point in a long-coming technology-driven reckoning on the nature of teaching and learning.

REFERENCES

Anderson, D. M., & Haddad, C. J. (2005). Gender, voice and learning in online course environments. *Journal of Asynchronous Learning Networks*, 9(1), 3–14.

Bonk, C. J., Kim, K. J., & Zeng, T. (2005, June). Future directions of blended learning in higher education and workplace learning settings. In C. J. Bonk & C. R. Graham (Eds.), *EdMedia+ innovate learning* (pp. 3644–3649). Waynesville, NC: Association for the Advancement of Computing in Education (AACE).

Burke, C. (2001). Women, guilt, and home computers. *Cyberpscyhology, Behavior, and Social Networking*, 4(5) 609–615.

Creswell, J. W., & Clark, V. L. P. (2017). *Designing and conducting mixed methods research*. Thousand Oaks, CA: Sage Publications.

Curran, C. (2008). Online learning and the university. In W. J. Bramble & S. Panda (Eds.), *Economics of distance and online learning: Theory, practice, and research* (pp. 26–51). New York, NY: Routledge.

De Giusti, A. (2020). Policy brief: Education during COVID-19 and beyond. *Revista Iberoamericana de Tecnología en Educación y Educación en Tecnología*, (26), e12.

Dube, B. (2020). Rural online learning in the context of COVID 19 in South Africa: Evoking an inclusive education approach. *Multidisciplinary Journal of Educational Research*, 10(2), 137–157.

Gilboy, M. B., Heinerichs, S., & Pazzaglia, G. (2015). Enhancing student engagement using the flipped classroom. *Journal of Nutrition Education and Behavior*, 47(1), 109–114.

Government of Kenya. (2020, September). Kenya basic education COVID-19 emergency response plan. Retrieved from https://www.education.go.ke/images/Kenya_basic_Education_COVID-19_Emergency_Response_Plan-compressed.pdf. Accessed on January 2, 2021.

Gunn, C., McSporran, M., Macleod, H., & French, S. (2003). Dominant or different? Gender issues in computer supported learning. *Journal of Asynchronous Learning Networks*, 7, 14–30.

Holt, D., & Challis, D. (2007). From policy to practice: One university's experience of implementing strategic change through wholly online teaching and learning. *Australasian Journal of Educational Technology*, 23(1), 110–131.

Kamal, A. A., Shaipullah, N. M., Truna, L., Sabri, M., & Junaini, S. N. (2020). Transitioning to online learning during COVID-19 Pandemic: Case study of a Pre-University Centre in Malaysia. *International Journal of Advanced Computer Science and Applications*, 11(6), 217–223.

Kamonde, M. (2003). *The diffusion, adoption and development of ICTs for research, teaching and communication in public universities in Kenya*. Doctoral dissertation, University of Nairobi.

Kathula, D. N. (2020). Effect of Covid-19 pandemic on the education system in Kenya. *Journal of Education*, 3(6), 31–52.

Kebritchi, M., Lipschuetz, A., & Santiague, L. (2017). Issues and challenges for teaching successful online courses in higher education: A literature review. *Journal of Educational Technology Systems*, 46(1), 4–29.

Kemp, S. (2021). Digital 2021: Kenya. Retrieved from https://datareportal.com/reports/digital-2021-kenya. Accessed on April 28, 2021.

Kennewell, S., Parkinson, J., & Tanner, H. (2002). *Developing the ICT capable school*. London: Routledge.

Kohnstamm, T. (2020, December 10). How Microsoft designed a campus with the evolution of work in mind. Retrieved from https://news.microsoft.com/features/israel-campus/

Kramarae, C. (2001). *The third shift: Women learning online*. Washington, D.C.: American Association of University Women Educational Foundation.

Latchem, C. (2014). Gender issues in online learning. In I. Jung, & C. N. Gunawardena (Eds.), *Culture and online learning: Global perspectives and research* (pp.126–136). Quicksilver Drive Sterling, VA: Stylus Publishing.

Macharia, J., & Nyakwende, E. (2009). Factors affecting the adoption and diffusion of internet in higher educational institutions in Kenya. *Journal of Language, Technology & Entrepreneurship in Africa*, *1*(2), 6–23.

Martinez, J. (2020). *Take this pandemic moment to improve education*. EduSource. Retrieved from https://edsource.org/2020/take-this-pandemic-moment-to-improve-education/633500

Moyi, P. (2020). Out of classroom learning: A brief look at Kenya's COVID-19 education response plan. *International Studies in Educational Administration (Commonwealth Council for Educational Administration & Management (CCEAM))*, *48*(3), 59–65.

Selvam, S. G. (2017). *Empirical research: A study guide*. Nairobi: Paulines Africa.

Simonson, M., Zvacek, S. M., & Smaldino, S. (2019). *Teaching and learning at a distance: Foundations of distance education* (7th ed.). Charlotte, NC: Information Age Publications.

Slimi, Z. (2020). Online learning and teaching during COVID-19: A case study from Oman. *International Journal of Information Technology and Language Studies*, *4*(2), 44–56.

Statistica. (2020). Retrieved from https://www.statista.com/statistics/1135785/university-enrollment-in-kenya/#:~:text=In%20the%202019%2D2020%20academic,year%20(2018%2D2019). Accessed on January 02, 2021.

Tondeur, J., Van Keer, H., Van Braak, J., & Valcke, M. (2008). ICT integration in the classroom: Challenging the potential of a school policy. *Computers and Education*, *51*(1), 212–223.

UN. (2020). Policy brief: Education during COVID-19 and beyond. Retrieved from https://www.un.org/development/desa/dspd/wp-content/uploads/sites/22/2020/08/sg_policy_brief_covid-19_and_education_august_2020.pdf. Accessed on January 02, 2021.

Vygotsky, L. S. (1987). Thinking and speech. In R. Rieber & A. Carton (Eds.), N. Minick (Trans.), *L. S. Vygotsky, Collected works* (Vol. 1, pp. 39–285). New York, NY: Plenum.

Waithaka, M. W. (2013). *Internet use among university students in Kenya: A case study of the University of Nairobi*. Doctoral dissertation, University of Nairobi.

Wallace, L. (2007). Online teaching and university policy: Investigating the disconnect. *International Journal of E-Learning & Distance Education/Revue internationale du e-learning et la formation à distance*, *22*(1), 87–100.

Waterhouse, S. A. (2004). *The power of Elearning: The essential guide for teaching in the digital age*. Boston, MA: Allyn & Bacon.

Williams, D., Coles, L., Wilson, K., Richardson, A., & Tuson, J. (2000). Teachers and ICT: Current use and future needs. *British Journal of Educational Technology*, *31*(4), 307–320.

World Bank. (2011). *Engendering ICT toolkit*. Washington, DC: World Bank.

CHAPTER 7

TRANSITIONING FROM PHYSICAL CLASSROOM TO DISTANCE EDUCATION DURING THE COVID-19 CRISIS: A LEBANESE CASE STUDY IN HIGHER EDUCATION

Ahmad Samarji

ABSTRACT

Distance education (DE) is neither a new concept nor process. Learning through postal correspondence can be traced back to more than 150 years. The avenues of DE have evolved from postal correspondence, videotaped lessons, electronic communications, to distance teaching higher education institutes. Up until the start of 2020, DE was an educational process of choice or preference. However, when WHO declared COVID-19 as a pandemic in March 2020, DE was no longer an option but rather the only choice and educational avenue for the majority of the universities worldwide; Lebanon is no exception. This chapter considered the case study of DE at Phoenicia University, Lebanon, studying instructors' attitudes and perceptions about some of the quality attributes of DE such as interactivity, inclusiveness, and immediacy prior to and after their first online semester. A mixed methods approach was adopted, where pre- and post-test surveys were administered with 54 instructors in Spring 2020. Semi-structured interviews were conducted with 12 instructors toward the end of that semester. This study found that the participants held a more positive stance when it came to instructor immediacy following their first online semester. On the contrary, instructors' attitudes and perceptions toward interactivity and inclusiveness did not significantly change between the pre- and post-test results, maintaining a less favorable stance of DE for these particular attributes in comparison to physical classroom education. The study concluded that overall, participants perceived DE as an efficient approach given the unprecedented crisis; nonetheless, the effectiveness of such an approach was challenged by many obstacles and limitations due to internet connection issues and the unreliable power infrastructure.

Keywords: Lebanon; higher education; higher education institutions; distance education; online education; online learning; online teaching; COVID-19 Pandemic

INTRODUCTION

Distance education (DE) is defined as "institution-based, formal education where the learning group is separated, and where interactive telecommunications systems are used to connect learners, resources, and instructors" (Simonson, Smaldino, Albright, & Zvacek, 2006, as cited in Schlosser & Simonson, 2009, p. 1). Moore (2013) describes DE settings as those occurring when the students and the teacher are separated by location, and sometimes by time, lacking face-to-face interaction. Simonson and Seepersaud (2019) assert that DE is characterized by four main features. The first feature is being institutionally based, differentiating DE from self-study. The second is the separation – geographically and sometimes in time zones – between the students and the instructor. The third feature is interactivity through telecommunications, where interaction can occur synchronously, at the same time, or asynchronously, at different times. The fourth component of DE is the availability of educational resources and their connectedness to the distance learning and teaching process, facilitating such a process between the instructor and the students (Simonson & Seepersaud, 2019).

To many instructors and educators, DE might seem a recent idea, concept, and process. Nonetheless, DE existed well before the introduction of Web 1.0 and Web 2.0 technologies (Moore, 2013). In reality, the concepts, processes, and modes of teaching, learning, and assessment in DE can be traced back to more than 150 years ago (Schlosser & Simonson, 2009). DE has evolved from correspondence study, electronic communications, to distance teaching universities (Schlosser & Simonson, 2009).

Over the past two decades and in the USA alone, online learning became significantly popular. This was best reflected and detailed in Allen and Seaman's (2013) report: "Changing Course: Ten Years of Tracking Online Education in the United States." Compared to 2002, when less than 50% of higher education institutions reported that online education was critical to their long-term strategic planning, Allen and Seaman (2013) found that in a decade, in 2012, this number jumped to become close to 70%. Additionally, they reported that the number of students taking at least one online course in 2012 increased by over 570,000 to a new total of 6.7 million, denoting an all-time high figure of 32% of all students in the USA (Allen & Seaman, 2013).

Online learning might not be as "distant" as DE as it can incorporate a minor face-to-face component versus a major online one; in other words, at least 80% of the course content needs to be delivered online as asserted by Allen and Seaman (2013). Nonetheless, for the general public, online learning is often interchangeably used to mean both online and DE. Hence, this chapter extracted data from Google Trends to see the worldwide popularity of "online learning" as a search term over the past decade. On Google Trends, the zone option "Worldwide" was selected, and the time range was customized to start on 01/01/2010 and conclude on 12/31/2020, covering 11 years: 10 years ranging from 2010 to 2019, inclusive, and the 11th year (2020) being the "pandemic year." Numbers collected via Google Trends represent

> search interest relative to the highest point for the given region and time. A value of 100 is the peak popularity for the term. A value of 50 means that the term is half as popular. A score of 0 means that there was not enough data for this term. (Google Trends, 2021)

The data collected from Google Trends were sorted and categorized to create yearly averages and are presented in Fig. 1.

Regardless of any substantial increase or growth in the number of created DE programs, offered online courses, and reported online enrollments over the past two decades, interest in online learning and DE has experienced an unprecedented, unimagined threshold during the COVID-19 pandemic, as clearly reflected by Fig. 1. The yearly averages detailed in Fig. 1 covered 132 months, out of which only April 2020, enjoyed a 100% peak search popularity for "online learning" (Google Trends, 2021). This is unsurprising, particularly in the month that followed WHO's declaration of COVID-19 as a pandemic and the transition to DE by the majority of education institutes all over the globe.

This chapter will investigate the experience of one of the Lebanese higher education institutions in transitioning from physical classroom to DE amid COVID-19 pandemic. The chapter will particularly investigate the perceptions and attitude of faculty members at Phoenicia University (PU), Lebanon, toward DE before and following the transition to online teaching and learning.

Before embarking on the case study analysis, it is essential to explore some literature review about DE prior to and during the pandemic.

DE PRE-COVID-19

In the last two decades (period ranging from 2000 to 2019) and as a result of the Web 1.0, Web 2.0, and Web 3.0 technologies, much of the attention was drawn toward promoting e-learning and online learning in higher education, where both terms were in some instances interchangeably used. Crook (2013) argues that e-learning as a term was first used in the late 1990s. The term was broadly employed by some authors to incorporate any form of learning that uses information and communication technology (ICT), while was confined by other authors to refer to online learning via the World Wide Web (Crook, 2013). As ICT tools

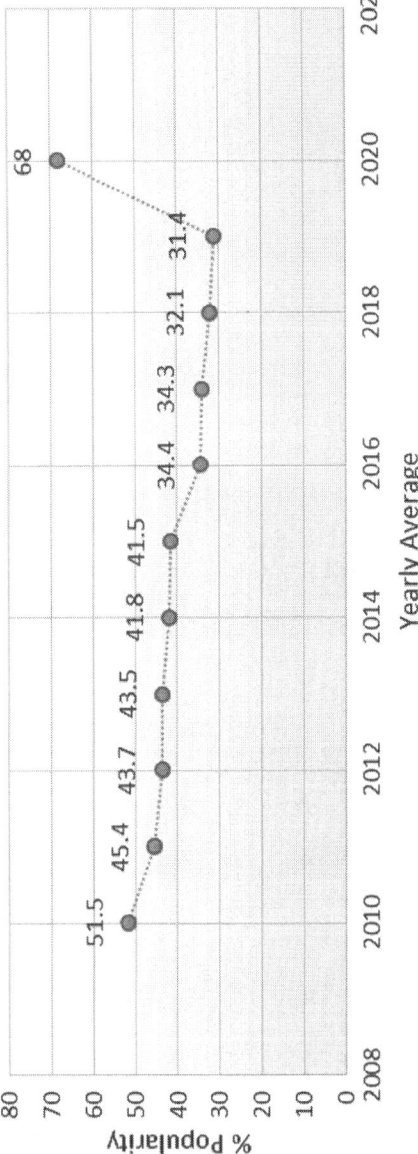

Fig. 1. Interest in "Online Learning" Over Time (Yearly Basis). Original data were collected from Google Trends (2021).

evolved in this period, e-learning started replacing earlier terms such as computer-assisted learning and computer-based training while contributing and witnessing the emergence of terms such as t-learning, learning through interactive digital television, and m-learning, learning through mobile devices (Crook, 2013).

DE benefited from the emergence of e-learning and ICT in education to transform its earlier avenues (e.g., correspondence, videotaped lessons, etc.) to new virtual platforms (Moore, 2013; Simonson & Seepersaud, 2019). A great deal of research in this period focused on the quality of DE. Many scholars and educators argued that DE cannot adopt the same quality assurance practices used in physical classroom education nor can it rely on the assumptions aligned with traditional educational settings (Stella & Gnanam, 2004). Quality in DE is not synonymous with excellence but rather refers to the "management of a continuous process aimed at bridging the gap between the expected effect (what ought to be learned) and the actual effect (what has been learned)" (Trentin, 2000, p. 17).

Defining the term "quality" in DE is a complex task that demands consideration of interwoven elements (Trentin, 2000). Hence, many scholars inquired into the various attributes of quality DE, some of which are: inclusiveness, immediacy, and interactivity. A recent study that focused on online programs offered by 16 Australian universities found that teacher immediacy along with an inclusive and interactive design, content, and delivery strongly contribute to a supportive and engaging online teaching and learning environment, leading to an increased student retention rates (Stone & Springer, 2019). A number of studies attributed students' dissatisfaction and inability to persist in virtual learning groups to the lack of interactivity, feelings of isolation and loneliness, and lack of instructor immediacy (Thurmond, Wambach, Connors, & Frey, 2002; Tu & McIsaac, 2002; Willging & Johnson, 2009). Another recent research highlighted the importance of ensuring inclusive teaching practices to decrease barriers and increase opportunities for diverse student populations within online learning environments (Cash, 2019).

Online teaching is not perceived by many teachers and instructors as smooth as physical classroom teaching but as a more demanding process (Cornelius, 2014). This explains the initial resistance revealed by some teachers and instructors at the start of an online teaching program (Redmond, 2011).

DE DURING COVID-19

The literature about DE during the COVID-19 pandemic is still limited as we are in the midst of the crisis. However, what simply defines DE during the COVID-19 pandemic is the fact that it was neither an option nor a matter of choice, but a forced process, forced by the coronavirus crisis. With governments and industries struggling with the pandemic, there was hardly any choice for the higher education sector but to transition all or most of its programs and courses from physical classroom settings to online delivery within a few days or weeks.

One of the recently published papers about the DE model adopted at one of the Turksih universities during the pandemic found that students' views about online learning were greatly impacted by resources, such as their ability to access online sessions via a computer or a laptop not only via their smartphones and having access to reliable internet connection aside from their mobile internet connection (Ince, Kabul, & Diler, 2020). Another study inquired into high school students' and teachers' perceptions of DE. The study (Hebebci, Bertiz, & Alan, 2020) found that both students and teachers held positive and negative opinions about DE. Sustaining educational activities in a planned and scheduled manner under extraordinary conditions was among the positives. In contrast, limited interactivity (unlike on-campus education), infrastructure problems, and lack of equipment were among the expressed remarkable negatives (Hebebci et al., 2020). A third study examined the attitudes of the academics in sports sciences toward DE during the pandemic. This study generated insights about the impact of a number of factors such as gender, professional seniority, and prior online teaching experiences on the attitude toward DE (Bingol, 2020). A fourth study focusing on online higher education via Open Universities Australia found that among the identified challenges reported by lecturers in their online delivery were having to cope with technical glitches, lack of immediacy, and difficulties with engagement (Chen, Dobinson, & Kent, 2020).

THE CONTEXT OF THIS CHAPTER

Simonson, Schlosser, and Orellana (2011) argue that the literature about DE has matured with numerous research studies and scholarly contributions. This argument holds true prior to the COVID-19 pandemic, as DE was a matter of choice, where each educational institution had the option to offer its programs or part thereof entirely or partially from a distance or through a blended approach. Many institutions continued to deliver their programs on campus explicitly.

Amid COVID-19, DE is no longer a matter of choice or preference; it is now the "no other educational option" that is compatible with governmental imposed health and protective measures, lockdown periods, and curfews. Such an unprecedented situation of "forced online teaching and learning" has created new challenges, opportunities, and a whole range of issues, inquiries, and discussion topics that urge more research.

This chapter will contribute to the emerging literature about DE during the COVID-19 pandemic by analyzing the case study of PU, Lebanon in transitioning from physical classroom education to DE in March 2020, following the Lebanese Ministry of Education and Higher Education's decision to stop physical and on-campus educational and academic activities. PU had to make all the logistic and academic planning and preparations, including training for faculty and staff and briefing students, to move to an online teaching and learning setting for the Spring 2020 semester in a matter of a couple of weeks. Training for the faculty and program coordinators included a series of workshops on how to prompt inclusiveness, promote instructor immediacy, and enhance interactivity in an online classroom setting and all the recommended pedagogical and curricular changes to offer a richer and more rewarding online academic journey.

A pre- and post-test questionnaires and semi-structured interviews were carried out to study instructors' pre-informed perceptions about DE prior to the start of the semester and any change in such perceptions toward the end of their online teaching and learning journey in this semester. As emphasized by literature, instructors were asked to evaluate online teaching and learning in terms of inclusiveness, interactivity, and immediacy. Additionally, instructors were asked to evaluate how smooth was DE in terms of planning, preparation, delivery, and assessment in comparison to physical classroom education and how effective was such a virtual educational experience.

METHODOLOGY

A case study is a common methodological approach across various fields, including education, that can use qualitative or quantitative data, or even combinations of them (Mills, Durepos, & Wiebe, 2009). Each approach has its advocates and opponents. The "epistemological view" of qualitative research in case study analysis is an "interpretative" one with an "inductive" line of reasoning, whereas, that of quantitative research is an "essentially empirical-analytic" one based on a "deductive reasoning" (Mills et al., 2009, p. 760). Hence, a mixed quantitative and qualitative approach will generally produce more valid, more reliable, and richer findings than what would solely be generated in either methods (Caracelli & Greene, 1997). Mixed methods research provides a "more complete picture by noting trends and generalisations as well as in-depth knowledge of participants' perspectives" (Creswell & Plano-Clark, 2017, p. 33). The mixed design of methods "provides strengths that offset the weaknesses of both quantitative and qualitative data" (Creswell & Plano-Clark, 2017, p. 9), facilitating the triangulation of results (Mertens, 2009).

Therefore, in our case study, a mixed methods approach was adopted to study the perceptions and attitudes of instructors toward DE prior to and toward the end of Spring 2020 semester, after transitioning nearly all courses to an online delivery setting.

The quantitative component in the methodology entailed a pre- and post-test survey that were sent to PU instructors across all colleges. A total of 54 instructors completed both the pre- and post-test questionnaires. The survey was designed to test some of the attributes of quality in DE emphasized in literature, such as inclusiveness, interactivity, and immediacy. Additionally, instructors were asked to evaluate how smooth was DE in terms of planning, preparation, delivery, and assessment in comparison to physical classroom education and how effective was such a virtual educational experience. The designed questionnaire was validated after consulting with two prominent educators in the field of DE. Following validation, the survey was finalized. A five-point Likert scale was used. Table 1 details the questions asked to the instructors.

Table 1. Pre- and Post-questionnaire (Quantitative Component).

Question 1	On a scale of 1–5, where 1 means much less interactive, 3 means as interactive, and 5 means much more interactive, how does DE compare to physical classroom education in terms of interactivity?
Question 2	On a scale of 1–5, where 1 means much less inclusive, 3 means as inclusive, and 5 means much more inclusive, how does DE compare to physical classroom education in terms of inclusiveness?
Question 3	On a scale of 1–5, where 1 means much less immediate, 3 means as immediate, and 5 means much more immediate, how does DE compare to physical classroom education in terms of instructor immediacy?
Question 4	In terms of planning, preparation, delivery, and assessment, and on a scale of 1–5, where 1 means much less smooth, 3 means as smooth, and 5 means much more smooth, how does DE compare to physical classroom education in terms of smoothness?
Question 5	On a scale of 1–5, where 1 means much less effective, 3 means as effective, and 5 means much more effective, how does DE compare to physical classroom education in terms of effectiveness?

The qualitative component was conducted through semi-structured interviews. Out of the 54 instructors who completed the pre- and post-questionnaires, 12 participated in short semi-structured interviews toward the end of the semester. Designing the semi-structured questions was informed by the results generated from the quantitative component. Table 2 details the semi-structured interview questions articulated to the 12 instructors.

Both the questionnaires and semi-structured interviews were administered and carried out in English.

DATA COLLECTION AND ANALYSIS

Instructor's attitudes, perceptions, and assessment of DE at PU during the pandemic was tested and evaluated via a mixed methods approach.

Quantitative Method

An online questionnaire was sent to all PU instructors across its six colleges prior to and toward the end of Spring 2020 semester. A total of 54 instructors fully completed both surveys. In addition to demographic questions and as detailed in Table 1, five questions were posed to test instructors' attitude and assessment of how interactive, inclusive, immediate, smooth, and effective was DE when compared to physical classroom education. All five questions were based on a

Table 2. Semi-structured Questions (Qualitative Component).

Question 1	In your own words and after delivering your courses online in this semester, how do you perceive DE?
Question 2	In your own words and after delivering your courses online in this semester and thinking about your previous teaching and learning experiences prior to the pandemic, how would you compare DE to physical classroom education?

five-point Likert scale. Using SPSS, a one-way ANOVA test was used to analyze the data at a significance level of 0.05.

Question 1 prompted participants to compare DE to physical classroom education in terms of interactivity. The one-way ANOVA test results are detailed in Table 3.

As the *p*-value (0.67) is >0.05, it is evident that there is no significant difference between the pre- and post-tests, and that the overall average of instructors' attitude toward the attribute of interactivity remained nearly the same, with a slight decline in the average toward DE being less interactive than physical classroom education.

Question 2 focused on testing instructors' perceptions on how DE compares to physical classroom education in terms of inclusiveness. The results are detailed in Table 4.

As the *p*-value (0.280) is >0.05, it is evident that there is no significant difference between the pre- and post-tests, and that the overall average of instructors' attitude toward inclusiveness in DE as compared to physical classroom education remained nearly the same, with a slight decline in the average in the post-test results toward DE being less inclusive than on-campus education.

Question 3 investigated instructors' pre- and post-perceptions of immediacy in DE compared to physical classroom education. The results are detailed in Table 5.

As the *p*-value (0.0426) is <0.05, it is evident that the mean value is significantly different between the pre- and post-tests and that the overall average of instructors' perception of the immediacy attribute in DE has increased from 2.32 to 2.77, and the median has jumped from 2 to 3, inclining toward being more comparable to that in physical classroom education.

Question 4 investigated instructors' pre- and post-perceptions of how smooth is DE in comparison to on-campus learning in terms of planning, preparation, delivery, and assessment. The results are detailed in Table 6.

Table 3. Collected Data – Question 1.

	Mean	Median	*P*-value
Pre-test	2.26	2	0.67
Post-test	2.16	2	

Table 4. Collected Data – Question 2.

	Mean	Median	*P*-value
Pre-test	2.55	2	0.280
Post-test	2.30	2	

Table 5. Collected Data – Question 3.

	Mean	Median	*P*-value
Pre-test	2.32	2	0.0426
Post-test	2.77	3	

Table 6. Collected Data – Question 4.

	Mean	Median	*P*-value
Pre-test	2.10	2	0.444
Post-test	2.23	2	

As the *p*-value (0.444) is >0.05, it is evident that there is no significant difference between the pre- and post-tests and that the overall average of instructors' post-perception of how smooth is DE in terms of planning, preparation, delivery, and assessment did not significantly improve and sustained its declination toward being less favorable.

Question 5 investigated instructors' pre- and post-perceptions of the effectiveness of DE compared to physical classroom education. The results are detailed in Table 7.

As the *p*-value (0.0151) is <0.05, it is evident that the mean value is significantly different between the pre- and post-tests and that the overall average of instructors' perception of the effectiveness of DE has increased from 2.26 to 2.84, and the median has jumped from 2 to 3, inclining toward being more comparable to that in physical classroom education.

Qualitative Method

Twelve instructors out of the fifty-four who completed the pre-and post-survey, participated in the semi-structured interviews. To comply with the research ethics requirements and keep participants' identities anonymous, the identity of the 12 interviewees were respectfully coded as P1, P2, P3, ..., P12.

The first open-ended question prompted interviewees to share their perceptions of DE after delivering their courses online in Spring 2020. Except for a few responses, the majority of the responses were generally positive toward DE. These positive responses were coded under two main themes.

The first theme reflected DE as "fun, novel experience. It is what the world is going towards nowadays" (P3). It is a "promising and great opportunity" (P7) and "serves the future of work and mobility as it gives learners the opportunity to study anywhere and at any time" (P11).

The second theme emphasized DE as the practical and efficient model during a crisis. Several participants emphasized DE as "a way to sustain a virtual educational bond when physical interaction is not possible" (P1) and "a great alternative during difficult times" (P9). DE is "very practical and efficient, especially in critical situations" (P5).

Nonetheless, the majority of the positive opinions/perceptions about DE were followed by conjunctive adverbs to "contrast" the preceding positive opinion. In

Table 7. Collected Data – Question 5.

	Mean	Median	*P*-value
Pre-test	2.26	2	0.0151
Post-test	2.84	3	

other words, the majority of the participants who expressed positive views and opinions about DE, employed a connecting adverb (e.g., but, however, instead, etc.) to contrast that the many attributes of DE are being limited and capped by the unreliable power and internet infrastructure in Lebanon. Examples of these contrasting comments are: "… but technically challenging given our infrastructure" (P7), "… instead, many of these great opportunities were capped by the limitations in the internet connectivity in our country" (P9), and "… however a challenging one in the Lebanese context" (P2).

The second open-ended question prompted interviewees to compare their current DE experience to their experiences with on-campus education prior to the pandemic. A number of participants asserted toward the end of the semester that DE experience was better than what they have expected. P11 argued that "I found it much better than what I expected. Aside from the power cuts and internet connection interrupts, all went good!." P5 asserted that "the training we received at the start of the semester was very useful, and I was able to apply some of the verbal and non-verbal immediacy techniques which smoothed the feeling of separation." The experience was "eye-opening" for P6 as the participant was able to "discover that so many online tools are available to facilitate learning online … and [to use] many websites and Apps to support students' understanding and help them apply the knowledge they've gained in different contexts."

On the contrary, a number of instructors were concerned that "the unstable internet connection and power outages made interactivity and inclusiveness more challenging, despite the many opportunities DE brings along" (P12). Likewise, P4 argues that "it was sometimes hard to ensure that all students are interacting with me when few students might drop out of the online meeting due to electricity or internet issues, challenges we never had to face while on-campus." Similarly, P6 who had an overall positive experience with DE admitted that "it was very difficult to encourage participation in class especially since some students did not have constant access to internet and electricity."

More than half of the participants emphasized that DE was not as smooth as physical classroom education as it required much more time and effort when it came to planning, preparation, delivery of specific content, and assessment practices. For instance, P8 commented "it requires double the effort in terms of planning, teaching, and assessment."

DISCUSSIONS AND FINDINGS

The quantitative data analysis showed no significant differences between the pre- and post-test results when it came to instructors' attitudes and perceptions toward interactivity and inclusiveness in DE compared to physical classroom education with a slight decline in the overall average in the post-test results, asserting their stance that DE was less interactive and inclusive than on-campus education. Data analysis from the qualitative component provided justifications to such a stance, as the majority of interviewees stated that the unreliable internet connection and power outages made it very challenging to make sure that all students were engaged and ensure inclusiveness. Additionally, quantitative data analysis revealed no significant change in instructor's attitude toward how smooth DE was, maintaining a stance that it was less smooth than physical classroom education. The qualitative component provided further details about this stance as the instructors found DE much more time and effort consuming in terms of planning their lessons/lectures, preparing online teaching and learning material, delivering the content, and administering online assessment tasks.

On the contrary, quantitative data analysis revealed a significant change in instructors' attitude and perceptions toward immediacy in an online setting, and the post-test results showed a positive change in their stance, leaning toward perceiving instructors' virtual presence in a DE setting as immediate as instructors' actual presence in a physical classroom. Semi-structured interviews revealed that such a positive change was attributed to the training that faculty received prior to starting their online teaching and learning journey, where both verbal and nonverbal immediacy techniques and approaches in a virtual setting were explored. The training also incorporated techniques and methods to promote interactivity and prompt inclusiveness; however, the poor internet and electricity infrastructures in Lebanon hindered instructors from making full use of these techniques and methods. Hence, the attributes of interactivity and inclusiveness were not as positively perceived as immediacy in DE.

Additionally, quantitative data analysis revealed a significant change between the pre-test and post-test means when it came to instructors' attitudes and perceptions about the effectiveness of DE in comparison to physical classroom education, leaning toward perceiving DE as effective as on-campus education. Nonetheless, the post-test mean increased to 2.84 and did not reach or exceed 3, where 3 was defined on the five-point Likert scale as "DE is as effective as physical classroom education." This also applied to all the other attributes, where the pre- and post-test means ranged between 2 and 3, never equaling nor exceeding 3. This clearly indicates that overall instructors perceived physical classroom education as more effective, immediate, interactive, inclusive, and smooth than online teaching and learning. However, the significant increase – though still below 3 – in instructors' average attitude toward effectiveness and immediacy in addition to the results generated from semi-structured interviews (e.g., P9's argument that many of the opportunities that DE could have brought were capped by the infrastructure) clearly suggest that participants found DE an efficient teaching and learning approach during the pandemic rather than an effective one. Additionally, in terms of quality and considering inclusiveness, immediacy, and interactivity as some of the major attributes of quality DE, data analyses from both the quantitative and qualitative components strongly suggest that the quality of such an online teaching and learning experience was negatively impacted in terms of interactivity and inclusiveness but positively impacted in terms of immediacy. Such a discrepancy between the quality features of DE map to the discrepancy between efficiency and effectiveness of such an experience. In other words, such an online teaching and learning experience was efficient in connecting and being immediate with the students and in delivering the content given the circumstances, but was not effective as physical classroom education due to the challenges with interactivity and inclusiveness (e.g., students dropping out of online meetings) and the capped online opportunities because of the poor infrastructure.

Findings from this case study will contribute to the emerging literature about DE amid COVID-19 and will inform future studies, discussions, and approaches post-COVID-19 about how to consider and balance between the effectiveness and efficiency of online teaching and learning and ensure that the attributes of quality DE are maintained.

LIMITATIONS

The results from this case study analysis are limited by the small sample size and the context, the Lebanese context. Generalizing of results from this study are limited to higher education institutes in countries who suffer similar issues in terms of poor internet connection and unreliable electricity and power infrastructure, for these two major issues significantly impacted participants' attitudes and perceptions toward DE.

ACKNOWLEDGMENTS

I would like to acknowledge the invaluable input of all the participants in this study, appreciating the time they dedicated to the study, while being very much occupied with transitioning to DE and striving to offer a rich and rewarding online academic journey during the unusual, uncertain, and unprecedented time of COVID-19.

REFERENCES

Allen, I. E., & Seaman, J. (2013). *Changing course: Ten years of tracking online education in the United States*. Newburyport, MA: Sloan Consortium.

Bingol, S. (2020). Attitudes of the academics in sports sciences towards distance education. *African Educational Research Journal, 8*(4), 799–805.

Caracelli, V. J., & Greene, J. C. (1997). Crafting mixed-method evaluation designs. *New Directions for Evaluation, 74*, 19–32.

Cash, C. (2019). *Analyzing faculty attitudes and actions surrounding distance education accommodations and inclusiveness based on UDL principles*. Doctoral dissertation, University of Central Florida. Retrieved from https://stars.library.ucf.edu/etd/6599

Chen, J. C., Dobinson, T., & Kent, S. (2020). Lecturers' perceptions and experiences of Blackboard Collaborate as a distance learning and teaching tool via Open Universities Australia (OUA). *Open Learning: The Journal of Open, Distance and e-Learning, 35*(3), 222–235.

Cornelius, S. (2014). Facilitating in a demanding environment: Experiences of teaching in virtual classrooms using web conferencing. *British Journal of Educational Technology, 45*(2), 260–271.

Creswell, J. W., & Plano-Clark, V. L. P. (2017). *Designing and conducting mixed methods research*. Thousand Oaks, CA: Sage Publications.

Crook, D. (2013). E-Learning. In G. McCulloch & D. Crook (Eds.), *The Routledge international encyclopedia of education* (pp. 670–673). Florence: Taylor & Francis.

Google Trends. (2021). *Explore: Online learning*. Google Trends. Retrieved from https://trends.google.com/trends/explore?date=2010-01-01%202020-12-31&q=online%20learning. Accessed on January 20, 2021.

Hebebci, M. T., Bertiz, Y., & Alan, S. (2020). Investigation of views of students and teachers on distance education practices during the Coronavirus (COVID-19) pandemic. *International Journal of Technology in Education and Science (IJTES)*, *4*(4), 267–282.

Ince, E. Y., Kabul, A., & Diler, I. (2020). Distance education in higher education in the COVID-19 pandemic process: A case of Isparta Applied Sciences University. *Distance Education*, *4*(4), 343–351.

Mertens, D. M. (2009). *Transformative research and evaluation*. NY: Guilford press.

Mills, A. J., Durepos, G., & Wiebe, E. (Eds.). (2009). *Encyclopedia of case study research*. Thousand Oaks, CA: Sage Publications.

Moore, M. G. (Ed.). (2013). *Handbook of distance education*. New York, NY: Routledge.

Redmond, P. (2011). From face-to-face teaching to online teaching: Pedagogical transitions. In *Proceedings ASCILITE 2011: 28th annual conference of the Australasian Society for Computers in Learning in Tertiary Education: Changing demands, changing directions* (pp. 1050–1060). Australasian Society for Computers in Learning in Tertiary Education (ASCILITE).

Schlosser, L. A., & Simonson, M. (2009). *Distance education: Definition and glossary of terms* (3rd ed.). Charlotte, NC: Information Age Publishing.

Simonson, M., Schlosser, C., & Orellana, A. (2011). Distance education research: A review of the literature. *Journal of Computing in Higher Education*, *23*(2–3), 124.

Simonson, M., & Seepersaud, D. J. (2019). *Distance education: Definition and glossary of terms*. Charlotte, NC: Information Age Publishing.

Simonson, M., Smaldino, S., Albright, M., & Zvacek, S. (2006). *Teaching and learning at a distance: Foundations of online education* (3rd ed.). Upper Saddle River, NJ: Pearson.

Stella, A., & Gnanam, A. (2004). Quality assurance in distance education: The challenges to be addressed. *Higher Education*, *47*(2), 143–160.

Stone, C., & Springer, M. (2019). Interactivity, connectedness and 'teacher-presence': Engaging and retaining students online. *Australian Journal of Adult Learning*, *59*(2), 146.

Thurmond, V. A., Wambach, K., Connors, H. R., & Frey, B. B. (2002). Evaluation of student satisfaction: Determining the impact of a web-based environment by controlling for student characteristics. *The American Journal of Distance Education*, *16*(3), 169–190.

Trentin, G. (2000). The quality–interactivity relationship in distance education. *Educational Technology*, *40*(1), 17–27.

Tu, C. H., & McIsaac, M. (2002). The relationship of social presence and interaction in online classes. *The American Journal of Distance Education*, *16*(3), 131–150.

Willging, P. A., & Johnson, S. D. (2009). Factors that influence students' decision to dropout of online courses. *Journal of Asynchronous Learning Networks*, *13*(3), 115–127.

CHAPTER 8

COVID-19 CHRONICLES IN EDUCATION: OVERCOMING GLOBAL PANDEMIC CHALLENGES IN TURKEY BY EMPOWERING EDUCATORS TO BECOME DIGITALLY LITERATE

Ayşegül Liman Kaban and Sinan Aşçı

ABSTRACT

Applying digital literacy skills in face-to-face or online classrooms started ringing the changes during the COVID-19 pandemic in recent months. Stating the obvious, well-planned distant learning experiences are different from courses offered online in response to a crisis or disaster. Every institution around the world has worked on preserving instruction throughout the COVID-19 pandemic. The extent to which educators being aware of their own and their students' digital literacy skills perceived how and what kind of information and communication technologies are used under such an emergency remote teaching and learning. The preparedness level of learners in using online information and communication technologies is a naturally regulated phenomenon because they are born to live a life of technology. Yet, educators have applied experience, and practical knowledge in face-to-face classroom settings remains a mere curiosity to remote teaching. This study was conducted to investigate educators' level of preparedness to use online information and communication technologies for their emergency remote teachings and their experiences from the field by focusing on moderating variables – asserted by Means, Bakia, and Murphy (2014) – like modality, instructor role online, online communication synchrony, source of feedback, and role of online assessments. Based on self-report scaled and open-ended questions in the same questionnaire, the participants were recruited online via convenience and accidental sampling, and the data were analyzed by using Statistical Package for Social Sciences software version 22.0 and thematic analysis. Within this study, how educators experience remote teaching during the global pandemic and what they prefer to carry out for the same effectiveness of the courses are discussed based on their digital literacy skills and digital readiness.

Keywords: COVID-19; emergency remote teaching; distance learning; digital readiness; educators' perception; digital literacy skills; digital inequalities; education

1. INTRODUCTION

The first cases of the COVID-19 pandemic were confirmed in Turkey in March 2020 when the Spring term had already started. As in many other countries, all the educational institutions quickly turned to emergency remote teaching by embracing remote forms of teaching and learning whereas school and university closures were announced. The global pandemic caused the cancelation of the on-campus classes, imposing schools at which classes were face-to-face to switch to remote learning in a very limited time. The COVID-19 pandemic created fear not only about the state of health but also the economic conditions for educators and learners about the uncertain circumstances of life, and at the same time COVID-19 lifted education to an "emergency matter" category (Williamson, Eynon, & Potter, 2020). These changes seem not to stand alone for a limited time, but to bring out long-term effects in educational settings. That's why the education sector, like the other sectors, shall get ready for the post-COVID-19 era which is frequently called the "new normal."

The expression "new normal" as a buzzword was first used in the business world and in the contemporary political landscape. The aim of such use was to take attention to the industrial economies and transform to normal after the global pandemic (El-Erian, 2010). Researchers all around the world have started debates on the online modality of instruction and implementation of the online modality in the post-COVID-19 new normal (Basilaia & Kvavadze, 2020; Mulenga & Marbán, 2020; Naciri, Baba, Achbani, & Kharbach, 2020; Sintema, 2020b). It is important to note that not that much attention is paid to the relationship between online modality, digital readiness, and educators' perceptions of themselves and on the learners in virtual classrooms.

To deal with this real challenge and experience a smooth change in the daily lives, a report titled "Education in a post-COVID world: Nine ideas for public action" was created by UNESCO in order to invite debate, engagement, and action by governments, organizations, civil society, educational professionals, and also learners. The report focuses in improving future learning methodologies and improving infrastructures that can cater for both face-to-face and remote modes of learning. These nine steps are detailed like

> committing to strengthen education as a common good; expanding the definition of the right to education so that it addresses the importance of connectivity and access to knowledge and information; valuing the teaching profession and teacher collaboration; promoting student, youth and children's participation and rights; protecting the social spaces provided by schools as we transform education; ensuring scientific literacy within the curriculum; protecting domestic and international financing of public education; advancing global solidarity to end current levels of inequality. (UNESCO, 2020, p. 1)

After classifying what is meant by emergency remote teaching and learning, its impact regarding the digital inequalities, the needs for digital readiness, and moderating variables, the chapter will focus on the first period of transferring the teaching experience online. The following section will present the research tools and the research processes to explain how data are collected on the field and the preliminary findings regarding the first days of the COVID-19 pandemic. In the final section, the experiences of educators for the first term of the COVID-19 pandemic in Turkey will be analyzed in order to show how the educators' perceptions and digital readiness pave the way for an easy transition regarding the variables detailed in this chapter.

2. LITERATURE REVIEW AND THEORETICAL BACKGROUND

2.1. A New Conceptualization of Teaching: Emergency Remote Teaching

A new approach, as a result of the COVID-19 pandemic, has emerged in education as a global norm at the beginning of 2020. Remote teaching, electronic learning, distance education, and online instruction are not brand new methods in education, but apparently, they are going to be transformed with the pandemic. Experts in this field of research and studies have already started debates on emergency remote teaching and a new pandemic pedagogy has become the center of the education sector. Coronavirus has activated

> "[…] the world's biggest educational technology (ed-tech) experiment in history. With 1.5 billion students out of school and hundreds of millions attempting to learn solely online, the experiment will reshape schools, the idea of education, and what learning looks like in the 21st century. (Anderson, 2020, p. 2)

When emergency remote teaching is compared with previous experiences that are planned from the start and designed to be online, it is a temporary shift of instructional delivery to a substitute delivery mode because of crisis conditions (Craig, 2020; Hodges, Moore, Lockee, Trust, & Bond, 2020). Hodges et al. (2020) also add that a well-designed online learning environment is different from courses which are offered online in response to a crisis or disaster.

All educational institutions suddenly moved their instruction online overnight, which might create a negative image for remote learning. Under these circumstances, no one has made the transition to online teaching by truly designing to take full advantage of the affordances and possibilities of online format (Hodges et al., 2020). As a result of this, online learning is believed to have lower quality than face-to-face learning environments although a collection of literature illustrates contrasting results.

2.2. The Impact of COVID-19 Pandemic on Digital Inequalities

Educational settings have not become available to all individuals rapidly during the COVID-19 pandemic because of technological exclusion. In other words, the advent of COVID-19 has thrown a spotlight on digital inequalities and social inequalities in learning environments. The usage of digital tools in educational settings causes some changes in paradigms that underpin the basics of digital literacy for tackling the new process providing new challenges (Aşçı, 2020). For this reason, we should take the first lesson of digital inequalities from the first period of the COVID-19 pandemic to entrench the basics of digital literacy, especially for young learners.

The children are called as digital natives, digikids, ikids, igeneration, digital childhoods, etc.; however, they are not magically skilled with technologies from birth (Liman Kaban & Karadeniz, 2021). On the one hand, many young individuals have access to the internet and other new technologies, on the other hand, there is an important amount of young individuals who are excluded. According to the UNESCO (2020) GEM report, 40% of the poor countries are not successful to assist learners throughout the COVID-19 crisis. In the same report, it was also mentioned that about 258 million children and youth were completely excluded from education, and poverty is the main encountered problem that prevents them from accessing education. While schools have closed owing to the COVID-19 pandemic, policymakers have realized that the rhetoric about young individuals is not correct, and many young individuals cannot participate in the educational settings. Not only in education but also in gender inequalities are often neglected when there is an epidemic (UNESCO, 2020). The recent United Nations (2020) report also puts emphasis on the same situation by claiming that learners who are influenced by school closures are the ones with poor digital skills and no access to the internet and hardware for distance learning.

Digital inequality has become another major concern nationally and internationally, so a timely understanding of how vulnerable individuals with less education, physical health problems, low literacy skills, and low level of internet skills is needed to enforce the existing inequalities.

2.3. Profiling the Needs for Digital Readiness

Digital readiness for any learning and teaching process in the internet age and during the COVID-19 pandemic is an international research domain because various success factors and enabling conditions are involved in conceptualizing and measuring the processes of education today. Following such an emergency remote teaching, macro- and micro-level perspectives on digital readiness start playing an essential role to reveal the reasons for mastering digital skills and to discuss the effectiveness of online education. According to Hong and Kim (2018), digital readiness implies knowledge of technological developments, skills, attitudes, and understanding for using digital technologies to fulfill the aims and expectations of education. Considering this general framework to define digital readiness, it can be inferred that it encompasses the purposeful use of digital skills for education and research works, the development of abilities on digital media use with the help of active participation in and critical consideration of digital culture, and lastly the practices of theoretical, operational, and evaluation-based digital literacy skills and some strategies to amend the educational basis. That's why it can be one of the key points between educators' remote teaching experience and their expectations on the outcomes of various courses.

Different digital readiness models, regarding the courses and the common purposes, have been detailed in five concepts such as information technology, technological, organizational, and environmental framework, operational technology, industrial internet of things, and unified theory of acceptance and use of technology.

- "Information Technology" (Pick & Azari, 2011) is defined as the use of hardware and software to transmit and/or retrieve information and to achieve functional goals.
- "Technological, Organizational, and Environmental Framework" focuses on the adoption of innovations from identifying the needs of deploying them (Tornatzky & Fleischer, 1990).
- "Operational Technology" (Gammage et al., 2011) refers to the use of hardware and software to monitor and/or alter physical systems, and to achieve business goals.
- "Industrial Internet of Things" is an intelligent, horizontal, and vertical connection of people and machines (Bauer, Pokorni, & Findeisen, 2019).
- "The Unified Theory of Acceptance and Use of Technology" (Venkatesh & Zhang, 2010) is about using an information system and the users' subsequent usage behavior as the only conceptualization focusing on users' intentions, which has been tested for gender, age, experience, and voluntariness of use.

Adopting macro- and micro-level perspectives on digital readiness leads to analyzing the experiences in a multi-dimensional way and revealing different digital competency frameworks. In other words, digital readiness can be discussed by addressing the readiness of organizations, regions, and countries (Beetham & Sharpe, 2007; Bui, Sankaran, & Sebastian, 2003) as macro-level perspective taken into consideration, and the knowledge, skills, and attitudes of educators and learners to support the effective and purposeful use of technology (Ala-Mutka, 2011) as exemplified in the micro-level perspective. According to Horrigan (2016), digital readiness includes "digital skills" and "trust," the two factors of which converge into the third dimension of digital readiness as "use." Therefore, it is necessary to specify the educators' perceptions about their own digital readiness to understand a plethora of needs to get involved in the distance teaching opportunities and affordances during the COVID-19 pandemic. The above-mentioned five concepts related to digital readiness can be applied to any kind of educational settings because of digitization in various fields of works.

2.4. Moderating Variables

Extending tangible variables means a lot in educational settings to comment on and analyze the data collected in field studies. Means et al. (2014) claim that online learning is divided into nine elements and these elements are modality, pacing, student–instructor ratio, instructor role online, student role online, online communication synchrony, pedagogy, the role of online assessments, and source of feedback. In this study, modality, instructor role online, online communication synchrony, source of feedback, and the role of online assessments were used. The assessment element was not involved because it focuses on the process and experiences.

As the teaching can be defined as emergency remote teaching, modality choice is not well designed. According to the United Nations (2020) report, the unequal division of the modalities of learning throughout school closures possibly build inequities in the longer term. In low-income settings where high-tech approaches are widely inaccessible, alternative "low-tech" approaches, such as radio or television, and, critically, "no-tech" approaches, such as printed resource distribution, are likely to be more viable (BETTSHOW, 2020).

There are two main online communication synchrony: asynchronous (diverse time and diverse place) and synchronous (same time and diverse place). Generally, when the learners are geographically dispersed, asynchronous online communication is preferred: however, during the COVID-19 pandemic, learners are not geographically dispersed so asynchronous and synchronous communication might be used to carry out effective teaching and learning environment online.

Remote learning is frequently seen as the synonym of content-driven self-study style in which the benefits are restricted for geographically dispersed participants. In remote teaching, there are three leading pedagogies which are called expository (transmission through audio or text), interactive (working with peers online), or independent practice. We found that studies in which students worked collaboratively online and those in which they worked with online explanations or lectures (expository pedagogy) produced learning outcomes that on average exceeded those of students in the corresponding face-to-face control group (Means et al., 2014).

Considering these pedagogies, it can be conveniently inferred that educators are the core of the learning process. In the school closures, teachers and education system leaders had to adapt their pedagogy to ensure the best outcomes for learners by online learning (BETTSHOW, 2020). According to the same report, in order to create an effective remote learning experience, a strong sense of teacher presence is needed (BETTSHOW, 2020). When several studies in the literature have been taken into consideration, the success of online learning is generally related to a supportive learning community (Garrison & Akyol, 2013). In a learning community which is formed collectively, the educators and the learners build and share knowledge, and they reply and reflect on each other: in other words, this kind of satisfying experience could be achieved with the help of collaboration. In the learning environment, interaction needs to be supplied between teacher, student, and the content. As claimed by Garrison et al. (2000), teaching presence is described as the design, facilitation, and direction of cognitive and social processes to support. In addition to this, Anderson et al. (2001)

claim that teaching presence is separated into three parts which are "instructional design and organization, facilitating discourse, and direct instruction."

Based on the ideal student–instructor ratio, there is no agreement about it while teaching online (Taft, Perkowski, & Martin, 2011). According to McCarthy and Samors (2009), having a small number of learners influence the learning process positively. In contrast, some researchers highlight that when the learners' achievement is the case, effective teaching strategies are more important than the size of the class (Ko & Rossen, 2010; Swan, 2002). In order to have interactive and collaborative online classes, the optimal learner number in each class should be between 15 and 30 (Grandzol & Grandzol, 2010; Orellana, 2006; Palloff & Pratt, 2007). Although previous studies have recognized that the class size is important to create an effective learning environment, the question of ideal class size still needs to be studied.

The National Education Technology Plan defines learner-centered instruction: "Technology-based learning and assessment systems will be pivotal in improving student learning and generating data that can be used to continuously improve the education system at all levels" (U.S. Department of Education, 2010, p. xi). Online assessments control the design of remote courses. For example, in systems which use mastery learning principles, the assessments are used to decide if the learner is ready to start a new learning objective (Means et al., 2014). When the adaptive systems are facilitated, assessments can be organized to supply information, differentiated instruction might be used. In remote learning environments, feedback is a feature that cannot be underestimated. When the immediate feedback used in the learning process, we might keep the score or inform the learning about the progress (Means et al., 2014).

3. METHODOLOGY

This study is to reveal the chronicles in the education process in order to see how to overcome the challenges in education among educators and why to empower educators to become digitally literate in Turkey. The study applies to the following developmental questions:

- whether there is any correlation between the educator's perceptions on their own and students' readiness and the factors such as the type of institution, the field of studies, daily internet usage, and experience in teaching online;
- whether there is any correlation between operational and technical settings and the factors such as the type of institution, the field of studies, daily internet usage, and experience in teaching online;
- lastly, whether there is any meaningful relationship between their perceptions and operational/technical settings.

In addition, to address these questions, this study is designed to better understand and examine the context of educators' experiences on emergency remote teaching and how this has been experienced in different settings based on their own stories which they revealed to explain how they have been dealing with such an emergency situation with the help of their institutions, colleagues, and platforms. In order to tackle these goals, a questionnaire was conducted to educators in Turkey, which is a common approach to get to know in studies of developing a general point of view. Despite the fact that self-reported studies do not possibly reflect the accurate situation, educators' perceptions reflected in the questionnaire spark off meaningful discussions to base the future research theoretically and practically.

A total of 238 educators (80.7% were female, 18.5% were male, and 0.8% did not want to respond) participated in this study, who were recruited via convenience (based on teaching online during the first wave of a pandemic) and accidental sampling through social media platforms; educators who are known to the researchers were contacted and asked if they accepted to share the questionnaire within their networks. Participants received no compensation for completing this questionnaire.

Participants completed a questionnaire for collecting the demographic (like their gender, age, and residential city) and the teaching experience information (like duration, type of institution, type of work, the field of studies, number of students, level of studies, and modality). The same participants filled in the questionnaire for knowing the internet habits based on a daily usage, pieces of training based on distance/online teaching, and platforms used in this period. In addition to these questions, five open-ended questions were added to get an insight into the transition of studies, environment effects, engagement strategies, continuity and integrity of assessment, and effects of face-to-face teaching interruptions.

The data collected through recruiting educators in Turkey into the questionnaire were analyzed by using Statistical Package for Social Sciences software version 22.0, and the answers collected in a quantitative way were analyzed by using thematic analysis. For the whole questionnaire, the reliability analyses were performed for the items related to "the educators' perceptions on their own and students' readiness" and "operational and technical settings." The Cronbach's alpha levels are 0.837 and 0.812, correspondingly. According to Akbulut (2010, as cited in Çoşkun & Aşçı, 2020), the reliability of scales are as follows: if the calculated Cronbach's alpha coefficient is $0.00 \leq \alpha < 0.40$, the scale is considered not reliable; if the calculated Cronbach's alpha coefficient is $0.40 \leq \alpha < 0.60$, the scale is considered to have low reliability; if the calculated Cronbach's alpha coefficient is $0.60 \leq \alpha < 0.80$, the scale is considered quite reliable; and if the calculated Cronbach's alpha coefficient is $0.80 \leq \alpha < 1.00$, the scale is considered highly reliable. Based on Cronbach's alpha levels, the questionnaire is *highly reliable*.

4. FINDINGS

4.1. Demographic Information

A total of 238 educators in Turkey participated in this study, 80.7% of whom were female, 18.5% were male, and 0.8% did not want to respond.

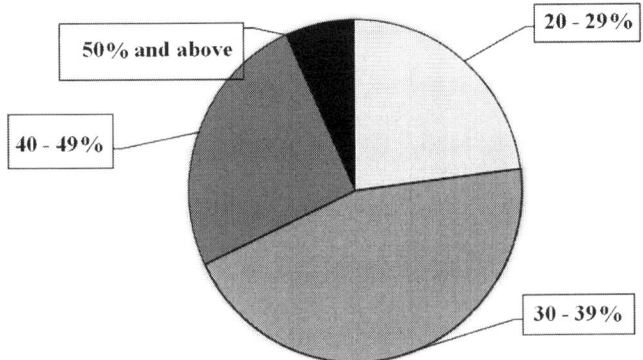

Fig. 1. Ages of Participants.

As seen in Fig. 1, 23.1% of the participants were in the age range of 20–29; 45% in the age range of 30–39; 25.2% in the age range of 40–49, and 6.7% were in the age range of 50 and above. Because there are seven geographical regions in Turkey, all the regions are aimed to cover, and 62.2% of participants in this study live in the Marmara Region as the most over-populated among the others.

In this study, participants are expected to work for different educational levels. Around 59% of the participants work for preschools, 37.4% for elementary schools, 17.6% for high schools, 37.8% for universities, and 1.3% for other institutions aiming at adults. Around 83.6% of the participants stated that they work full-time, and 16.4% do their jobs part-time.

As seen in Fig. 2, 49.6% of the participants work for public institutions, 45% for private institutions, and 5.4% for semi-public semi-private (foundation) institutions. Among these participants, 71.8% carry out their teaching activities in social sciences, 15.5% in applied sciences, and 12.6% in physical sciences.

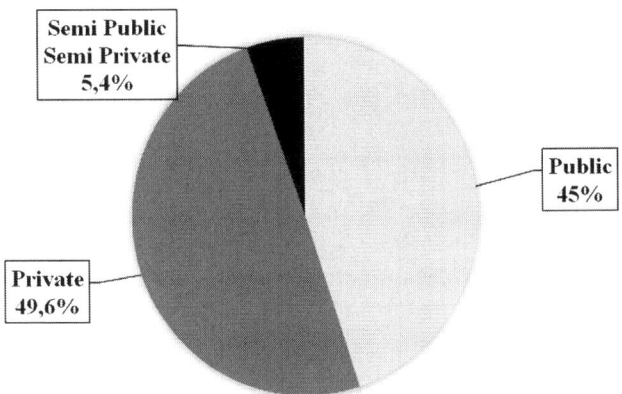

Fig. 2. Types of Institution.

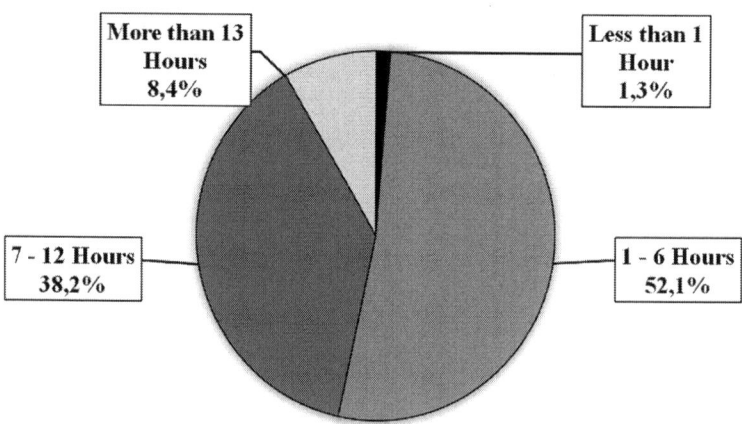

Fig. 3. Daily Internet Usage.

There are different years of experiences that the participants reflect on perceiving the situation during the COVID-19 pandemic. Around 4.6% of the participants have experienced in teaching for less than 2 years, 23.9% for 2–5 years, 29% for 6–10 years, 29.8% for 11–20 years, and 12.6% for more than 20 years. In addition to their teaching experiences in physical settings, 91.6% moved any of the lessons to an online platform during the COVID-19 pandemic while only 8.4% of the participants did not do it.

When the daily internet usage averages of the participants are asked, it is seen (see Fig. 3) that 1.3% spend on the Internet less than 1 hour, 52.1% between 1 and 6 hours, 38.2% between 7 and 12 hours, and 8.4% more than 13 hours. Under these circumstances, the online teaching experience is another concern to understand the field and the chronicles of educators. That's why participants are asked to reveal their experience in online teaching. Around 7.1% of the participants have experienced online teaching for less than 1 week, 57.6% for 2–4 weeks, 3.8% for 7–11 weeks, 23.9% for 1–6 months, 3.8% for 1–3 years, 1.3% for 4–5 years, and lastly, 2.5% for more than 5 years. As seen in numbers, most of the participants started teaching online just after the global pandemic.

4.2. Transition to Emergency Online Teaching

Considering these years of online teaching experience, the transition process from face-to-face teaching to online is another point of concern to see the instant experience for emergency online teaching. As seen in Fig. 4, 60.5% of participants had less than 1 week to transfer their materials into the online platforms, 33.2% did in 1–2 weeks, 3.8% did in 3–4 weeks, and 2.5% for 1–2 months.

Considering the modality about how the participants have taught, 34.5% stated that they have been making use of synchronous affordances, 9.7% with asynchronous affordances, and 55.9% have been working with both. Among the participants using synchronous affordances, 47.9% share the synchronous recording, and the rest do not. Different modalities based on communication

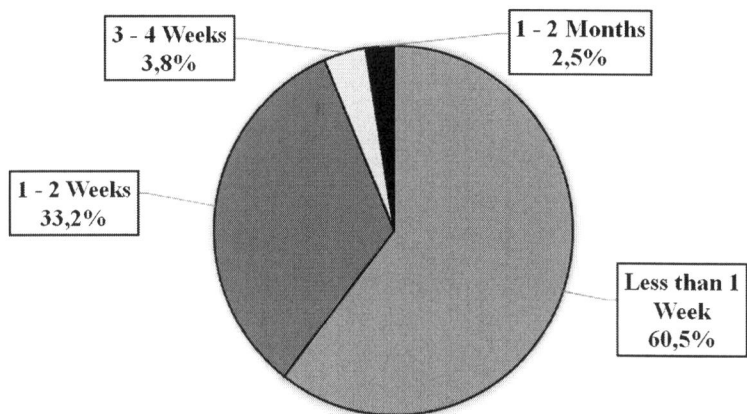

Fig. 4. Duration Assigned for Transferring Their Jobs.

affordances can be thought of how teacher and student experience the educational setting. For example, the synchronous or asynchronous teaching and learning experiences change the immediate feedback opportunity.

Looking at the numbers of the learners in the classrooms as seen in Fig. 5, 10.5% of them consist of 2–10 individuals, 34.5% with 11–20 individuals, 30.3% with 21–30 individuals, 13% with 31–50 individuals, 9.7% with 51–100 individuals, and 2.1% with more than 100 individuals.

Whether the participants have been trained about distance/online teaching before transferring their classrooms online or not is a significant point to discuss the details about how they have been experiencing it. Only 14% of the participants have not taken any training or assistance to complete the process in a suitable way: however, the rest has got some assistance through online interactive materials (7.6%), consultation with an educational technologist (14.9%), online

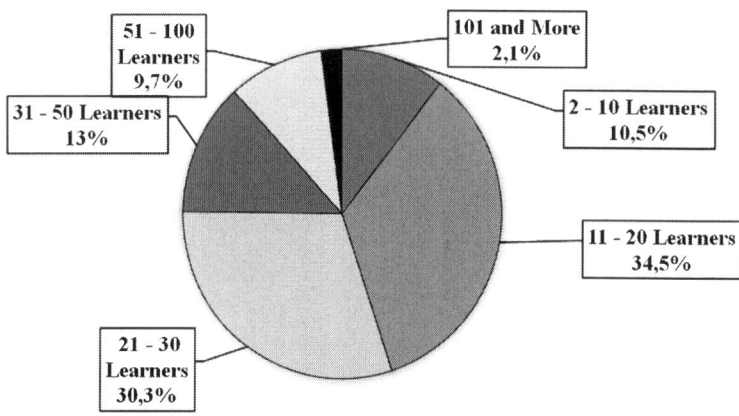

Fig. 5. Number of Learners in the Classroom.

non-interactive materials (28.2%), and online pieces of training (29.2%). Getting trained about the immediate and ongoing processes is assumed by the educators to make themselves feel comfortable enough while they teach online in an unexpected way.

The technological allowances or devices which the participants have been using to deliver their courses change a lot according to their own outcomes and general purposes. They have been using conferencing platforms (71.6%), learning management systems (6.6%), asynchronous discussion forums (2.7%), collaborative documents (5.3%), recording and sharing their own videos (5.2%), and sharing videos recorded by other professionals (7.1%). The remaining share (1.5%) is that the participants use other technologies they can reach at that moment according to the availability.

4.3. The Educators' Perceptions and Their Operational/Technical Settings

As seen in Table 1, 62.6% of the participants feel ready to teach their courses online, but only 20.6% do not feel ready. When their students' situations are asked, on the contrary, 37.8% of the participants think that their students are not ready to transfer their studies online. Less than the disagreement, 30.7% think that their students are ready to do their studies online. Following readiness based on any thoughts they have got according to their environments, only 14.2% of the participants do not feel confident in using technological devices to support online teaching, but a great majority of them agree on feeling confident enough to carry out their teachings online.

As seen in Table 2, 68.1% of participants agree on the fact that their internet connection is fine enough to carry out online courses. In addition to this, most of them disagree or do not have any idea about their students' internet connection quality. Based on the device owning, more than half of the participants own a good computer to connect the online courses and carry out their teachings online.

4.4. The Relationship between Teaching Experience, Students' Participation, Continuity, and Emergency Remote Teaching

The participants are asked to rate their experience about whether the transition to emergency remote teaching affects their teaching experience, whether the

Table 1. Educators' Perceptions of Themselves and Their Students.

	Completely Disagree	Disagree	Neither Agree Nor Disagree	Agree	Completely Agree
I feel ready to teach my classes remotely/online	5.9	14.7	16.8	43.3	19.3
I think my students are ready for distance/online learning	10.5	27.3	31.5	24.8	5.9
I am confident in using technology to support distance/online teaching	7.1	7.1	11.8	45.4	28.6

Table 2. Educators' Thoughts on Their Operational/Technical Settings.

	Completely Disagree	Disagree	Neither Agree Nor Disagree	Agree	Completely Agree
My internet connection is fine	10.9	8.0	13.0	42.9	25.2
I have got a good computer (laptop or desktop)	9.7	12.6	9.7	37.0	31.1
Most of my students have got a good internet connection	10.9	22.3	30.7	29.4	6.7

transition to emergency remote teaching affects their students' participation, and whether the continuity/integrity of the assessment of students' learning has been affected or not. Nearly all of participants think that their teaching experience has affected the transition process, and their students' participation and the continuity/integrity of assessment have been also affected on average.

4.5. Correlation Analysis

In this study, correlation analysis has been applied to understand the relationship between "the educators' perceptions of themselves and their students" and "the educator's thoughts on their or their students' operational/technical settings." In addition to this, the analysis has been applied to understand this general relationship and its dimensions, like:

- the type of institution;
- the field of studies;
- daily internet usage;
- the online teaching experience; and
- the duration assigned to transfer their jobs online.

According to Baş (2013, as cited in Çoşkun & Aşçı, 2020), correlation coefficients changes between -1 and $+1$ ($-1 \leq r \leq +1$): it refers to "very weak" if between 0.00 and 0.25, "weak" if between 0.26 and 0.49, "moderate" if between 0.50 and 0.69, "strong" if between 0.70 and 0.89, and "very strong" if between 0.90 and 1.00. When this relationship is positive, it refers to a linear relationship; however, it refers to a non-linear relationship if negative.

According to the correlation analysis results, as seen in Table 3, there is a positive meaningful relationship between the type of institution and the educator's thoughts on their or their students' operational/technical settings ($r = 0.239$; $p < 0.001$). In addition, there is a negative meaningful relationship between the field of studies and the educators' perceptions of themselves and their students ($r = -0,136$; $p = 0.03$).

Considering the daily internet usage of educators, there is a positive meaningful relationship with both the educator's thoughts on their or their students' operational/technical settings ($r = 0.209$; $p < 0.001$) and the educators' perceptions of

Table 3. Correlation Analysis of Educators' Perceptions on Themselves and Thoughts on Their Operational/Technical Settings.

	Correlations	Perceptions	Thoughts
Gender	Correlation coefficient (r)	0.086	0.051
	Sig. (p)	0.186	0.438
Age	Correlation coefficient (r)	−0.022	0.020
	Sig. (p)	0.733	0.760
Region	Correlation coefficient (r)	−0.018	0.119
	Sig. (p)	0.779	0.068
Educational level	Correlation coefficient (r)	0.108	0.014
	Sig. (p)	0.096	0.827
Type of institution	Correlation coefficient (r)	0.034	**0.239****
	Sig. (p)	0.598	0.000
Field of studies	Correlation coefficient (r)	**−0.136***	−0.028
	Sig. (p)	0.036	0.667
Teaching experience	Correlation coefficient (r)	−0.010	−0.019
	Sig. (p)	0.873	0.774
Daily internet usage	Correlation coefficient (r)	**0.166***	**0.209****
	Sig. (p)	0.010	0.001
Online teaching experience	Correlation coefficient (r)	**0.250****	**0.132***
	Sig. (p)	0.000	0.042
Duration for transferring their jobs online	Correlation coefficient (r)	**0.133***	**0.140***
	Sig. (p)	0.040	0.031
Teaching platforms	Correlation coefficient (r)	0.098	0.081
	Sig. (p)	0.133	0.215
Number of students	Correlation coefficient (r)	0.123	0.093
	Sig. (p)	0.059	0.151
Assistance/training to transfer online	Correlation coefficient (r)	−0.053	−0.085
	Sig. (p)	0.417	0.192
Perceptions of themselves and their students	Correlation coefficient (r)	1	**0.517****
	Sig. (p)		0.000
Thoughts on operational/technical settings	Correlation coefficient (r)	**0.517****	1
	Sig. (p)	0.000	

**. Correlation is significant at the 0.01 level (2-tailed).
*. Correlation is significant at the 0.05 level (2-tailed).

themselves and their students ($r = 0.166$; $p < 0.001$). In addition to the daily internet usage, online teaching experience is also a concern for grounding the discussion about transferring the studies and jobs online in an urgent way. When online teaching experience is taken into consideration, there is a positive meaningful relationship with the educators' perceptions of themselves and their students ($r = 0.250$; $p < 0.001$) and the educator's thoughts on their or their students' operational/technical settings ($r = 0.132$; $p = 0.04$).

To transfer the courses and reflect the experience which the educators gained, there is more or less some time to allocate for completing the tasks before starting to teach online. As understood from the data, there is a positive meaningful relationship between the time assigned for transferring their jobs online and the educators' perceptions of themselves and their students ($r = 0.133$; $p = 0.04$) or the educator's thoughts on their or their students' operational/technical settings ($r = 0.140$; $p = 0.03$). All in all, considering the data collected through the questionnaire, there is a positive meaningful relationship between the educators' perceptions of themselves and their students and the educator's thoughts on their or their students' operational/technical settings ($r = 0.517$; $p < 0.001$).

4.6. Themes Asserted by the Participants

In this study, while analyzing three open-ended questions, thematic analysis was used. The data from the open-ended questions were coded and categorized into similar groups by determining the major themes and sub-themes of the coding process. These categories were used to construct a matrix of major themes, which were sorted by the researchers under specific headings. The researchers and two field experts in the field coded the data separately to supply interrater reliability. The interrater reliability between the coders was 90%, and Miles and Huberman (1994) states that 80% agreement on 90% of codes is sufficient.

In the questionnaire, three open-ended questions were asked to understand the reflections of the COVID-19 pandemic on teaching. In the study, it is found out that there were some tools which teachers used to continue emergency remote teaching. Table 4 was created with the answers of the participant educators.

When this table is analyzed, it is possible to conclude that participants prefer synchronous video conferencing sessions to reach the students.

Many participants also stated that the curriculum needs to be designed. According to digital pedagogy principles, curriculums and instruction need to be organized.

The statements below assist these findings:

> [...] Distance education is not planned. Neither tutors nor students are ready. What will happen at the end of the process? For example, will those who complete the courses remotely be deemed successful, in other words, will they pass the class and therefore receive their diploma? What will happen to those who do not continue distance education? Everyone says something good, but no one says anything good in private conversations. Distance education has a physical negative impact on the teacher and the student; like a headache, the level of anxiety in psychology increases. (A Secondary School Teacher)

> [...] The new age pushes us to integrate technology in education. We all needed to get out of our shells and the children already adapted to this situation. (University Instructor)

Table 4. Emergency Remote Teaching Tools.

Learning Management System	Video Conferencing Tools	Pre-recorded Videos	Web Tools
Google Classroom	Zoom	YouTube videos	Powerpoint slides
Moodle	Adobe Connect	Record my video	Google document
Blackboard	Microsoft Teams	Powerpoint slides and audio	Kahoot, Quizziz, Genially
EBA		Khan Academy	Flipgrid
WhatsApp		Vitamin Öğretmen	Padlet
		Tonguç Academy	Mindmeister
			Storyboard

Participants have not only focused on the academic process, but the other concerns have become visible to all individuals who start caring about all the experiences. That's why digital inequality has been another issue in a remote learning environment according to the experiences collected in the questionnaire.

The statements below support this claim:

> [...] Not all students have access to the internet. Those who come from the village by public transportation cannot even reach the eba support point because the service does not work due to the pandemic. There is no bus anyway. I work in Kalecik. There is no local bus. I can hardly go to school from Akyurt with the other buses going to and from Ankara. I am crowded and there are buses in very few hours. The students in the village had great difficulty. Continuity and integrity cannot therefore be achieved. It cannot be provided even in lessons. (Even I am very scared that I will catch a virus on the bus. What should the children do even if there is a bus?). (Primary School Teacher)

Novelty effect is another concern that comes out in the study. Participants reflecting their experience in the open-ended questions frequently mention the decreasing participation in the online video conferencing sessions. Novelty effect might be claimed as the reason for this decreasing motivation and participation. "Novelty effect" (Metcalf et al., 2019) was explained as development in learning when new technology was introduced, attributable to increased interest in the new technology that tended to diminish as students became more familiar with it.

The statements below support these findings:

> [...] At first participation was high, but after some time, fewer students started to come. (High School Teacher)

> [...] Students were more motivated at the beginning but they are increasingly losing motivation. (Secondary School Teacher).

> [...] The fact that the online learning environment, which is far from interaction, cannot be adapted successfully. (High School Teacher)

> [...] My students are also in a different mood and motivation, as the conditions we are indirectly affecting people's psychology and health, and change our lifestyles and routines. The communication and needs of each of them have changed with their family. The environments that are suitable for studying and preparing for lessons are limited. It does not seem possible for such a difference to be a minimum standard measurement. (University Instructor)

When all these ideas are examined, participants stated several major concerns which were educators' thoughts on their operational/technical settings, educator, and student problems as detailed in Table 5.

5. DISCUSSION AND CONCLUSION

Effective communication strategies are the heart of emergency remote teaching. The center of any educational process is the human relationship between a student and a teacher (UNESCO, 2020). Teacher presence remains significant as we face the potential for protracted or periodic school closures in many regions of the world to control the spread of the virus. Central to effective remote teaching or learning is the establishment of teacher presence, whereby

Table 5. Themes Extracted through the Experience Participants Explained.

Educators' Thoughts on Their Operational/Technical Settings	Issues (Faced by Educators)	Issues (Faced by Students)
- Internet access - Computer	- Well-being - Increased workload - Demanding curriculum goals - Hardships on feedback giving - Ethics of examination - Teacher education (how-to training on effective feedback, testing and assessment, class management, and effective technology integration) - Management problems	- Well-being - Participation - Not knowing how to learn - Absence of experience on remote learning - Not having self-regulation - Lack of parental experience - Spending time in front of a device

teachers actively engage with their students through different forms of dialogue, activities, and assessment, and through meaningful contact (where possible) with pupils and parents. These forms of engagement are also critical for safeguarding, especially for vulnerable children (BETTSHOW, 2020). Schools are also places where we can encounter others, not like ourselves, others whom we learn from, others who expand our understanding of the global tapestry of ways of being human (UNESCO, 2020). As understood with these statements from different reports and articles, because of the COVID-19, educators' well-being ought to be considered. To support this well-being for both educators and learners, some concerns for the needs should be addressed under specific circumstances.

The results of this research show that there is a relationship between the type of institution, daily internet usage, online teaching experience, and the time assigned for transferring their teachings online between their perceptions and thoughts on different factors. In addition, we can infer that there is a relationship between the educators' perceptions of themselves and their students and the educator's thoughts on their or their students' operational/technical settings. By looking at these items closely with the help of open-ended questions, educators and students experience the same process within more or less similar aspects. That's why whatever is provided to tackle the transition process to the educators should be also available for learners and parents. By doing so, the equality issues can be coped with.

Any training program needs to be conducted to let everyone in this scenario get benefits at the same level. According to Penfold (2020), teacher professional development programs need to be blended, and he summarizes six features of these programs. These features overlap with the findings of this research. Educators ought to be informed by the latest evidence on adult learning and post-COVID-19 teacher professional programs need to be concerned with blended synchronous (real-time) and asynchronous (self-paced) lessons. These programs can also use video to demonstrate and share good practice and ensure that educators demonstrate a strong sense of "presence." Establishing familiar routines that can be sustained and offering a central repository of high-quality resources are another feature of post-COVID-19 teacher education.

The restrictions of the COVID-19 do not influence only the common lifestyle but also the curriculum at any level of educational settings. Most of the participant educators in this research reveal that there is a necessity to reduce the learning outcome in the curriculum into a new normal not to feel and make the learners feel overloaded. In this way, the amount of time which is spent in front of the screen is automatically reduced. According to Romano, Papa, and Saulle (2012), reducing curriculum outcomes facilitate the adoption of the curriculum in various subjects while designing an instruction. If an example should be given, while teaching math, science, literature, and history, subjects can be combined with scientific inventions and literary works during each term. For this reason, while creating the curriculum, we need to consider three important steps (Print, 1993) in general. The first one is significance. The criteria of significance can be applied in conditions where content is deliberated in terms of how fundamental it is to the theme under study. Where the content is contemplated as valuable to the subject, it is deemed significant, thus recommended for inclusion in a curriculum. The second one is relevance. Outcomes need to be correlated with community values, principles, and issues that might facilitate learners to be good citizens. The last one is utility. Educators who create a curriculum ought to acknowledge two effective perspectives of the learning outcomes: now and the future. As there are some outcomes that learners need to acquire now and there are also others which they need to acquire to be prepared for the future. During these days with the concerns of COVID-19, educators focus on the matters related to general education principles at the level of their teaching experience.

Since the beginning of the COVID-19 outbreak, educational settings are involved in unlocking a chance for flexibility in their goals, but the "new normal" in the educational settings cannot make the educators and learners see the relevancy, flexibility, and how their presence is responsive enough to tackle the transition process. The majority of challenges experienced by the educators illustrate the important degree of constraint: however, various opportunities are also evolved. To tackle not COVID-19, but teaching during COVID-19 needs to take some efforts on maximizing the utilization of digital technologies so that both educators and learners can get ready for a digital-oriented environment, especially by determining national policies to include various individuals from diverse backgrounds and experiences for effective delivery of education.

REFERENCES

Akbulut, Y. (2010). *Sosyal bilimlerde SPSS uygulamaları (SPSS applications in social sciences)*. İstanbul: İdeal Kültür Yayıncılık.

Ala-Mutka, K. (2011). Mapping digital competence: Towards a conceptual understanding. Seville: Institute for Prospective Technological Studies (IPTS), European Commission, Joint Research Centre. Retrieved from http://ftp.jrc.es/EURdoc/JRC67075_TN.pdf

Anderson, J. (2020). The coronavirus pandemic is reshaping education. *Quartz*. Retrieved from https://qz.com/1826369/how-coronavirus-is-changing-education/?fbclid=IwAR0_yZ_hf_5VGWSlua EwKpzdoD0YxSExGpSbZNAB8EHAH_ER_qSrUi5EgQ. Accessed on March 30, 2021.

Anderson, T., Rourke, L., Garrison, D., & Archer, W. (2001). Assessing teaching presence in a computer conferencing context. *Journal of Asynchronous Learning*, 5, 1–17.
Aşçı, S. (2020). *Bullying in the internet age*. Bern: Peter Lang D.
Basilaia, G., & Kvavadze, D. (2020). Transition to online education in schools during a SARS-CoV-2 Coronavirus (COVID-19) pandemic in Georgia. *Pedagogical Research*, 5(4), em0060. doi:10.29333/pr/7937
Baş, T. (2013). *Anket: anket nasıl hazırlanır?, Anket nasıl uygulanır?, Anket nasıl değerlendirilir? (Questionnaire: how to prepare? How to apply? How to analyze?)*. Ankara: Seçkin Yayıncılık.
Bauer, W., Pokorni, B., & Findeisen, S. (2019). Production assessment 4.0 – Methods for the development and evaluation of Industry 4.0 use cases. *Nature*, 793, 501–510. doi:10.1007/978-3-319-94196-7
Beetham, H., & Sharpe, R. (2007). *Rethinking pedagogy for a digital age: Designing for 21st century learning*. New York, NY: Routledge.
BETTSHOW. (2020). Learning in a crisis. Retrieved from https://www.bettshow.com/white-paper-learning-in-a-crisis. Accessed on March 30, 2021.
Bui, T. X., Sankaran, S., & Sebastian, I. M. (2003). A framework for measuring national e-readiness. *International Journal of Electronic Business*, 1(1), 3–22. https://doi.org/10.1504/ijeb.2003.002162
Craig, R. (2020). What students are doing is remote learning, not online learning: There is a difference. Retrieved from https://www.edsurge.com/news/2020-04-02-what-students-are-doing-is-remot-learningnot-online-learning-there-s-a-difference
Çoşkun, D., & Aşçı, S. (2020). Shared selves on social media: Examining the relationship between real and ideal selves of generation-Y Instagram users in Turkey. *Athens Journal of Mass Media and Communications*, 6(4), 229–254. doi:10.30958/ajmmc.6-4-2
El-Erian, M. A. (2010). *Navigating the new normal in industrial countries*. Washington, DC: International Monetary Fund.
Gammage, B., Plummer, D. C., Valdes, R., Mcgee, K., Potter, K., Tan, S., Aron, D., Hunter, R., Heiser, J., Prentice, B., Alvarez, G., Basso, M., Fiering, L., & Dulaney, K. (2011). Gartner's top predictions for IT organizations and users, 2011 and beyond: IT's growing transparency. *Managing*. doi:G00208367.
Garrison, D., Anderson, T., & Archer, W. (2000). Critical inquiry in a text-based environment: Computer conferencing in higher education. *The Internet and Higher Education*, 2, 87–105.
Garrison, D. R., & Akyol, Z. (2013). Toward the development of a metacognition construct for communities of inquiry. *The Internet and Higher Education*, 17, 84–89.
Grandzol, C. J., & Grandzol, J. R. (2010). Interaction in online courses: More is not always better. *Online Journal of Distance Learning Administration*, 13(2), 1–18.
Hodges, C., Moore, S., Lockee, B., Trust, T., & Bond, A. (2020). The difference between emergency remote teaching and online learning. EDUCAUSE Review. Retrieved from https://er.educause.edu/articles/2020/3/the-difference-between-emergency-remote-teaching-and-online-learning
Hong, A. J., & Kim, H. J. (2018). College students' digital readiness for academic engagement (DRAE) scale: Scale development and validation. *Asia-Pacific Education Researcher*, 27(4), 303–312. https://doi.org/10.1007/s40299-018-0387-0
Horrigan, J. (2016). Digital readiness gaps. Internet and Technology, 20 September 2016. Pew Research Centre. Retrieved from https://www.pewresearch.org/internet/2016/09/20/the-meaning-of-digital-readiness/. Accessed on June 12, 2020.
Ko, S., & Rossen, S. (2010). *Teaching online: A practical guide*. New York, NY: Routledge.
Liman Kaban, A., & Karadeniz, S. (2021). Children's reading comprehension and motivation on screen versus on paper. *SAGE Open*, 11(1), 1–11. doi:10.1177/2158244020988849
Means, B., Bakia, M., & Murphy, R. (2014). *Learning online: What research tells us about whether, when and how*. New York, NY: Routledge Taylor & Frances.
Metcalf, S. J., Chen, J. A., Kamarainen, A. M., Frumin, K. M., Vickrey, T. L., Grotzer, T. A., & Dede, C. J. (2019). Transitions in student motivation during a MUVE-based ecosystem science curriculum: An evaluation of the novelty effect. In K. Becnel (Ed.), *Emerging technologies in virtual learning environments* (pp. 96–115). Hershey, PA: IGI Global. doi:10.4018/978-1-5225-7987-8.ch005
McCarthy, S. A., & Samors, R. J. (2009). *Online learning as a strategic asset*. APLU-Sloan National Commission on Online Learning. Retrieved from http://sloanconsortium.org/publications/survey/index.asp

Miles, M. B., & Huberman, A. (1994). *Qualitative data analysis: An expanded sourcebook*. Thousand Oaks, CA: Sage Publications.

Mulenga, E. M., & Marbán, J. M. (2020). Is COVID-19 the gateway for digital learning in mathematics education?. *Contemporary Educational Technology*, *12*(2), ep269. doi:10.30935/cedtech/7949

Naciri, A., Baba, M. A., Achbani, A., & Kharbach, A. (2020). Mobile learning in higher education: Unavoidable alternative during COVID-19. *Aquademia*, *4*(1), ep20016. doi:10.29333/aquademia/8227

Orellana, A. (2006). Class size and interaction in online courses. *The Quarterly Review of Distance Education*, *7*(3), 229–248.

Palloff, R. M., & Pratt, K. (2007). *Building online learning communities: Effective strategies for the virtual classroom*. San Francisco, CA: Jossey-Bass.

Penfold, C. (2020). *Remote teacher professional development: six principles for effective programmes*. Education Development Trust. Retrieved from https://www.educationdevelopmenttrust.com/our-research-and-insights/commentary/remote-teacher-professional-development-six-princi

Pick, J. B., & Azari, R. (2011). A global model of technological utilization based on governmental, business-investment, social, and economic factors. *Journal of Management Information Systems*, *28*(1), 49–84. doi:10.2753/mis0742-1222280103

Print, M. (1993). *Curriculum development and design*. Sydney: SRM Production Services.

Romano, L., Papa, L., & Saulle, E. (2012). *Awesome lesson ideas to integrate science across the curriculum*. Teach Hub. Retrieved from http://www.teachhub.com/integratescience-across-curriculum

Sintema, E. J. (2020b). E-learning and smart revision portal for Zambian primary and secondary school learners: A digitalized virtual classroom in the COVID-19 era and beyond. *Aquademia*, *4*(2), ep20017. doi:10.29333/aquademia/8253

Swan, K. (2002). Building learning communities in online courses: The importance of interaction. *Education, Communication, & Information*, *2*(1), 23–49.

Taft, S. H., Perkowski, T., & Martin, L. S. (2011). A framework for evaluating class size in online education. *The Quarterly Review of Distance Education*, *12*(3), 181–197.

Tornatzky, L. G., & Fleischer, M. (1990). *The process of technology innovation*. Lexington, MA: Lexington Books. doi:10.1016/S0925-5273(98)00075-9

UNESCO. (2020, March 26). *Global education coalition*. UNESCO. Retrieved from https://en.unesco.org/covid19/educationresponse/globalcoalition

United Nations. (2020). Policy brief: Education during COVID-19 and beyond. Retrieved from https://unsdg.un.org/resources/policy-brief-education-during-covid-19-andbeyond

U.S. Department of Education. (2010). Office of Communications and Outreach, Guide to U.S. Department of Education Programs, Washington, D.C. https://www2.ed.gov/programs/gtep/gtep2010.pdf

Venkatesh, V., & Zhang, X. (2010). Unified theory of acceptance and use of technology: U.S. vs. China. *Journal of Global Information Technology Management*, *13*(1), 5–27. doi:10.1080/1097198X.2010.10856507

Williamson, B., Eynon, R., & Potter, J. (2020) Pandemic politics, pedagogies and practices: Digital technologies and distance education during the coronavirus emergency. *Learning, Media and Technology*, *45*(2), 107–114. doi:10.1080/17439884.2020.1761641

CHAPTER 9

SELF-DIRECTED LEARNING COMPETENCIES – A KEY TO SUCCESS IN ONLINE LEARNING: A LITHUANIAN CASE STUDY

Rasa Poceviciene

ABSTRACT

March 30, 2020 is a day of qualitative changes in the Lithuanian education system. This day in history – at least in the history of education – will record the day when mass distance learning began in the entire Lithuanian education system. All educational activities from kindergarten to higher and adult education were organized at a distance. In fact, the idea of distance learning was not so new in Lithuania. The first steps in developing a distance learning system in Lithuania were taken 25 years ago, but before the pandemic, it was more the exception than the norm and, of course, it had never been global. But in Spring 2020, all educational institutions (in general education during 2 weeks, in higher – even only during 2–3 days) were transformed from contact to distance learning. From a few-month perspective, it can be said that, despite all the circumstances, this transformation has been quite successful. In order to better understand the reasons for this quite sufficiently successful transition, it would be worthwhile to briefly review the organization of distance learning in Lithuania until the 2020 pandemic.

Keywords: Self-directed learning competencies; new literacies of students amid COVID 19; teaching/learning in a distance; success in online learning; higher education amid quarantine; self-directed learning competencies in distance education

DISTANCE LEARNING IN LITHUANIA BEFORE THE PANDEMIC

In general, the beginning of distance learning in Lithuania can be related to the end of the twentieth century – the beginning of the twenty-first century. The technologies that emerged in the country at that time already enabled the learning content to be brought outside the educational institution. In 1995, the ideas of distance learning in higher educational institutions were implemented by the distance learning centers operating in universities. Almost at the same time, the first steps of distance learning were done in schools of general education. The network of Lithuanian schools was created in which the distance learning system via "virtual classroom" operated. The Fotonas School of Young Physicists, the School of Young Programmers, and the Lithuanian National Academy of Students based their activities on the principles of distance learning. Elements of distance learning have also been introduced at the level of formal general educational curricular. But in practice, this has been more the exception than the rule. Distance learning was mainly oriented and mostly appointed to students with various health problems, special educational needs, participating in the training of highly skilled athletes, who could not attend schools regularly, preparing for international olympiads, international student mobility or exchange programs, as well as for those who temporarily lived abroad and those who have been temporarily deprived or restricted of liberty. In that time, special conditions have been set for schools wishing to organize distance learning. The school had to manage and administer a virtual learning environment with the necessary tools to organize the educational process. Members of the school community also had to be prepared. Students had to have access to appropriate information technology, and teachers to have mastered distance teaching and adapted the educational process to a virtual learning environment and to be able to use other informational computer technologies. Prior to the COVID-19 pandemic, distance learning services in Lithuania were provided only by more than 50 different educational institutions, and only a few schools in the country had officially recognized curricular (Distance learning or organization of learning in a distance?, 2020).

In higher education, the situation was similar. Although distance learning was used more widely than in general education, here also distance learning was more the exception than the rule. On the contrary, there have been many different projects, seminars, courses, and conferences for distance education during those two decades. Teachers improved their skills by preparing distance courses, creating the necessary infrastructure for their implementation, and developing relevant competencies. However, it must be acknowledged that at the beginning more attention was paid to the technological aspect of distance learning, but later it was realized that the creation of a qualitative distance learning course is possible only by combining technological, didactic, and psychological principles.

Thus, if by 2020 distance education was intended for a very small part of Lithuanian students and was provided by a relatively small number of teachers, at the beginning of 2020, the situation changed and distance teaching/learning became the norm, a daily practice for every Lithuanian student and teacher.

Distance education from a rather unusual phenomenon quickly became a common practice. This is partly due to the experience gained by some teachers and students in the past and, in particular, to the relatively high level of technological preparedness achieved before the pandemic. For this reason, with the start of the first quarantine, it was only necessary to complete some of the technological preparation activities required for global distance teaching/learning. It was possible to do it quickly and with high quality also due to the sufficiently well-developed IT infrastructure and IT culture in Lithuania (Table 1).

As we can see, even before the pandemic, 76.7% of the population had a personal computer; more than 80% of them had internet and broadband internet access. And those numbers were constantly growing. The absolute majority of young people (98.0/98.3/98.0%) even before the pandemic have used smart phones (Table 2).

Table 1. Households Having Personal Computers and Internet Access (Database of Indicators, 2020).

Location	Computers		Internet Access		Broadband Internet Access	
	2019	2020[a]	2019	2020[a]	2019	2020[a]
City and village	76.7	76.7	81.5	82.1	81.4	81.8
Cities	82.4	84.1	85.6	87.2	85.6	87.2
Towns	79.2	79.8	83.2	83.9	83.2	83.8
Other towns	74.2	72.5	79.3	78.3	79.3	78.1
Village	70.9	69.9	77.7	78.1	77.2	77.4

[a]First quarter (before the quarantine).

Table 2. Persons Who Have Used a Smartphone (Database of Indicators, 2020).

Age of the Respondents	2020 Years
All persons aged 16–74	77.5
16–24	98.0
16–29	98.3
25–34	98.0
35–44	93.0
45–54	79.9
55–64	61.5
65–74	34.5

DISTANCE LEARNING IN LITHUANIA AT THE BEGINNING OF QUARANTINE IN SPRING OF 2020

At the beginning of 2020, the COVID-19 pandemic spread, the Minister of Education, Science and Sport (MESS) has established that until the end of the quarantine period, all the levels of Lithuanian educational system are carried out by distance learning organizing. This was the rule for the entire Lithuanian educational system. And if before the pandemic schools must confirm their technical and academic preparedness for distance education, now, at the time of the transition of all students in the country to the way of organizing distance education, a rare school met all the established criteria for the organizing of such education. The new order no longer regulated either the target groups of students or the requirements for the technical and educational base of the school as it was before the pandemic (Distance learning or organization of learning in a distance?, 2020).

Measures have been taken to adapt to the new situation as quickly as possible. First, existing legislation has been supplemented. Another important step was to take care of creating technical and technological conditions for all Lithuanian students to organize distance learning. Through the efforts of MESS and other education administrators, tablets and laptops and tools for children with special educational needs were purchased, borrowed, and distributed to students and teachers. It was for general education. For higher education, the institutions themselves try to solve all such problems. All educational institutions had free access to teaching platforms (Google G-Suite for Education, Microsoft Office 365, and Moodle). At the same time, other necessary elements of the organizing of distance learning were taken care of – the content of education, the competencies of teachers and learners, etc. An internet portal "Distance learning (s)" was set up to share information, digital resources, and good practice (but more for general education than for higher education); models for the organizing of teaching and learning at a distance or by combining the distance and daily educational process was developed; and training for teachers to improve their competencies to work remotely has started (Distance learning or organization of learning in a distance?, 2020).

According to Research of Vytautas Magnus University researchers: Lithuanian schools passed the quarantine exam (2020), in the survey conducted in May 2020, 81.6% of principals of educational institutions said they had conducted short distance courses for teachers on the use of various online tools and platforms. Two-thirds of those surveyed said that teachers' technical capacity to work from home had been improved and that they had received regular technical support. About 45.6% of the principals said they had prepared instructions for teachers on the use of online tools, and 41.1% as well as general didactic guidelines also.

After the first uncertainty, the Lithuanian educational community quite quickly adopted their behavior to the new circumstances. Lithuanian teachers improved their education in various ways by becoming specialists in the field of distance learning. The transfer of the teaching process to the virtual space took place in response to the emerging needs. Some normative acts and methodological materials were prepared during the summer till the new schooling year which in Lithuania begins on September 1 (e.g. "Distance Learning/Education Guide for General Education, 2020" for general education). The purpose of this guide was to summarize the experience of organizing distance education during the first quarantine and to provide recommendations for the new schooling year. In the guide not only the basics of distance learning were described and the general recommendations for the organization of distance learning were presented, but also the specific features of distance education at different levels (primary, basic, and secondary education) of the educational system were analyzed and even some concrete demands for the organizing of education in a distance were discussed.

It must be acknowledged that higher education did not receive such attention and such methodological support. Maybe because they were more prepared for distance education even before the pandemic. As it was mentioned, higher education in Lithuania already before the quarantine had a much higher level of experience in the organization of distance learning than general education.

On the contrary, despite all the efforts and support for teachers, the full potential of distance education itself was far from being exploited. According to the analysis of theoretical content, in general, distance teaching/learning can be understood as a way, a form, or a strategy of teaching/learning, and it could be organized on the level of way, form, or strategy; but only on the strategy level, all the possibilities of distance education can be realized fully. Only then it can meet all the goals and only such level of distance education enable the implementation of all the principles of self-directed learning (Table 3).

Table 3. Functional Purposes of Distance Learning.

Types of Distance Learning	Description
As a way	Correspondence and audiovisual transmission of the content of a certain part of the educational material (e.g. lecture)
As a form	A certain way of teacher–student interaction that ensures their mutual connection and is used as an alternative to traditional classroom teaching
As a strategy	An individual way for students to organize and use their specific opportunities to learn effectively in order to give them more freedom to manage the learning process

Source: Melnikovas (2017).

Despite all the efforts made, the results of the surveys show that teachers lacked certain skills, which prevented them from making a full and successful transition to organizing education at a distance.

In addition to the partially low level of digital literacy (the opinion of a quarter of respondents themselves, especially elder ones), a similar proportion of teachers also faced problems in developing or adapting teaching materials to distance teaching/learning. For a relatively large proportion (over 40%) of teachers, it was not clear enough how to maintain students' interest and motivate learning in online education, what could be left from contact teaching/learning process (study methods, evaluation procedures, methods and criteria, etc.) and what couldn't, what are the new opportunities in a distance and online education, how it is possible to use them instead to try to adopt that from contact education, and what skills are necessary for students and teachers in online education. The answers to those questions could be based on the analysis of the other surveys that were organized quite quickly after the first quarantine – in the summer of 2020. One such survey was conducted by the Lithuanian Students' Union (LSU) (Studies during Quarantine, 2020).

In order to better understand the results of the research, it would be expedient in a few words to present the higher education system in Lithuania. As elsewhere, in Lithuania, there are three levels of studies: bachelors, masters, and doctoral. However, unlike in other European countries, masters and doctoral studies in Lithuania are currently carried out exclusively at universities. Meanwhile, bachelor's level studies in Lithuania are implemented according to two types of study programs: colleges (in other words, applied science universities; professional bachelor's) and universities (bachelor's) (For Pupils and Students, 2020).

Professional bachelor's degree programs in colleges are more focused on professional activities and the applied nature of research conducted in those institutions. University undergraduate programs, meanwhile, are more academic, and the nature of university-based research is more fundamental than applied. All the other demands related to studies organization and quality are very similar and are not so important for the main topic of this book.

The survey of the LSU was conducted in 2020. From May 15 until June 15, 1120 bachelor and master students participated. The study sample was random. Respondents were randomly selected from LSU databases (Studies during Quarantine, 2020).

The main conclusions were made after analyzing the data:

- When lectures were canceled at higher education institutions, they were mostly organized online (90% at universities and 81% at colleges). This means that during the first quarantine, it was not distance learning, but more online education. For this reason, it would be more accurate and correct to use the terms "online learning" when referring to distance learning during the first quarantine, but not to "distance learning" or "distance education." In particular, the simultaneous and synchronous virtual communication between teacher and students and the use of special learning platforms is a very attractive but optional feature of distance learning. It was unnecessarily forgotten that asynchronous education can take place in addition to synchronous one. This means that distance teaching/learning also takes place when there is a mismatch in time between the delivery of teaching/learning material and the learning based on it. In fact, this option is very important and even more characteristic and in line with the very essence of distance learning. After all, one of the main goals of distance education is to create an education system enabling society to participate in lifelong learning at the right time, in the right place, and at the right pace for every learner.
- Based on the results of the survey, students were quite positive about the teachers' qualification to organize studies at a distance. About 33% of respondents think that all teachers and 36% of respondents think that majority of them have enough technical skills to organize studies remotely. Nearly 80% of teachers regularly provided course assignments (resources for reading, homework, etc.); almost 75% answered students' questions in a timely manner and provided feedback on completed assignments; 72% informed students how the course exam would be organized and executed, and nearly 63% were open to students' suggestions for improving studies in a distance.

- And although many students agreed that during the lectures in a distance they acquired necessary knowledge and skills, one-third of students (both at universities and colleges) think that their practical skills because of online education are lower than they would be in contact education.
- Evaluating the workload, nearly half of the students' mentioned that the workload increased, to a third – has not changed.

The general satisfaction in education in a distance is presented in Table 4.

And although in general it can be said that the students were satisfied with the organization of distance learning, the quality of the lectures satisfied them more than the quality of the seminars. And this, I think, is natural, because synchronous online education creates sufficient conditions for teaching and for the lectures, but it is not so suitable for the development of practical skills due to technological peculiarities alone. In addition, it showed the challenges that teachers faced when teaching online, when they tried to continue the usual contact teaching only on another platform – online. This situation of confusion can be confirmed by the fact that about 22% university students and even 44% students in colleges had difficulty assessing the quality of the seminars. Most likely, they could not assess the quality of the distance seminars precisely because they were completely different from the contact-organized seminars. However, it should be noted that such a situation was only during the first quarantine (Spring 2020). For the second one, teachers were already more prepared in both technical and didactic aspects. They have already learned new opportunities to activate students in online teaching/learning, to organize group work, discussions, practical works, to find new and suitable for online education tools and methods for evaluation, and so on (Daukilas & Kasperiūnienė, 2011; Haddad, Ferreira, & Faria, 2014; Simonson, Smaldino, Albright, & Zvacek, 2008). They were already more prepared for new forms of teaching/learning, methods, and technologies, and had more or less adapted online curricular.

And only later, after seminars and courses, in many cases organized by the universities and colleges themselves (learning in the organization and on the workplace) and recommendations, they realized that they needed to use other methods, techniques and methods than they used in contact education by the aim to achieve the same learning outcomes. But it is great that the support teachers provided to the students, as well as the information and support provided by the higher education institution's administration, was sufficient and appreciated by the students (Table 5).

More challenges had to be overcome during the preparation of the final work (preparation of the final work and public presentation in the qualification committee is a mandatory part of the study program) – 24% university students and 43% students in colleges had to change the topic of the thesis, research methods, research sample, and so on due to quarantine and without the possibility to physically visit companies and other organizations. This was more characteristic for students in colleges, due to their greater focus on practice and applied models of study and research. Also, it could be said about engineering, technological studies as well as medicine and execution of professional practices in those fields

Table 4. General Satisfaction in Education in a Distance.

Level of Satisfaction	Very Satisfied		Rather Satisfied		Rather Dissatisfied		Completely Dissatisfied		No Opinion	
Type of institution	University	College	University	College	University	College	University	College	University	College
Organization of lectures	19	16	48	48	22	18	8	14	4	4
Organization of seminars	15	12	38	28	17	8	9	8	21	44
Teachers' support	23	20	53	56	15	14	3	6	6	5
Information and support provided by the HEI[a]	24	23	39	47	15	12	11	9	11	9

[a]Higher educational Institution.

Table 5. Level of Satisfaction of Students.

Level of Satisfaction	Totally Agree		Rather Agree		Rather Disagree		Totally Disagree		No Opinion	
Type of institution	University	College	University	College	University	College	University	College	University	College
I was quick to adapt to the new learning experience	34	36	**38**	**41**	18	13	7	8	4	4
I think I will learn well the things taught this semester	15	18	26	25	**30**	**27**	19	19	10	11
My academic achievements due to distance learning have improved	8	14	22	28	**34**	22	18	16	18	20

Note: Bold indicates the highest values during all the periods.

that they also had more challenges than social sciences and humanities (Studies during Quarantine, 2020).

But all those changes and challenges were more or less manageable. And if to look at what factors – knowledge, skills, abilities, competencies, and attitudes – allowed managing them, it is obvious that the most important there were the abilities and skills of managing of your teaching/learning process. This can be illustrated by the results of one of the surveys. Together with other researchers, the survey was organized by the author of the chapter in one of the five largest colleges in Lithuania – Šiauliai State College. The survey was implemented in June 2020. The survey was qualitative and this allowed the researchers to gain a deeper understanding of the factors of success and failure of online education during the first quarantine. A total of 85 students of social sciences and business and management, as well as 16 teachers of humanities and social sciences, participated in this survey.

The difficulties raised for the students are presented in Table 6.

Table 6. Difficulties Raised for the Students During the First Quarantine.

Difficulties	Only at the Beginning	During All the Periods	There Were No Problems At All
Quality of internet at home	20.3	10.1	69.6
Possession of hardware and software	18.8	7.2	72.5
Stress	29	**26.1**	46.4
Fear of IT and cameras	21.7	**21.7**	58
Theoretical material and practical tasks are not clear and suitable for distance learning	2.6	15.9	59.4
Difficulties of adaptation to the changes of workload and regime	21.7	**20.3**	59.4
Being not able for self-motivation	18.8	11.6	66.7
Being not able to plan your time	17.4	8.7	68.1
Too many tasks	14.5	**20.3**	65.2
Too short time for executing the tasks	15.9	18.8	62.3
Too often provision of new tasks	14.5	13	69.6
Too complex, too difficult tasks	14.5	18.8	62.3
The same tasks for all (no possibility to choose)	13	**23.2**	60.9

Note: Bold indicates the highest values during all the periods.

It should be mentioned that most of the students stated that they had no problems and difficulties at the beginning or end of the quarantine. The results in the table show quite well that most of the difficulties raised at the beginning of online education in 3.5 months have been overcome. Some of them still remained quite big (like *Stress* and *difficulty adapting to workload and regime changes*), others are the same (like *IT and camera fears*), others are even bigger (*Too many tasks* and *the same tasks for everyone*) (*none options*).

In response to another question, students stressed that among all the factors that helped them the most to overcome all the challenges and difficulties, there was good organization of online studies by teachers (58%) and academic support for students (31.9%). Also, distance learning experience (14.5%), skills of time management (30.4%), and independent work (46,4%) are the factors that had positive influence on the students' success in online education.

Teachers' opinions about their experience in online education are presented in Table 7.

Here, we also see that at the beginning there were more challenges and difficulties, especially didactic, but later majority of them were overcome. Reflecting on their success and failures, teachers mentioned that the ability to quickly adapt themselves to new working conditions (66.7%), experience in distance education and time management skills (60%), didactic knowledge of distance education and seminars (53.3%), and openness for innovations (46.7%) were the most important factors to achieve success.

Table 7. Teachers' Opinions about Their Experience in Online Education during the First Quarantine.

Challenges Overcame/ Did Not Overcame	Aspects	Items
Challenges overcame successfully	Technical	• Technological problems (new IT tools, programs, etc.) • Insufficient technical capabilities available at home (cameras, etc.) • Distrust of your computer literacy knowledge and skills
	Didactic	• Lack of didactic knowledge and skills of distance teaching/learning • Too short time to prepare for quality work with students • Adaptation of materials and tasks to distance learning • Coordination of contact and distance learning • Lack of general practical advice for working in a distance • Creation of new and different educational environments that meet the interests of students • Maintaining the role of the teacher as a policy-maker and consultant rather than a source of information • Quality assurance and monitoring of the performance of practical tasks (e.g. through videos, etc.) • Organization of internships for students and development of students' practical skills in social partner companies in a distance • Too much information and variety about the organization of distance learning
	Psychological	• Fear of technology, video cameras
Challenges did not overcame successfully	Technical	• Quality of internet services during congestion in the homes of study participants • Disruptions due to different technical capabilities of students/teachers
	Didactic	• Changes in the workload and regime (without clear separation of work and rest time) • Maximum assurance of compliance with the rules of academic ethics, academic integrity, and internet etiquette • Too much information and variety about the organization of distance learning
	Psychological	• Intensity of distance teaching/learning and significantly increased workload • Greater personalization of the study process

SELF-DIRECTED LEARNING COMPETENCIES IN DISTANCE AND ONLINE EDUCATION

From all that what already is said, it becomes the clear idea that some competencies and skills are needed for the more successful online education, distance teaching/learning, and even for all forms of education. And those skills and competencies could be related to the ability of every learner to manage his or her own learning process, to be able to regulate himself or herself. In other words, every learner who would like to achieve success, especially online, in distance education, needs to have self-directed learning competencies.

The self-directed learning concept and the idea itself indeed are not very new. Already M. Knowles (1983) wrote that in its broadest meaning,

> "self-directed learning" describes a process by which learners take their initiative (without or with small support from others) in diagnosing their learning needs, formulating learning goals, identify human and material resources for learning, choosing and implement appropriate learning strategies, and evaluating learning outcomes.

But, till now this concept is more oriented to non-formal adult education. Nowadays and especially in education in a distance, online education, distance teaching/learning context, more and more clear that we need to enable our learners, our students to manage their learning process by themselves, because even physically we have no any possibility to do this. Students are not in the classrooms anymore and we as the teachers need to divide the responsibilities on the educational process and the success. So, announced by M. Knowles (1983) and developed by the other scientists (Brockett & Hiemstra, 1991; Candy, 1991; Kazlauskienė, Gaučaitė, Masiliauskienė, & Pocevičienė, 2013; Kazlauskienė, Gaučaitė, & Pocevičienė, 2015, 2016; Kazlauskienė, Masiliauskienė, Gaučaitė, & Pocevičienė, 2010; Poceviciene, 2014, 2019; Sumuer, 2018), self-directed learning competences are more and more important in twenty-first century and not only in online education, but in all.

All the more so as more and more opinions are heard that distance learning will continue even after a pandemic and quarantine. It is likely that not to the same extent as now, but the experience and skills gained to work remotely, the infrastructure, and the legal, material, and didactic basis created for distance and online education should not be forgotten. All the more so as a significant number of students and teachers are in favor of distance learning, see its many advantages and already have ideas on how to manage or overcome existing limitations. According to most, distance learning would be a great opportunity to study for those who, due to various reasons (disability, remoteness, nature of work, need to care for children, elderly or disabled people at home, etc.), cannot attend the studies. It would not only increase the availability of studies, but also improve their quality, for example, inviting a lecturer, a real expert, and specialist in his/her field, from abroad for one or two lectures. Also, one of the most valuable features of online education is that students can access the course and study it at any time convenient to them, in any place convenient to them, and for as long as they need it, without direct and synchronous contact with teachers. On the contrary, it is clear that in order to learn independently, even remotely and asynchronously, students need to know how to organize and manage their learning and time, how to motivate themselves, and so on. In other words, they need self-directed learning competencies. Teachers also need to know how to organize studies for self-directed learners, how to develop those skills for students, how to prepare online courses for this purpose, and, in general, what are the main guidelines and criteria for a qualitative online course in higher education.

Another aspect is that in many cases, even in higher education, teachers will have to devote time and effort in developing their competencies for their students, as this has still not been done in general education.

Attention and need to develop self-directed learning competencies is also based on the learning paradigm that focuses on the learner, but not on the teacher. Such competencies are necessary for the future labor market. In the TOP list of the competencies that will be necessary for the employee in 2030 according to the World Economic Forum: The Top 10 Skills You'll Need for the Future of Work (2020), there are many skills related to self-directed learning, for example, judgment and decision making, active learning, learning strategies, deductive reasoning, complex problem solving, etc.

ESSENCE AND CONCEPT OF SELF-DIRECTED LEARNING COMPETENCE

The following self-directed learning abilities are most often distinguished (Kazlauskienė et al., 2010, 2013, 2015, 2016; Knowles, 1983; Pocevičienė, 2014, 2019):

- *Ability to analyze your knowledge in various fields and understand what you already know, have learned, are able to do, and what more needs to be learned.* All these not only help to learn purposefully, but also has a positive effect on learning motivation, strengthens and maintains a positive attitude toward learning, and so on. A student with this ability is not afraid of its scope when given a new task; won't worry about not being able to do it or running out of time, and so on. On the contrary, he will first review the submitted material, analyze it in terms of knowledge/ignorance, and see that if some of the information provided is in fact already known. And that means he won't have to re-learn them unless he will not remember them. The other information somewhere else will be heard, read, known, but not fully and so on. And, finally, the new, unknown information, but in any case, it will be a smaller amount of information that learning will take more time. Naturally, such an analysis will increase the learner's motivation; he will realize that the task could be completed and that it may not require much effort.
- *Ability to analyze one's own learning process and oneself as a learner*, that is, understand which personal qualities, features, and abilities help and which hinder successful learning; what is the personal learning style; and so on. This ability provides excellent prerequisites for achieving the desired learning

outcomes through optimal time and effort, as this ability not only helps to understand which personal qualities and abilities help and what hinders successful learning; but also finds out what the personal learning style is and how to learn according to a certain learning style. Because every learning style has its own learning technologies that are most acceptable for that learner and that enable the learner to achieve good study results with optimal (not too many, not too less) efforts and time.
- *Ability to set our own learning goals and objectives, even when working in an audience, with others, and a teacher.* The ability enhances learning motivation, especially self-motivation because when learning to achieve one's individual learning goals, engagement is always higher. After all, when we learn for ourselves and by ourselves, it is always easier to overcome various learning difficulties and obstacles.
- *Ability to plan your learning time.* It not only helps to achieve learning outcomes on time but also teaches how to manage one's learning process, to learn systematically, and consistently. And this, in turn, evokes positive emotions, increases self-confidence, motivation to learn, and so on.
- *Ability to choose appropriate and high-quality learning content*, even if it is routinely provided by a teacher, not only increases interest in teaching/learning, but also makes it relevant and meaningful. After all, we always prefer to learn what we are interested in, what seems useful, and so on. On the contrary, more and more diverse information, including in terms of quality, reaches learners online, through the media, etc., so that a teacher or a book is no longer the only source of information. Learners often have to choose the necessary, correct, reliable, and high-quality information themselves. Here, it becomes very important to know on the basis of which criteria we can select the right, reliable, and correct information.
- *Ability to manage information*, that is, not only to find appropriate and reliable sources of information, to select the necessary material, but also to manage it, assess its completeness, reliability, accuracy, and combine information obtained from different sources, and construct new knowledge, etc.
- *Ability to choose appropriate learning strategies, methods, tools, learning resources, environment*, etc. It helps the learner complete tasks and achieve learning goals in the optimal time with optimal cost.
- *Ability to act purposefully to achieve the set tasks*, that is, to link new learning materials with existing ones, to learn from experience and through experience, and so on.
- *Ability to motivate oneself or more exactly to enable students to find the meaning* – their own meaning – of learning, of their studies. This idea is based on existentialist ideas of V. E. Frankl (1992) that the only stimulus for a person to act and to live is his/her ability to discover meaning in what he/she does and how he/she lives. Based on this philosophy, it could be argued that even in the educational process, there is no point in motivating students from the outside (because each person has a unique and individual meaning and the way to find it), and a learning environment needs to be created for them to discover their own meaning and only that meaning will motivate them.

- *Ability to reflect*, to reflect on and/or evaluate their learning process and results in terms of set goals or other selected criteria, to identify the reasons for success and failure. This ability is treated as one of the basic, essential self-directed learning skills. It is also very much needed for the ability to anticipate opportunities and strategies for improving one's learning process.
- *Ability to anticipate opportunities and strategies for improving one's learning process*. In summary, self-directed learning is learning in which the learner, even when learning together with others, is ready and able to independently set individual learning goals, adjust them according to need and/or situation, plan and organize their learning process, solve the problems of various kinds, to reflect on one's own learning experience and to evaluate the results obtained and the process itself, and to manage the further course of one's own learning process on the basis of those reflections and assessments (Kazlauskienė et al., 2010, 2013, 2015, 2016; Pocevičienė, 2019, 2014).

DEVELOPMENT OF SELF-DIRECTED LEARNING COMPETENCE

To develop the skills and competence, first of all, we need to change our viewpoint from a teaching to a learning paradigm. It should be mentioned that at the theoretical level in Lithuania as in many other countries this shift is done already. But in the educational practice not fully – only some separate elements, some innovations that could be related to the self-directed learning, but there is no systematic approach here, especially in higher education. For example, in every study program according to the regulation of Centre for Quality Assessment in Higher Education in Lithuania (Study Programme Assessment, 2020) study results are formulating in five aspects: *knowledge and its application, research skills, special abilities, social abilities*, and *personal abilities*, there is no systematic approach to the social and personal abilities and their development. In the Descriptors of the Study Field's (2020), there are recommendations on what exactly abilities, skills, and competencies could be developed for specialists in different study fields, and the set of possible skills and competencies are suggested, but self-directed learning competence is not yet involved in it. Of course, this competence could be related and understandable under such competencies as being able to learn the subjects of the area of professional activities independently or improve and increase professional competence independently through lifelong learning. On the contrary, it could be understood why it is not presented in those descriptors. For implementing self-directed learning competence into the curricular, it is necessary to overcome some objections and to create the necessary conditions. The most important ones are the following:

- Creation of free choice opportunities and shared and conscious responsibility of all the partners of the educational process. In practice, it means that on all steps of the educational process (from the study plan to the assessment of

the achieved study results), students have the possibility to make their own decision and choice, but it also means that after they have chosen or made a decision they become responsible for the results.
- Atmosphere of trust among all the members of the educational process – from students to teachers, administration of higher educational institution even to stakeholders in the society or labor market.
- Changes in the planning of educational activities in every subject and course. Changes in planning mean that it should be done from exactly the beginning of any educational activity and made focus at first on the activities of students (learning, student-centered paradigm), but not a teacher's (teaching paradigm). It means to plan the activities of students at first and only then think about what could or should be the actions of the teacher. It also means that in this system teacher is not the only resource for studies anymore or the main conductor of all the curricular. All studies are the co-operation and co-work of students and teachers in all phases (planning, organizing, commanding, coordinating, and controlling; McLean, 2011) of management of any process. This idea is fully in line with the ECTS concept (a standard means for comparing academic credits in Europe and in the cooperating countries, that is, the "volume of learning based on the defined learning outcomes and their associated workload of student") (What is the European Credit System (ECTS), 2020).
- Recognition of the individuality and uniqueness of everyone and knowing yourself as a learner and your own learning styles (from *learning styles according to the way information is processed till David Kolb's experiential learning styles and learning styles according to H. Gardner's theory of multiple intelligence, etc.*). It is obvious that every person has his/her personal learning style – the way to gather, work with, and share the information. And the possibility to work according to this personal learning style saves efforts and time everyone needs for learning and studying, and also motivate more and involve students in the study process. The purpose for a teacher is to recognize that each person has a personal learning style, which is determined by the peculiarities of physical, mental, social development, and to create the teaching/learning environment (also in online and distance education) suitable for all learning styles, the environment of universal design in what every student could freely choose the best for him/her the ways and the methods, strategies, and the model of studying. Also to accept the philosophy, the attitude that everyone can learn, study, do, etc., but it could be that only in his/her unique way. Self-directed learning not only encourages consideration of each learner's learning style but also provides excellent opportunities to individualize and personalize teaching.
- Self-directed learning is inseparable from reflective learning. According to P. Jarvis (2001), reflection reveals to a person what learning problems he has and is a moment that promotes learning. By reflecting, the learner can get to know himself/herself better, improve activities and relationships with the environment, take a new look at the accumulated knowledge and experience, reflect

on activities in the past, and reflectively perform activities here and now. Reflective learning promotes active and conscious commitment, provides opportunities to evaluate and change beliefs and assumptions, and applied theories that directly influence actions. Meta-cognitive self-reflection – self-assessment of one's abilities and shortcomings, problem-solving strategies, emotions (e.g. fear of excessive demands) should be the main tool of reflection and the main activity in the entire educational process.

Summarizing the above thoughts, it can be said that the ability to learn for self-directed today is necessary due to the accelerating forth industrial revolution. Different technologies and digitalization in all aspects of our life in near future will be no longer an exception, but rather a tradition and a norm.

Already now approximately a year from the beginning of the pandemic more and more often it is possible to hear the opinion that we will never come back to the previous world. It means that once technologies as well as online, distance, and other similar models of education came to our life, they will be our reality. At the same time, it means that for our students to be successful in their studies and later in the labor market, which may become more and more global, need to become self-directed learner as earlier as possible.

Changing workplaces also highlights the need for self-directed learning competencies and skills. This is especially relevant in co-working spaces as well as in online working or working in a distance. Until recently described as a novelty, these co-working spaces and working in a distance are becoming increasingly popular, but only those who are able to manage their working time and activities, who are able to work and motivate themselves to work on their own, without external impulses or control, that is those who have self-directed learning (learning), will be able to work in such places.

And distance education is a great opportunity to develop these competencies. Only it must be organized according to certain didactic principles, because distance education is not only technology but also education, and above all, learning that also has its own principles and theories, and which in the case of distance learning is fundamentally different from working in classrooms. And the first such principle, from didactic attitude, is the realization that distance learning is primarily learning and it fundamentally changes our activities. It changes not only externally but also internally.

REFERENCES

Brockett, R. G., & Hiemstra, R. (1991). *Self-direction in adult learning: Perspectives on theory, research, and practice*. London: Routledge.

Candy, P. C. (1991). *Self-direction for lifelong learning: A comprehensive guide to theory and practice*. Oxford: Jossey-Bass.

Database of Indicators. (2020). Retrieved from https://osp.stat.gov.lt/statistiniu-rodikliu-analize?indicator=S4R029#/ (in Lithuanian).

Daukilas, S., & Kasperiūnienė, J. (2011). *Design and implementation of e-learning courses*. Kaunas. Retrieved from http://dspace.lzuu.lt/bitstream/1/497/1/e_mokymo_kursu_projektavimas_ir_realizavimas_metodika.pdf (in Lithuanian).

Descriptors of the Study Field. (2020). Retrieved from https://www.skvc.lt/default/lt/kokybes-uztikrinimas/krypciu-aprasai (in Lithuanian).
Distance Learning/Education Guide for General Education. (2020). Retrieved from https://www.emokykla.lt/upload/nuotolinis/Nuotolinio%20mokymo%20Vadovas_3.pdf (in Lithuanian).
Distance learning or organization of learning in a distance? (2020). *Analysis of educational problems*, 2020, November, No. 8 (186). ISSN 2669-0977. Retrieved from Nuotolinis-mokymas_Svietimo_problemos_analize.pdf (in Lithuanian).
For Pupils and Students. (2020). Retrieved from https://www.smm.lt/web/lt/mokiniams-ir-studentams (in Lithuanian)
Frankl, V. E. (1992). Man's search for meaning. Retrieved from https://edisciplinas.usp.br/pluginfile.php/3403095/mod_resource/content/1/56ViktorFrankl_Mans%20Search.pdf
Haddad, M., Ferreira, N., & Faria, A. (2014). The use of educational technologies in distance education – Enabling the appropriation of teaching and learning process. *Open Journal of Social Sciences*, 2, 54–58. Retrieved from https://pdfs.semanticscholar.org/3f40/3a1dae3ebd56228e4be7cfd0562ab18c329f.pdf
Jarvis, P. (2001). *Learning paradoxes*. Kaunas: VDU (in Lithuanian).
Kazlauskienė, R., Gaučaitė, E., Masiliauskienė, R., & Pocevičienė, R. (2013). Self-directed education oriented to the innovative decisions: As challenge and possibility for student and teacher. In *Childhood and Education – 2013, Papers of scientific practical conference*, Šiauliai, pp. 65–75. ISBN 978-9955-32-193-4 (in Lithuanian).
Kazlauskienė, A., Gaučaitė, R., & Pocevičienė, R. (2015). Implementation of the self-directed learning system in general education schools: Analysis of manifestation of changes. *Journal of Education and Training*, 2(1), 155–167. ISSN 2330-9709.
Kazlauskienė, A., Gaučaitė, R., Pocevičienė, R. (2016). Preconditions for sustainable changes in didactics applying self-directed learning in the general education school. *Journal of Teacher Education for Sustainability*, 18(2), 105–118. doi:10.1515/jtes-2016-0018. ISSN 1691-4147. eISSN 1691-5534.
Kazlauskienė, A., Masiliauskienė, E., Gaučaitė, R., Pocevičienė, R. (2010). Organizing of self-directed learning at school as educational innovation: Context of Bologna processes. *Mokytojų ugdymas: mokslo darbai*, 15(2), 71–79. ISSN 1822-119X (IndexCopernicus nuo 2008) (in Lithuanian).
Knowles, M. S. (1983). *Self-directed learning. A guide for learners and teachers*. Englewood, NJ: Cambridge Adult Education.
McLean, J. (2011). Fayol – Standing the test of time. *Manager: British Journal of Administrative Management*, 74, 32–33. ISSN 1353-5188.
Melnikovas, A. (2017). Potential of distance education as a means of the Lithuanian armed forces' peacetime functional performance enhancement. *Factors of Modern Society Education*, 2, 125–136 (in Lithuanian).
Poceviciene, R. (2014). Learning to learn competency as the necessary condition for quality of students' independent work. *Studijos šiuolaikinėje visuomenėje: mokslo darbai [Studies in Modern Society: Academic Papers]*, 5(1), 52–60. ISSN 2029-431X (in Lithuanian).
Poceviciene, R. (2019). Self-directed learning for adult educators by the electronic platform for adult learning in Europe. Opportunities and challenges. In I. B. Alfonso, L. M. Fernández-Martínez, R. Suárez-Álvarez (Coordinadores), *Vulnerabilidad y cultura digital. Riesgos y oportunidades de la sociedad hiperconectada* (pp. 389–408). Madrid: Editorial DYKINSON. ISBN 978-84-1324-647-5
Research of Vytautas Magnus University researchers: Lithuanian schools passed the quarantine exam. (2020). Retrieved from https://svietimas.vdu.lt/vdu-mokslininku-tyrimas-lietuvos-mokyklos-karantino-egzamina-islaike/ (in Lithuanian).
Simonson, M., Smaldino, S., Albright, M., & Zvacek, S. (2008). *Teaching and learning at a distance* (3rd ed.). Upper Saddle River, NJ: Pearson Education Inc.
Study Programme Assessment. (2020). Retrieved from https://www.skvc.lt/default/lt/kokybes-uztikrinimas/kvsp/programu-vertinimas- (in Lithuanian).
Studies during Quarantine. (2020). Retrieved from LSS tyrimas.pdf (in Lithuanian).
Sumuer, E. (2018). Factors related to college students' self-directed learning with technology. *Australasian Journal of Educational Technology*, 34(4). Retrieved from file:///C:/Users/Asus/Downloads/3142-Article%20Text-12981-2-10-20170911.pdf

What is the European Credit System (ECTS)? (2020). Retrieved from https://www.study.eu/article/what-is-the-ects-european-credit-transfer-and-accumulation-system

World Economic Forum: The Top 10 Skills You'll Need for the Future of Work. (2020). Retrieved from https://www.coorpacademy.com/en/blog/learning-innovation-en/world-economic-forum-the-soft-skills-to-prepare-employees-for-the-future-of-work/

CHAPTER 10

WHICH ATTITUDES HELPED THE ACADEMICS TO OVERCOME THE DIFFICULTIES OF ONLINE EDUCATION DURING COVID-19?

Veronika Végh, Klára Soltész-Várhelyi and Henriette Pusztafalvi

ABSTRACT

Hungarian school communities also faced with the challenging situation posed by COVID-19 in March 2020. The transition to emergency remote teaching could be affected by many factors. The attitudes of educators are important as their decisions largely determined the methods of digital education. In the present study, 147 high school teachers and 58 academics' data were analyzed. Academics were more likely to maintain interactions during their courses, and they preferred to make their own material for the lessons, while high-school teachers more often borrow material from pre-existing sources. The authors also found that the effect of self-efficacy on resilience is mediated through the intention to create teaching materials and through the willingness to adopt them as well. It can be concluded that the assistance cannot be one-dimensional, as teachers of different ages, with different IT competencies, teaching at different levels of education, teaching different subjects, have different needs and need to be supported in different ways.

Keywords: Emergency remote teaching; education during coronavirus; Hungarian teachers; teachers; academics; digital teaching; coronavirus

INTRODUCTION

As in many parts of the world, Hungarian school communities also had to face the unexpected challenges posed by the transition from traditional classroom settings to distance learning to reduce the risks of COVID-19 in March 2020. In addition to public education, the changes also affected universities. The universities' reaction to this challenge was diverse (Crawford et al., 2020), some universities didn't have a response at all, while others switched totally to digital education. It is important to emphasize that the implemented form of online education cannot be considered as digital education in the classical sense of the term. As Flores and Gago (2020) described the situation, it was an "unprecedented emergency educational response" (p. 2). It was not a pre-organized educational network, but a sudden transition (Rapanta, Botturi, Goodyear, Guàrdia, & Koole, 2020), and the aim was to provide available, temporary access to teaching materials (Hodges, Moore, Lockee, Trust, & Bond, 2020). Consequently, in the present study, we use the term emergency remote teaching (ERT) referring to the immediate digital teaching during COVID-19. Many professionals have examined how tertiary education was affected by the quick transition to ERT both from the students and from the teachers' perspectives. Studies show that university students and educators had mixed feelings about the consequences of lockdown and ERT. On the one hand, students perceived more flexibility in terms of time and environment, collaborated more with their peers, and became more self-reliant (Daroedono et al., 2020; Donitsa-Schmidt & Ramot, 2020; Salleh, Ghazali, Ismail, Alias, & Rahim, 2020). Their confidence was reported to be higher during ERT than in the traditional teaching settings, and the application of new teaching methods, the usage of many learning resources, mock quizzes, and the immediate feedbacks were also perceived positively and their fear of failing has been eliminated in this pandemic situation (George, 2020). On the other hand, students may have lacked the necessary equipment for online learning or they had a poor internet connection. Furthermore, university students felt that their concentration and content understanding was also hindered. Students reported maintaining self-discipline challenging and they missed interactions, input from lecturers, and support. The perceived workload was also reported to be higher (Daroedono et al., 2020; Quezada, Talbot, & Quezada-Parker, 2020, Salleh et al., 2020).

Reviewing the sources of the successful transition to ERT, it depended on four major areas: (1) how education was organized despite the shortness of time, (2) what educational materials were available, (3) how and to what extent educator was available and if the interaction was maintained, and (4) the difficulties of assessment and feedback have been resolved.

Having alternative plans for new situations, well-organized cooperation among professionals are key features of the smooth transition. It is important to present students with a variety of learning resources, and reliable workbooks, and to encourage students to support their learning from online and offline sources (Bao, 2020; George, 2020). The "personal" presence of the teacher in ERT is important, students appreciate the availability of visual tutors and the consultations with the course lecturer (Bao, 2020; George, 2020).

The examination of the attitudes of educators is important as well because their decisions largely determined the methods of digital education during this period and knowing the individual teaching practices may contribute to see a clearer picture of a successful, smooth transition.

It is worth examining what teacher attitudes have made teaching more successful during ERT, and also what factors helped teachers to stay in good mental state during the transition, as only a teacher with good mental health status can teach and support their students effectively. Therefore, in addition to students' experiences, it is also important to learn how teachers experienced the first wave of ERT.

TEACHERS' PERCEPTIONS DURING COVID-19

It was reported that the teachers had mixed emotions about ERT. Purwanto et al. (2020) reported positive aspects, like more flexibility, no office hours, no need for transportation; therefore, people experienced less stress and lower costs; and negative aspects, as people's work motivation seemed to be lower and the home office costs were increasing. Besides, tremendous work-related stress has been placed on academics during these months and their mental health status could have been affected (Holmes et al., 2020). The mental health incidents increased as a consequence of the pandemic (Gritsenko et al., 2020). Mental stress has also had an impact on teachers' health status. Scientific data show an association between increased stress and increased vocal symptoms in case of university professors during the transition to online education (Besser, Lotem, & Zeigler-Hill, 2020). Teachers' level of anxiety has been affected by their age, gender, educational level, and status, their level of fear and worries, the institute location, and the availability of information (Li et al., 2020). Their role as a teacher and their self-image was also affected negatively (Varea & González Calvo, 2020), as well as their personal lives (Watermeyer, Crick, Knight, & Goodall, 2020). Teachers' perceived institutional and collegial support, their preparedness and confidence level, the accessibility of the necessary technological aids, and how their workload was impacted have varied at large among teachers (Watermeyer et al., 2020).

An individuals' resilience is determined by several protective and risk factors. High self-efficacy or altruistic behavior are known to be protective factors. In the case of teachers, both risk and protective factors can arise from their work like school administration, colleagues, and students. It is a challenging task for the future to rethink the concept of teachers' resilience and to observe it from several perspectives and find the patterns that can help teachers to "strive not just survive" (Beltman, Mansfield, & Price, 2011). While self-efficacy is a relatively constant trait of a person, resilience is a dynamically changing state, therefore it is important to monitor it continually especially in times when teachers are exposed to huge distress.

The purpose of this study is to examine teachers' attitudes toward education that have had an impact on their ability to cope with the difficulties posed by ERT and to maintain their mental health during COVID-19. In the first half of the study, we mapped the attitudes of academics toward online education. In the second half of the chapter, we examined how these attitudes are related to the academics' self-efficacy and how much they helped to maintain resilience in the first period of online education.

METHODS

The online questionnaire collected data about educators' opinions on the transition to ERT. We examined the teachers' demographic data, their ERT practices, and their personal feelings in this situation. E-mails with the research details were sent to school directors in primary and secondary education and to the head of institutions or faculties in tertiary education. Approximately, one-fifth of Hungarian schools and institutions were contacted, and the location of the contacted schools was evenly distributed geographically. The directors were asked to forward a letter to the educators asking them to complete our questionnaire. Completion of the questionnaire was voluntary and anonymous. Totally, 767 answers arrived back from teachers between 5th June and 29th June from primary, secondary, and tertiary education levels. In the present study, academics and high school teachers' answers have been analyzed. In Hungary, high school typically lasts for four years (from age 14/15), where students are prepared for further studies. From the secondary level of education, students can continue their studies at tertiary levels. The age of university students typically ranges from 18/19 to 24/25 years. Compared to primary school and vocational high school teachers, teachers who are teaching in high school show higher resemblance to university lecturers in a sense that the material taught is more theoretical and the teaching methods are more similar.

In the present study, we examined the data of 147 high school teachers and 58 academics. There was no significant difference in age between the two groups (High school teachers: $M = 49.08$, $SD = 9.389$, $Min = 25$, $Max = 67$ and Academics: $M = 47.31$, $SD = 10.183$, $Min = 25$, $Max = 69$). The gender ratio is different; the proportion of women among high school teachers is significantly higher (Female: 107/73%; Male: 40/27%), but this proportion is balanced among academics (Female: 29/50%; Male: 29/50%). Differences in the gender ratio should be kept in mind during the analysis when interpreting the effects of the institution type.

RESULTS

Attitudes Toward ERT and Their Characteristics

In the questionnaire, we asked the educators about their attitudes toward ERT, and analyzed the responses using principal component analysis with direct Oblimin rotation. As a result, we obtained seven main components, of which three are important for the present chapter. One scale is related to the importance of interaction, and it included items such as whether the educators sought personal communication through online interfaces and tried to maintain interactivity during their lessons during ERT. The reliability of the scale was good,

$\alpha = 0.735$. Two scales were related to the digital teaching materials used during ERT. The scale of "Intention to create their own materials" measured the extent to which the educators created their own digital teaching materials (presentations, digital worksheets, and tests) during the pandemic. The reliability of the scale was good, $\alpha = 0.795$. The items of the "Willingness to borrow materials" scale consisted of items related to the adopted digital presentations and worksheets. The reliability was acceptable, $\alpha = 0.620$. Based on the component score coefficients of the principal components analysis, the values of the non-standardized items were weighted, and the weighted items were averaged, resulting in scales whose means remained comparable with each other. Direct Oblimin rotation was set to Delta $= 0$ to allow correlations between scales. This setting usually results in weak- or medium-strength correlations between components.

The perceived importance of interaction positively correlated with both the intention to create teaching materials ($r = 0.269$) and the willingness to borrow them ($r = 0.118$), and surprisingly, the scales related to the creation and adoption of teaching materials were also positively correlated with each other ($r = 0.181$). Further analysis of the correlations revealed that both scales are correlated positively with desirable psychological attributes such as resilience ($r_{creat} = 0.331$; $r_{adopt} = 0.258$), well-being ($r_{creat} = 0.212$; $r_{adopt} = 0.259$), and self-efficacy ($r_{creat} = 0.309$; $r_{adopt} = 0.269$), and negatively correlated with the perceived stress during ERT ($r_{creat} = -0.209$; $r_{adopt} = -0.208$). They were also positively correlated with ERT-related attitudes that indicates successful transition to ERT such as the perceived efficiency ($r_{creat} = 0.324$; $r_{adopt} = 0.243$), sufficient technical conditions ($r_{creat} = 0.220$; $r_{adopt} = 0.225$), positive attitude toward the info-communicational technologies ($r_{creat} = 0.368$; $r_{adopt} = 0.326$), and the perceived potential for improvement provided by ERT ($r_{creat} = 0.205$; $r_{adopt} = 0.128$). These correlations allow us to conclude that the creation and adoption of teaching materials during ERT cannot be considered as contradictory processes, but rather as alternative solutions to the difficulties of transitioning to ERT. They both can be considered as a successful method to cope with the sudden need for a large amount of digital materials. Therefore, both dimensions were problem-solving focused ways of overcoming the difficulties of teaching during COVID-19.

Differences in Attitudes

We used a 2-way ANOVA to analyze the effect of the institution type and gender on the extent to which educators maintained the interaction during classes. In general, the academics were more likely to maintain interaction during their lessons, $F(1,201) = 14.959$, $p < 0.001$, Part. $\eta^2 = 0.069$ (Fig. 1, Part A). The interaction between institution type and gender was also significant, $F(1,201) = 4.893$, $p < 0.028$, Part. $\eta^2 = 0.024$, and it stemmed from the fact that while there was no difference between men and women at university, $F(1,201) = 0.052$, $p = 0.819$, Part. $\eta^2 < 0.001$; in high school, men maintained the interaction less during their lessons $F(1,201) = 12.332$, $p = 0.001$, Part. $\eta^2 = 0.058$.

Regarding the teaching materials, using a 3-way ANOVA test, we examined the effect of institution type and gender on creation and adoption of digital

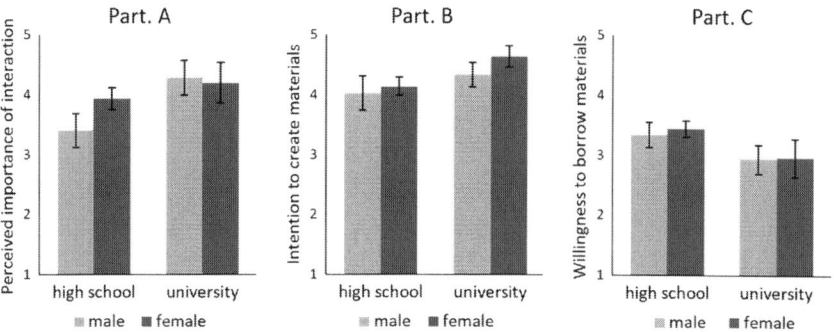

Fig. 1. Differences between Institution Types and Gender in the Attitudes of Perceived Importance of Interaction, the Creation and Adoption of Digital Materials.

materials. We found that academics preferred to create the digital materials themselves, $F(1,201) = 10.166$, $p = 0.002$, *Part.* $\eta^2 < 0.048$ (Fig. 1, Part B), while the high school teachers were more likely to adopt the already prepared digital materials, $F(1,201) = 17.454$, $p < 0.001$, *Part.* $\eta^2 < 0.080$ (Fig. 1, Part C). The effect of gender and the interaction terms associated with it were not significant.

The Mediating Role of These Attitudes between Self-efficacy and Resilience

Both the intention to create and the willingness to adopt digital materials can be seen as forms of coping methods. The intention to maintain interaction during ERT also appeared as a component of successful teaching. Therefore, we hypothesized that these attitudes will be influenced by the educators' self-efficacy. We also hypothesized that those who successfully coped in any way with the problems that occurred during ERT felt more resilient in the situation. We used mediation analysis to examine whether self-efficacy had a direct effect on the educators' resilience during ERT and/or an indirect effect through the use of successful coping mechanisms. We included the institution type and the age of the educators as moderating variables into the mediation. Originally, gender was also included into the model, but we did not find a significant moderating effect, so it was omitted from the final model. The models used in the analyses are shown in Fig. 2.

In the next part, we present three models, in which we mediate the effect of self-efficacy on resilience through (1) the intention to create digital teaching materials, (2) the willingness to adopt them, and (3) the importance of maintaining interaction during ERT. We also examine the moderating effect of age and institution type on the mediating pathway, thus developing a double-moderated mediation analysis. Due to the complexity of these models, the separate discussion of the results and their interpretation makes it very difficult to understand the phenomenon, so unlike the classical structure of articles, we present the statistical analysis and their explanations together.

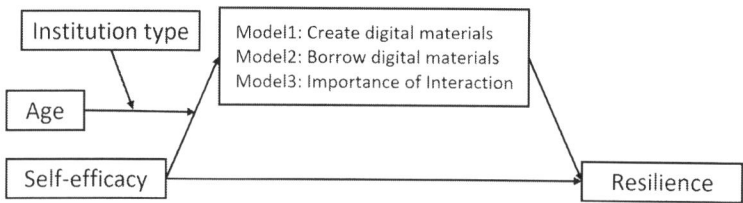

Fig. 2. Schematic Representation of the Three Double-moderated Mediation Models.

Effect of Self-efficacy on Resilience

Self-efficacy alone explains resilience well, a relationship that is not surprising since these two psychological concepts are closely related (Path c in Tables 1–3). Resilience cannot be seen as a constant personality trait of a person, but as a dynamically changing state that is constantly shaped by the person's beliefs and living conditions. Resilience feeds on two sources, for someone to be resilient, they need to be persistent and resourceful. Resourcefulness means that the person believes in being able to find the right solution in every situation, in which belief is driven by the person's self-efficacy. In all of our three models, self-efficacy affects resilience partly directly (Path c′ in Tables 1–3), partly indirectly, through the intention to create digital materials and the willingness to adopt them and the perceived importance to maintain interaction (Path ab in Tables 1–3). Their job is a significant part of a teacher's life, so understandably, the successes and the perceived efficiency in their work had an impact on their resilience, thus the significant indirect effects. Nevertheless, the quarantine situation under COVID-19 posed challenges for the teachers not only in their work but also in other areas of their life, so understandably, the educator's self-efficacy affected their resilience outside the field of education as well, thus the significant direct effect.

The Mediating Pathway through the Intention to Create Digital Materials

Analyzing the parts of the mediating pathway (Table 1), it can be said that self-efficacy fundamentally increases the educators' intentions to create digital learning materials (Path a). Including age and institution type as moderating variable into the mediation model, we found a significant main effect of age, in general, older educators are less likely to create their digital materials. The main effect of institution type is also significant, as academics are more likely to create their digital teaching materials. The three-way interaction between self-efficacy, age, and institution type is also significant.

Looking at Fig. 3 Part A, the 3-way interaction stems from the following patterns. In case of young people, the intention to create their digital materials is at a similar level in university and high school, and self-efficacy has a positive effect of similar strength on it. However, in case of older educators, we see a difference between academics and high school teachers. The lack of self-efficacy in high school teachers leads to a marked decrease in the intention to create digital

Table 1. Mediation Analysis Modeling the Effect of Self-efficacy on Resilience through the Attitude of Intention to Create Digital Materials Moderated by Institution Type and Age.

Path	Outcome	Predictors		β	SE	p	LLCI	ULCI
c (total)	Resilience	Self-efficacy		0.747	0.046	<0.001	0.638	0.852
a	Creating materials	Self-efficacy		0.243	0.060	0.000	0.124	0.361
		Institution		0.367	0.141	0.010	0.089	0.645
		Age		−0.241	0.061	0.000	−0.362	−0.120
		Self-eff * Inst.		−0.138	0.131	0.294	−0.398	0.121
		Self-eff * Age		0.070	0.066	0.294	−0.061	0.200
		Inst. * Age		0.208	0.132	0.116	−0.052	0.468
		Self-eff * Inst. * Age		−0.253	0.121	0.039	−0.492	−0.013
		Cond. effects						
		High sch.	Younger	0.138	0.116	0.236	−0.091	0.368
			Middle	0.288	0.071	0.000	0.147	0.429
			Older	0.438	0.116	0.000	0.210	0.666
		University	Younger	0.257	0.124	0.039	0.013	0.501
			Middle	0.138	0.111	0.215	−0.081	0.358
			Older	0.020	0.161	0.900	−0.297	0.337
b	Resilience	Creating materials		0.124	0.052	0.018	0.021	0.226
c' (direct)	Resilience	Self-efficacy		0.713	0.048	0.000	0.617	0.808
ab (indirect)	Resilience	Self-efficacy						
		High sch.	Younger	0.017	0.019	−	−0.012	0.061
			Middle	0.036	0.019	−	0.004	0.077
			Older	0.054	0.028	−	0.006	0.115
		University	Younger	0.032	0.021	−	0.001	0.080
			Middle	0.017	0.013	−	−0.001	0.048
			Older	0.003	0.013	−	−0.024	0.033

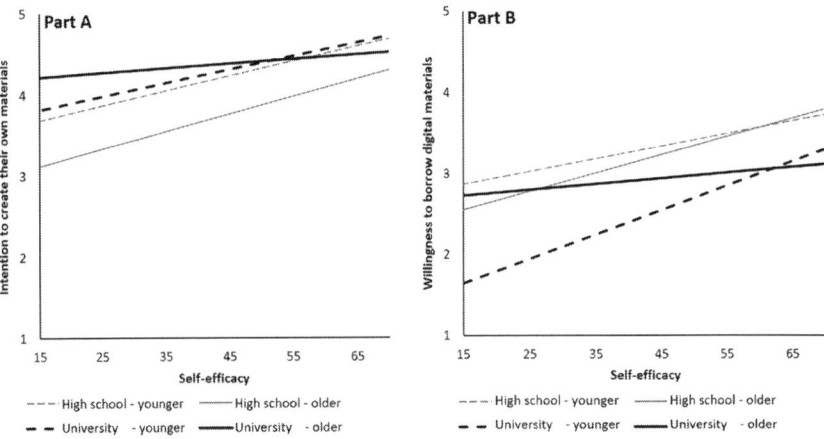

Fig. 3. Moderating Effect of Institution Type and Age in the "Path a" Part of the Mediation Analyses. Part A: Moderating Effects on the Intention to Create Digital Materials. Part B: Moderating Effects on the Willingness to Borrow Digital Materials.

materials. Even those who feel self-efficient fall behind their younger colleagues but for teachers whose self-efficacy is low, the lag is tremendous. We see a completely different pattern among older academics. In case of low self-efficacy, older academics have a higher intention to create digital materials than any of the other groups, but in the case of high self-efficacy, it drops below the value of young educators.

The Mediating Pathway through the Willingness to Adopt Digital Materials

We found that the effect of self-efficacy on resilience is mediated through the willingness to adopt teaching materials as well (Table 2). The mediation is partial; besides the indirect route (Path ab), the direct route is also retained (Path c'). As we have seen previously, the adoption of teaching materials can also be a positive way how educators dealt with the sudden need for digital materials during ERT. Thus, educators who successfully incorporated external materials into their lessons were also able to experience themselves to be efficient in their work during ERT and thereby maintain their resilience through positive reinforcement.

We found a moderating effect of age and institution type on the mediating pathway. The main effect of self-efficacy is significant, self-efficient people tend

Table 2. Mediation Analysis Modeling the Effect of Self-efficacy on Resilience through the Attitude of Willingness to Borrow Digital Materials Moderated by Institution Type and Age.

Path	Outcome	Predictors		β	SE	p	LLCI	ULCI
c (total)	Resilience	Self-efficacy		0.747	0.046	<0.001	0.638	0.852
a	Borrowing materials	Self-efficacy		0.287	0.062	<0.001	0.164	0.409
		Institution		−0.751	0.146	<0.001	−1.038	−0.464
		Age		0.031	0.063	0.628	−0.094	0.156
		Self-eff * Inst.		−0.079	0.136	0.559	−0.347	0.188
		Self-eff * Age		0.054	0.068	0.434	−0.081	0.189
		Inst. * Age		0.054	0.136	0.693	−0.215	0.323
		Self-eff * Inst. * Age		−0.266	0.125	0.035	−0.513	−0.018
		Cond. effects						
		High sch.	Younger	0.178	0.120	0.139	−0.058	0.415
			Middle	0.315	0.074	<0.001	0.169	0.461
			Older	0.452	0.119	<0.001	0.216	0.687
		University	Younger	0.369	0.128	0.004	0.117	0.621
			Middle	0.224	0.115	0.053	−0.003	0.450
			Older	0.079	0.166	0.635	−0.249	0.406
b	Resilience	Borrowing materials		0.064	0.050	0.205	−0.035	0.163
c' (direct)	Resilience	Self-efficacy		0.731	0.048	<0.001	0.636	0.826
ab (indirect)	Resilience	Self-efficacy						
		High sch.	Younger	0.017	0.007	–	0.005	0.033
			Middle	0.020	0.007	–	0.008	0.034
			Older	0.023	0.008	–	0.009	0.040
		University	Younger	0.030	0.014	–	0.007	0.064
			Middle	0.017	0.011	–	0.001	0.043
			Older	0.005	0.015	–	−0.020	0.040

to incorporate more external sources into their own teaching materials. The main effect of institution type is also significant, adoption of materials is less common among academics than high school teachers. The main effect of age is not significant.

Analyzing the interactions introduces more details into the relationships seen above (Fig. 3, Part B). Among high school teachers, when self-efficacy is high, age does not affect the willingness to adopt external materials, both younger and older teachers are willing to do so. Teachers with low self-efficacy adopt less materials, and this decline is particularly prevalent in the older generation. In general, academics are less willing to adopt digital materials than high school teachers. Self-efficacy increases the willingness among academics as well, but in contrast to high school teachers, among academics, the younger ones are those, who are more prone to the decrease in their willingness as self-efficacy decreases.

Discussing the Results of Moderated Mediations Related to the Creation and Adoption of Digital Materials

In public education, and accordingly in high school education, the curriculum is mainly uniform in all schools in Hungary. There are state-defined textbooks that are typically available for all students, and teachers could be sure that students had these textbooks at home during the quarantine. The use of digital (PowerPoint) presentations during lessons were not present all the time in Hungarian high schools before COVID-19; therefore, presumably high school teachers did not have their full digital material reservoir at the beginning of ERT. However, there were several educational websites where the entire materials were available. These sites existed and were well-known even before COVID-19, and they were mostly used by students in preparation for their exams. During the ERT, high school teachers could rely on the textbooks and websites and accordingly were less compelled to create their own digital curriculum. Those, especially older teachers, who use ICT tools less confidently, presumably did not create their own digital presentations during the first wave of ERT but used these already existing sources for their lessons.

The teachers who wanted to provide further assistance beyond the compulsory curriculum to their students, might have sought digital materials in addition to the textbooks and the well-known educational websites. This behavior might be more typical for teachers with high self-efficacy, while those with lower self-efficacy were more likely to stick to the minimum required, compulsory curriculum and rely more on available textbooks and websites during the already stressful period of COVID-19 and the ERT. It is also understandable why older teachers with lower self-efficacy were particularly prone to a decrease in their willingness to search for additional digital materials as these teachers are likely to be less at home in the online world, so it may have been particularly challenging for them to find these extra digital materials.

University curricula cannot be considered general at all. Accordingly, no generally available digital materials were present at the beginning of the ERT that could have been adopted by the academics in their entirety. Many academics did not even need them. Over the past decade or two, there has been a shift in university education, with blackboard education increasingly being replaced by digital (PowerPoint) presentations. The changes are slow and still in progress. Among the younger academics, there is almost no one who would not make digital presentations for their lectures and even for their practical courses. Among the older academics, several have switched to digital presentations, but there are still some who have remained with the traditional lectures at the blackboard.

Educators with low self-efficacy were presumably having content with the already prepared digital presentations that they had been using before ERT. They might have relied on their already existing digital presentation in the same manner, as high school teachers with low self-efficacy relied on textbooks and well-known websites. Academics who did not already have digital materials before the pandemic were forced to make them quickly or to adopt materials from others. In the latter case, most likely, it was not the digital presentations that were adopted by the academics, but the official university notes and transcripts of other courses similar to their own.

In contrast, academics with high self-efficacy might have recognized that the ERT posed additional difficulties for their students and sought to supplement their – probably already existing – digital materials with additional sources that can help students with the successful mastery of the curriculum in this new situation. They might have been willing to produce such materials but were neither reluctant to take them from external sources.

For high school educators, who have rarely used digital teaching materials before ERT but were able to rely on textbooks, continuing with textbooks during ERT required the least changes compared to their usual teaching methods. While this solution may seem to place the least burden on the educator, transferring traditional teaching methods to digital education without changes is not necessarily effective. It does not make up for the lack of support provided by personal education. As a result, the teacher may experience inefficiencies, slower student progress, and poorer performance compared to the pre-ERT period. Such teachers may have felt less effective during ERT. Lack of sense of self-efficacy can negatively affect their resilience. Additionally, perceiving the inefficiencies and failures during ERT may develop an attitude in them that digital education is not successful. A negative attitude toward ERT can lead to a higher sensitivity toward ERT-related difficulties, correspondingly resulting in greater perceived stress, thus further reducing the teacher's resilience.

The case of academics who based their education entirely on their previously made digital presentation during ERT is similar. In the traditional education system, the role of PowerPoint presentations is to support the verbal information-transmission, but due to limited communication opportunities, under ERT, these presentations had to become the primary carriers of information. Presentations that were made for traditional classes were not sufficient during ERT. The ineffectiveness of this form of education was probably felt by all academics.

Teachers with higher self-efficiencies presumably responded to these inefficiencies by modifying their digital curricula, adapting them to online education and supplementing them with additional digital materials. Due to the urgency of the task, in addition to or instead of creating new materials, they could also look for reliable online resources to support their students' learning. Whether these materials have been created by the academics or adopted by them does not matter in the sense that both behaviors can be considered a problem-solving-focused approach and they can effectively help students to learn the curriculum. Presumably, these teachers felt less inefficiencies and experienced more success during ERT, which led to higher resilience. Amidst the already stressful period of COVID-19, it may seem like an extra burden to compile supplementary digital materials in addition to the compulsory curriculum. Yet, those who found the energy within themselves for these extra commitments were able to experience greater success in the transition to digital education.

The Mediating Pathway through the Intention to Maintain Interaction during ERT

In this model, we examined the effect of self-efficacy on resilience through the intention to maintain interaction during ERT. Age and institution type were included into the model as moderating factors on the mediating pathway (Table 3). The mediation is partial, in addition to the direct effect of self-efficacy (Path c'), the indirect pathway is also significant (Path ab).

Table 3. Mediation analysis modeling the effect of self-efficacy on resilience trough the attitude of perceived importance of interaction during ERT moderated by institution type and age

Path	Outcome	Predictors		β	SE	p	LLCI	ULCI
c (total)	Resilience	Self-efficacy		0.747	0.046	<0.001	0.638	0.852
a	Import. of	Self-efficacy		0.176	0.061	0.005	0.055	0.297
	interaction	Institution		0.346	0.144	0.017	0.061	0.63
		Age		−0.065	0.063	0.300	−0.189	0.058
		Self-eff * Inst.		0.137	0.134	0.310	−0.128	0.402
		Self-eff * Age		0.204	0.068	0.003	0.07	0.338
		Inst. * Age		0.097	0.135	0.475	−0.169	0.363
		Self-eff * Inst. * Age		−0.302	0.124	0.016	−0.546	−0.057
		Cond. effects						
		High sch.	Younger	−0.157	0.119	0.189	−0.391	0.078
			Middle	0.15	0.073	0.042	0.006	0.294
			Older	0.456	0.118	< 0.001	0.223	0.689
		University	Younger	0.286	0.126	0.025	0.037	0.536
			Middle	0.273	0.114	0.017	0.049	0.497
			Older	0.26	0.164	0.115	−0.064	0.584
b	Resilience	Import. of interac.		−0.029	0.053	0.586	−0.132	0.075
c' (direct)	Resilience	Self-efficacy		0.753	0.048	< 0.001	0.659	0.848
ab (indirect)	Resilience	Self-efficacy						
		High sch.	Younger	0.004	0.012	–	−0.013	0.035
			Middle	−0.004	0.009	–	0.001	0.013
			Older	−0,013	0.026	–	0.007	0.031
		University	Younger	−0,008	0.017	–	0.004	0.027
			Middle	−0.008	0.016	–	0.004	0.025
			Older	−0.007	0.018	–	0.003	0.028

Regarding the moderations on the indirect route (Path a of Table 3 and Fig. 4), the main effect of self-efficacy was significant, individuals with higher self-efficacy were more likely to try to maintain interaction during ERT. The main effect of institution type was also significant, academics were more inclined to maintain interaction than high school teachers, and this difference is especially present among educators with high self-efficiency. Age had a moderating effect only among high school teachers, as older teachers with low self-efficacy were explicitly lagging behind in terms of maintained interaction. No such effect of age was observed among academics.

Discussing the Results of Moderated Mediation Related to the Intention to Maintain Interaction during ERT

The use of video conferencing applications was new to most teachers and students. Although almost everyone has used such applications for personal purposes, this kind of use of video conferencing tools in education was completely new to many educators, with large-scale lectures not held online before. They were inexperienced in how to maintain communication with the students in these lectures, or even how to provide an opportunity to do so without the lecture falling into chaos. They had to learn technical skills like how to share a screen and even find applications that are capable for that. Practical courses using special

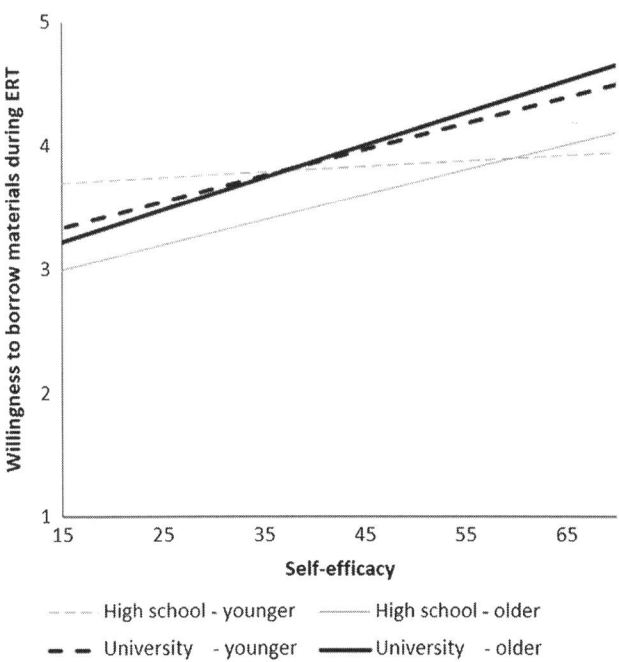

Fig. 4. Moderating Effect of Institution Type and Age on the Perceived Importance of Interaction during ERT in the "Path a" Part of the Mediation Analysis.

tools and software were forcibly turned into theoretical courses, as the software and tools were only available at the schools/universities. Thus, many educators switched to exclusively frontal education.

The moderating effect of age in the sample of high school teachers can probably be explained by the fact that approximately in the last two decades there has been a change in the methodology of Hungarian public education as well. The previous methodology, which predominantly emphasized frontal education, was slowly replaced by more modern, alternative methods, which, among other things, emphasized the importance of interaction. Because young teachers learned this methodology during their education, they were more likely to maintain interaction during ERT as well, regardless of their self-efficacy. In contrast, among older teachers who learned primarily the methodology of frontal education, those with low self-efficacy retained the form of frontal education in ERT as well, while teachers with high self-efficacy were more likely to incorporate opportunities for interaction into their lessons even before ERT, and made efforts to maintain them during the ERT as well. In contrast, academics do not undergo pedagogical training during their university years, so the methodological change in education over the past two decades is not clearly visible in their educational style either. Accordingly, in the educational style of academics, their personal preferences, their personality, and among other things their self-efficacy are more expressed.

GENERAL DISCUSSION AND CONCLUSION

Following the quarantine in May 2020, numerous articles have been published on how effective or ineffective online education has been, what methods and applications have proved successful, and how this form of education can be made more effective in the future. Most of the articles approached the effectiveness of the implemented online education through the experiences and performance of the students. However, it is also worthwhile to look at the effectiveness of online education from the educators' point of view and examine how they experienced the period of ERT, as truly effective education requires teachers who have the skills and knowledge to teach online and are in a good mental state to provide good quality education. The aim of our research is to examine how ERT has affected the mental state of teachers. In addition to the resilience presented here, we examined the stress experienced by teachers and the extent of their burnout specifically related to ERT. Examining the impact of ERT on the mental state of teachers is important in several ways. A short-term consequence could be that the teachers' performance is affected by their mental well-being during the period when digital education is taking place. Although ERT lasts only a short time relative to a person's career, the long-term effect of it may be that the deterioration in mental well-being happening during ERT (e.g., decreased resilience and increased burnout) may take a long time to reverse. Additionally, people who suffer from burnout are also at greater risk of leaving their careers, which can exacerbate the already present shortage of teachers. In our studies, we have shown that the educators' attitudes toward ERT has a significant effect on their well-being. In this study, we demonstrated how teachers' self-efficacy had an impact on their willingness to find problem-solving-focused responses to the needs and problems associated with the transition to digital education, thereby making their education more effective, which in turn has had an impact on the teachers' resilience. It is important to help teachers successfully overcome the difficulties of ERT, with state regulations, university-level regulations, formal and non-formal teaching aids, with software and with websites where teaching aids can be collected. However, the results presented here also show that this assistance cannot be one-dimensional, as people of different ages, different IT skills, teaching at different levels of education, teaching different subjects, have different needs and need to be supported in different ways.

ACKNOWLEDGEMENTS

The authors would like to thank all teachers who participated in the survey and filled in the questionnaire voluntary.

FUNDING DETAILS

All authors have declared that no financial support was received from any organization for the submitted work.

DISCLOSURE STATEMENT

The authors declare no potential conflict of interest.

REFERENCES

Bao, W. (2020). COVID-19 and online teaching in higher education: A case study of Peking University. *Human Behavior and Emerging Technologies*, 2(2), 113–115. doi:10.1002/hbe2.191

Beltman, S., Mansfield, C., & Price, A. (2011). Thriving not just surviving: A review of research on teacher resilience. *Educational Research Review*, 6(3), 185–207. doi:10.1016/j.edurev.2011.09.001

Besser, A., Lotem, S., & Zeigler-Hill, V. (2020). Psychological stress and vocal symptoms among university professors in Israel: Implications of the shift to online synchronous teaching during the COVID-19 pandemic. *Journal of Voice: Official Journal of the Voice Foundation*, S0892-1997(20)30190-9. https://doi.org/10.1016/j.jvoice.2020.05.028.

Crawford, J., Butler-Henderson, K., Jurgen, R., Bashar, M., Glowatz, M., Burton, R., ... Lam, S. (2020). COVID-19: 20 countries' higher education intra-period digital pedagogy responses. *Journal of Applied Learning & Teaching*, 3(1), 9–28. doi:10.37074/jalt.2020.3.1.7

Daroedono, E., Siagian, F., Alfarabi, M., Cing, J., Arodes, E., Sirait, R., ... Hutabarat, R. (2020). The impact of COVID-19 on medical education: Our students perception on the practice of long distance learning. *International Journal of Community Medicine and Public Health*, 7(7), 2790–2796. doi:10.18203/2394-6040.ijcmph20202545

Donitsa-Schmidt, S., & Ramot, R. (2020). Opportunities and challenges: Teacher education in Israel in the Covid-19 pandemic. *Journal of Education for Teaching*, 46(4), 586–595. doi:10.1080/02607476.2020.1799708

Flores, M., & Gago, M. (2020). Teacher education in times of COVID-19 pandemic in Portugal: National, institutional and pedagogical responses. *Journal of Education for Teaching*, *46*(4), 1–10. doi:10.1080/02607476.2020.1799709

George, M. L. (2020). Effective teaching and examination strategies for undergraduate learning during COVID-19 school restrictions. *Journal of Educational Technological Systems*, *49*(1), 23–48.

Gritsenko, V., Skugarevsky, O., Konstantinov, V., Khamenka, N., Marinova, T., Reznik, A., & Isralowitz, R. (2020). COVID 19 fear, stress, anxiety, and substance use among Russian and Belarusian university students. *International Journal of Mental Health and Addiction*, 1–7. Advance online publication. doi:10.1007/s11469-020-00330-z

Hodges, C. B., Moore, S., Lockee, B. B., Trust, T., & Bond, M. A. (2020). The difference between emergency remote teaching and online learning. Retrieved from https://vtechworks.lib.vt.edu/handle/10919/104648

Holmes, E. A., O'Connor, R. C., Perry, V. H., Tracey, I., Wessely, S., Arseneault, L., ... Bullmore, E. (2020) Multidisciplinary research priorities for the COVID-19 pandemic: A call for action for mental health science. *Lancet Psychiatry*, *7*(6), 547–560. doi:10.1016/S2215-0366(20)30168-1

Li, Q., Miao, Y., Zeng, X., Tarimo, C. S., Wu, C., & Wu, J. (2020). Prevalence and factors for anxiety during the coronavirus disease 2019 (COVID-19) epidemic among the teachers in China. *Journal of Affective Disorders*, *277*, 153–158.

Purwanto, A., Asbari, M., Suryani, P., Cahyono, Y., Fahlevi, M., & Mufid, A. (2020). Impact of work from home (WFH) on Indonesian teachers performance during the Covid-19 pandemic: An exploratory study. *International Journal of Advanced Science and Technology*, *29*(05), 6235–6244.

Quezada, R. L., Talbot, C., & Quezada-Parker, K. B. (2020). From bricks and mortar to remote teaching: A teacher education programme's response to COVID-19. *Journal of Education for Teaching*, *46*(4), 472–483.

Rapanta, C., Botturi, L., Goodyear, P., Guàrdia, L., & Koole, M. (2020). Online university teaching during and after the Covid-19 crisis: Refocusing teacher presence and learning activity. *Postdigital Science and Education*, *2*, 923–945. doi:10.1007/s42438-020-00155-y

Salleh, F. I. M., Ghazali, J. M., Ismail, W. N. H. W., Alias, M., & Rahim, N. S. A. (2020). The impacts of COVID-19 through online learning usage for tertiary education in Malaysia. *Journal of Critical Reviews*, *7*(8), 147–149.

Varea, V., & González Calvo, G. (2020). Touchless classes and absent bodies: Teaching physical education in times of Covid-19. *Sport Education and Society*, 1–19. doi:10.1080/13573322.2020.1791814

Watermeyer, R., Crick, T., Knight, C., & Goodall, J. (2020). COVID-19 and digital disruption in UK universities: Afflictions and affordances of emergency online migration. *Higher Education*, 1–19. doi:10.1007/s10734-020-00561-y

ABOUT THE AUTHORS

A. W. Janitha C. Abeygunasekera is a Senior Lecturer at the Department of Accounting, Faculty of Management and Finance, University of Colombo, Sri Lanka with more than 10 years of teaching experience. She obtained her Bachelor of Business Administration degree (specialized in Finance) from the University of Colombo and the Master of Business Administration degree from the Postgraduate Institute of Management, Sri Lanka. In 2019, she finished her PhD degree in Performance Measurement and Business Process Management at the Queensland University of Technology, Australia. Further, she is a Fellow of Higher Education Academy, UK, and received the SEDA accreditation from the UK for her Certificate in Teaching in Higher Education obtained from the University of Colombo. Currently, she is also the Project Coordinator of the AHEAD-ELTA-ELSE-DP (Enriching Learning, Teaching, Assessment, and English Language Skills Enhancement Development Project) of the Department of Accounting. The World Bank finances this project, and it attempts to develop the English language, research, and employability skills of undergraduates. Further, she is leading the team "Teaching, learning, and assessment development" in the Internal Quality Assurance Cell of the Faculty of Management and Finance, University of Colombo. She has teaching interests in accounting, auditing, and research methods and research interests in a range of areas, including accounting and financial reporting, performance measurement, auditing, business process management, small and medium scale enterprises, big data and analytics, and teaching and learning. She has published and presented in international journals and conferences, organized international research conferences, and served in various capacities such as a reviewer, track chair, and editorial committee member. Further, she had reviewed research papers in many international journals.

Stanislaus Agava is currently the Chief Librarian at Tangaza University College (TUC), Nairobi, Kenya. He holds a Master of Library and Information Science from Kenyatta University. He also holds a Master of Information Technology from the University of Pretoria in South Africa where is he is currently pursuing a PhD in Information Studies. His PhD thesis is on data literacy with the aim of developing a data literacy framework for researchers in Kenyan Universities. He also teaches information literacy skills at TUC. He is a husband and father to two children.

Muhammad Shajjad Ahsan is currently working as a Professor of the Department of Drama at Jahangirnagar University, Dhaka, Bangladesh. He has taught across a range of core undergraduate and postgraduate courses on Screenwriting, Media Production, Film Studies, Television Studies, Directing for Media, and Research

Methodology. His main research interests are in the areas of media education, workforce development, and technology integration for the creative and cultural industries in Bangladesh. Through his research he usually puts forward various policies for consideration or discussion on media industry and practices. Currently, he has developed a keen interest in working on the educational policy issues.

Atm Shafiul Alam is currently an Assistant Professor at the School of Electronic Engineering and Computer Science, Queen Mary University of London, UK since 2019. He received his BSc (Hons) degree with first class in Information and Communication Engineering from the University of Rajshahi, Bangladesh, the MSc degree with distinction in Telecommunications and Computer Networks Engineering from the London South Bank University, UK, and the PhD degree in Wireless Communications from The Open University, Milton Keynes, UK. Before joining at the Queen Mary University of London, he worked on several European and UK funded projects as a Research Fellow for the 5G Innovation Centre, University of Surrey, UK, and the University of Bradford, UK. His research interests include the areas of intelligent wireless communications and networks, in particular, smart energy and spectrum-efficient radio resource management for 5G and beyond, Internet of Things, the emerging applications of machine learning in wireless communications for verticals such as smart grids, intelligent transport systems, smart cities and homes, and industrial automation. He is also interested in technology-driven teaching and learning, and he is currently a Fellow of Higher Education Academy (FHEA).

Sinan Aşçı is an Assistant Professor in the Department of New Media at Bahçeşehir University, and he is working as a PDRA and Adjunct Professor for SDI Munich. He completed his BA in English Language Teaching at Anadolu University (2010) and was an exchange student in British and American Studies at the University of Pardubice in Czechia (2008). He received his MA degree in General Journalism at Marmara University (2013) with a thesis on the representation of lesbian, gay, bisexual, and transgender individuals in newspapers in Turkey and the USA. Then, he earned his PhD in Media and Communication Studies from Galatasaray University (2018) with a thesis work focusing on "cyberbullying and youth in Turkey" under the supervision of Prof. Dr Michel Bourse. He has been teaching media courses both in Turkey and Germany, providing services as an editor and manuscript reviewer of peer-reviewed journals, and doing research on social media, social media and kids, cyberculture, digitization, digital journalism, and digital literacy.

Md. Ashrafuzzaman is an Assistant Professor at the Department of Education, Bangabandhu Sheikh Mujibur Rahman Digital University, Bangladesh. He has been working around 11 years in the fields of teacher education, training and educational research with different universities and organizations. In 2014, he received an MPhil degree in English Language Education from the Institute of

Education and Research, University of Dhaka. He has also completed his BEd (Hons) and MEd from the same institute. He has published many research articles in national and international journals. His focuses of research are teachers' training programs, underprivileged children's education (sex workers, transgender, and slum children), English language education, classroom practice, teaching methods and techniques, assessment and feedback practice, blended and online learning, and information and communication technology in education.

Patrick Blessinger, EdD, is an Adjunct Associate Professor of Education at St. John's University, a Math and Science Teacher with the New York State Education Department, and Chief Research Scientist of the International Higher Education Teaching and Learning Association (in consultative status with the United Nations). He is the editor and author of many books and articles and he is an Educational Policy Analyst and contributing writer with UNESCO's Inclusive Policy Lab, University World News, The Hechinger Report, The Guardian, and Higher Education Tomorrow, among others. He teaches courses in Education, Leadership, and Research Methods and he serves on doctoral dissertation committees. He founded and leads a global network of educators focused on teaching and learning and he is an expert in inclusion, equity, leadership, policy, democracy, human rights, and sustainable development. He provides professional development workshops to teachers and professors and regularly gives presentations and keynote addresses at academic conferences around the world. He has received several educational awards, including: Fulbright Senior Scholar to Denmark (Department of State, USA), Governor's Teaching Fellow (Institute of Higher Education, University of Georgia, USA), and Certified Educator (National Geographic Society, USA).

Nelab Haidari works with United States Agency for International Development (USAID/Kabul) as the Program Assistant. She is in the second year of her MBA program at the American University of Afghanistan (AUAF). During her Bachelor's degree at AUAF, she won Presidents High-honor, Business Excellence NEWCO, and Best Mentor of The Year Awards. She also championed women empowerment, cultural exchange, and youth development in her role as US Embassy Kabul's Advisory Council Emerging Leader, CHAMPs Peer Mentor, and AUAF Arête Business Club President. Moreover, she is an independent researcher. Her interest lies in social and economic topics in Afghanistan, women and youth empowerment.

Madina Ibrahimi is an MBA student at the American University of Afghanistan. Her Bachelor's degree is in Business Administration with a focus on Management. She is an independent researcher, interested to write about social and economic subjects in her country, Afghanistan, in areas such as education, economics, entrepreneurship, and women empowerment. She also has more than five years of experience in business administration and coordination. She currently works as Client Liaison Senior Officer at Turquoise Mountain Foundation, where she connects Afghan carpet producers to international customers around the globe. Further, she is the Co-founder and an English teacher at Alef Course, a free online education platform.

Md Tariqul Islam is an Assistant Professor at BRAC Institute of Educational Development (BRAC IED), BRAC University. His research interest largely focuses on the sociology of education with particular attention to the global citizenship experience of young students in the globalized world. He earned his PhD in Education from Deakin University, Australia. He received his Bachelor (Hons) and Master's in Education from the University of Dhaka, Bangladesh. As a Researcher, he worked with several national and international organizations, for example, BRAC, NAEM, FREPD, UNESCO, UNICEF, ActionAid. His current research focuses on education for global citizenship, higher education and employability, education in emergencies, teaching and learning in higher education, teachers' professional development, information and communication technology in education, educational inclusion and exclusion, education for sustainable development, and play for learning and socio-emotional development.

Ayşegül Liman Kaban works as a Lecturer at Bahçeşehir University. In 2013, she completed her Master's degree in Emotional Contagion in Teacher–Student Relations at Marmara University. Between 2013 and 2016, she was the Editor of the IATEFL TEASIG Newsletter. She has been the Editor of IATEFL Learning Technologies since September 2016. In 2020, she finished her PhD degree in the field of Educational Technologies. She studied the effects of electronic reading experiences (printed book, on-screen reading, gamified reading, and personalized reading) and the influence of reading comprehension, motivation, and retention. Since 2009, he has been giving speeches about technology use in education, game, game-based learning, gamification at various national and international conferences, and continues teacher education. She has written two children's books, *Oyun Canavarı* and *Defne'nin dijital kimliği*, on game addiction and internet security. She is the Consultant of the Media Literacy Association in Turkey.

Arif Mahmud is a Lecturer in Education Studies at the University of Roehampton and a Senior Fellow of the Higher Education Academy. He has graduated from the School of Oriental and African Studies with a BA in Arabic and Islamic Studies. After graduating, he obtained a CELTA and traveled around the world teaching in different higher educational institutions. In 2013, he completed his MA in Education (Psychology) from the UCL IOE, and subsequently completed his PhD in 2018, with his thesis focusing on the role of emotional intelligence in the development of adolescents' social and emotional abilities and academic performance. His research interests lie in social and emotional learning and teaching, mental health, and eradicating inequalities in education for minority populations.

Nandita Mishra is senior lecturer at Department of Economic and Industrial Development (IEI), Linköping University (LiU), Sweden. She is a researcher and academic for over two decades. She is Ambassador to International Integrated Reporting Council (IIRC) London. She was awarded most innovative faculty in 2019 by the Center for Education Growth and Research. She is a Cost and Management Accountant by profession with a doctorate in corporate governance. She is also contributing to ICAI's Sustainability Reporting Standard Board as special invitee. She also tutors PhD scholars & students of master's degree based out in India and abroad.

Judith Pete is a Kenyan, currently working as a Lecturer and Research Coordinator at Tangaza University College of the Catholic University of Eastern Africa. She is an Open Education Scholar and champion in Open Education Resources (OER), Open Education Practices (OEP), and Online Education; who has achieved excellent academic prowess, with the most recent being a PhD in Management Science and Technology from the Open University in Netherlands. She has passion for continuous learning and professional development. She also studied MBA in Financial Management and Bachelors in Sustainable Human Development. She is actively involved in open research, training, leadership, management, policy issues, fund raising, and humanitarian support. She is very passionate about climate change having recently enrolled for an online course on Climate Change: from Science to Lived Experiences. Apart from being reliable team leader, she has an admirable public relations skill, which has helped her in building strategic partnerships globally. Her publications have focus on OER, OEP, diversity, equity and inclusion, gender justice rights, and financial inclusion which can be accessed through https://scholar.google.com/.

Rasa Poceviciene is an Associate Professor and Head of the Management and Communication Department at Siauliai State College. She holds a PhD in Social Sciences (Educology). She has more than 25 years of working experience (as a teacher (an academic), researcher, and manager) in higher education. She is also one of the creators of the self-directed learning system for general education schools, an expert of Electronic Platform for Adult Learning in Europe for the Siauliai region, an expert of the Lithuanian Study Quality Assessment Center, member of the scientific committee of scientific journal index, Comunicación, reviewer of international and national scientific journals, author of more than 80 scientific articles in international and national journals in areas of self-directed learning, creating, and implementing innovations as well as learning innovations, distance learning, intercultural communication, learner cognition, problem-solving management, and skills, relations between freedom and responsibility in the education, ensuring and improving the learner-centered teaching/learning process, knowledge management, and education for entrepreneurship and leadership. Results of the researches are permanently presented at international and national conferences and journals. Dissemination of these ideas is also carried out by creating and executing original courses and leading seminars, training, working in national and European projects, consulting and implementing innovations in practice, also working with student's in-home university as well as in other European universities (according to Erasmus+ programme).

Henriette Pusztafalvi is an Educator, an Associate Professor at the University of Pécs, Hungary. She is a Habilitated Doctor (PhD). She has a strong interest in interdisciplinary and multidisciplinary research in education and health sciences. Her main areas of interest include prospective and retrospective studies of health education, health behavior, and methodological renewal of health education. She is the Supervisor of several doctoral students with whom she researches various fields of health science, for example, health value, health behavior, and attitude of people with special needs. She believes in constant development, learning about new, effective educational methods are of great importance to her.

Mohammed Gul Sahibbzada is in his last semester of MBA (finishing in May 2021) at AUAF, and is the Founder, Chairman, and Chief Executive Officer of Kainaat Group of Companies – KGC: www.kainaatgroup.af. He has done his Bachelor in Management and Computer Science. He attended professional courses in human rights, journalism, public administration, and computer science. He writes news articles for national and international newspapers on political, economic, and social issues. He worked as Senior Official at UN and international non-governmental organizations, and built schools and paved roads out of his own resources in villages in Kunduz province. In addition to creating employment for scores of people, he has helped many enterprises get work and running.

Ahmad Samarji is currently the Dean of the College of Arts and Sciences and the Head of the Education Department at Phoenicia University, Lebanon. He is an Associate Professor in STEAM Education, Forensic Science Education, and Distance Education. He is the HETL Country Director for Lebanon. He served as an ICT Pedagogical Officer of the Australian Federal Government Project "Teaching Teachers for the Future." The project emphasized ICT capabilities in teacher education across four disciplines: Mathematics, Science, English, and History. Between 2012 and 2015, he served as the Vice President of the Mathematical Association of Victoria. In his ongoing inquiry into learning and teaching, he pays particular attention toward humanizing higher education, internationalizing the curriculum, and promoting student-centeredness. He views the curriculum as a complex conversation among all stakeholders, the most major of whom are students. Additionally, he supports peer (student) learning and teaching across various courses as a win–win combination for both the mentors and mentees, as well as the higher education institute. He asserts and continuously researches the effectiveness and the importance of adopting a spectrum of pedagogical approaches (project-based learning, problem-based learning, team-based learning, individualized learning, etc.) to respond to the complex human cognitive architecture and knowledge inquiry.

Sahaya G. Selvam is an Associate Professor of Psychology at the Institute of Youth Studies, Tangaza University College, Catholic University of Eastern Africa, Nairobi, Kenya. He holds a PhD in Psychology, from the University of London, UK. Originally from India, he has been serving as a Catholic Priest in

Eastern Africa since 2021. In addition to his Master's degree in Philosophy, prior to his PhD, he completed an MA degree in Psychology of Religion also at the University of London. Besides his focus on character-virtues, he brings together his academic background in philosophy and psychology to the field of education. Having been a Lecturer from the age of 24, and having engaged in academic administration for several years, he contributes passionately to pedagogy in the twenty-first century.

Enakshi Sengupta works with the American University of Afghanistan as the Director – Centre for Teaching and Learning and Associate Professor of the Business Department. She brings 25 years of experience working both in the corporate world and in the academic environment. She is a PhD holder from the University of Nottingham and has completed her MBA from the same university. She also has a Master's degree in English Literature from Calcutta University and two undergraduate degrees in English literature and Education. She has several professional diplomas in marketing and public relations from the UK. She also works as the Associate Editor of the book series Innovations in Higher Education Teaching and Learning, Emerald Publishing and has to date worked as the Lead Editor and Lead Author of 23 books under this series. She is also the Managing Editor of *Journal of Applied Research in Higher Education* from Emerald Publishing. She has contributed several journals and book chapters for Routledge, Springer, Palgrave, and Cambridge Publishing. She has been lauded with several international award which includes: 2021: Outstanding Faculty Award by Comparative and International Education Society's Study Abroad and International Students Special Interest Group (SIG); 2019: Editor's Choice Award – *Journal of International Students*; 2017: Emerald Literati Award: Outstanding Reviewer for *Journal of Applied Research in Higher Education*; 2016: India CSR Author Award for the book *Essentials of Corporate Social Responsibility* and also for Outstanding Contribution in the field of Corporate Social Responsibility in India.

M. Mahruf C. Shohel is currently working at the Doctoral College, University of Surrey. He is an Academic Researcher with special interests in education, childhood studies, international development and social science research methods including education for sustainable development, learning journey, teacher education, mobile technologies, ecological systems theory, school transition, language learning, and visual methods. He worked for several British universities including the universities of Aberystwyth, Cambridge, Glasgow, Leicester, Manchester, Sunderland, Sussex (Institute of Development Studies) and Bucks New University. His current research focuses on education in emergencies, teaching and learning in higher education, students learning journey, teachers' professional development in the global south, emerging technologies in education, English language teaching and learning, childhood poverty and educational exclusion, sustainable development and global citizenship.

Klára Soltész-Várhelyi is a Data Scientist working in the field of Humanities and Social Sciences as a Researcher and Statistician. She also works as a

Teaching Assistant at the Institute of Psychology of the Pázmány Péter Catholic University, Hungary, teaching Statistical and Methodological Subjects. She graduated in Psychology and Cognitive Sciences. She studied Computer Science and Data Visualization as well. She considers the free sharing of information to be essential for the development of science, therefore she regularly gives open lectures on methodological topics, has more than 500 freely available tutorial videos and numerous tutorial documents. She runs her own business as a Statistical Consultant under the name stathelp.hu.

Veronika Végh is a Biologist (MSc), Biology-English teacher (MA), and she holds a Doctorate degree in Health Sciences from the University of Pécs, Hungary. Her research interests primarily focus on education, the role of education in health development. Since 2014, she has been teaching Biology in English at an international secondary school in Hungary, both in the Hungarian education system and in international graduate training preparing her students for the International Baccalaureate.

Elaha Yousufi is an MBA student at the American University of Afghanistan, an independent researcher, and an entrepreneur. She has a Bachelor's degree in Computer Science and her current focus is business administration and management. She has more than eight years of experience in national and international organizations, and government entities in Afghanistan. She currently runs a business of her own in IT and Logistic Services under the name of Narwan Group of Companies and works as Counselor for the Ministry of Industry and Commerce.

NAME INDEX

Acharya, D. 7, 30, 32, 46
Achbani, A., 116
Adams, D., 59
Adanır, G. A., 15
ADB, 14
Agha, R., 46
Ahmad, L., 8
Ahsan, M. S., 32
Ainsworth, S., 32
Akbulut, Y., 122
Akyol, Z., 120
Alam, A. S., 50
Alam, A. T. M., 7, 30, 32, 46
Ala–Mutka, K., 119
Alan, S., 106
Albright, M., 102, 141
Alfarabi, M., 154
Alias, M., 154
Alif, A. R., 33
Al–Jabir, A., 46
Allen, I. E., 102–103
Allo, M. D. G., 59
Alsafi, Z., 46
American Psychological Association, 44
Anderson, D. M., 97
Anderson, J., 133
Angelucci, M., 46
Angrisani, M., 46
Anwar, N., 7, 30, 32, 46
Anwar, S. B., 33
Arodes, E., 154
Aron, D., 119
Arseneault L., 155
Asbari, M., 155
Aşçı, S., 118, 122, 127

Asnur, L., 30–31
Assocham, 46
Azari, R., 119
Aziz, K., 60

Baba, M. A., 116
Baiza, Y., 71
Baker, J. D., 24
Bakia, M., 9, 12, 116
BANBEIS, 32
Baniamin, H., M., 32
Bao, W., 154
Barac, M, 45–46
Barura, A., 33
Baş, T., 127
Basilaia, G., 116
Bauer, W., 119
Baumer, S., 31
Bedford, W., 26
Beetham, H., 119
Beltman, S., 155
Benbasat, I., 63
Bennett, D. M., 46
Bennett, S., 31
Benson, S., 15
Berezhna, S., 33
Berry, A., 30
Bertiz, Y., 106
Besser A., 155
Bharuthram, S., 59
Bigirwa, J. P., 60
Bingol, S., 106
Bittanti, M.
Black, P., 23
Blankenberger, B., 5
Bligh, B.

Bond, A., 15, 27, 117, 154
Bonk, C. J., 97
Borup, J., 40
Botturi, L., 154
Bowen, J. A., 5
Boyatzis, R. E., 35–36
Boyd, D., 31
Boyd, K. C., 61, 63
Bozkurt, A., 14, 15, 25
Braun, V., 35
Breiter, A., 32
British Educational Research Association, 36
British Psychological Society (BPS), 36
Brockett, R. G., 145
Brookhart, S. M., 23
Buckley, S., 42
Budhrani, K., 25, 44
Buheji, A., 46
Buheji, M., 46
Bui, T. X., 119
Bullmore E., 155
Burke, C., 97
Burton, R., 154
Butler–Henderson, K., 154
Byrne, M. M., 25

Cahyono, Y., 155
Candy, P. C., 145
Caracelli, V. J., 107
Carlson, B., 32
Cash, C., 105
Castán, J., 59
Cernerud, L., 59
Chai, K. K., 44
Challis, D., 86
Chaloux, B., 26
Chang, T.–W., 60
Chen, C., 42
Chen, J. A., 130
Chen, J. C., 106
Chima, A., 31
Chou, C., 42
Chowdhury, A. F., 33

Chowdhury, S., 33
Cing, J., 154
Clark, L., 41
Clark, V. L. P., 87, 89
Clarke, V., 35
Clinton, S., 26
Clow, D., 32
Clune, A., 32
Cluskey Jr., G. R., 26
Cody, R., 31
Coles, L., 86
Connors, H. R., 105
Conole, G., 32
Coppola, N. W., 24
Cornelius, S., 105
Çoşkun, D., 122, 127
Council, M. L., 30
Craig, R., 117
Crawford, J., 151
Creswell, J. W., 17
Crick, T., 155
Crockett, L., 31
Crook, D., 105
Crowne, S., 32
Cuban, L., 32
Cui, Y., 30
Curran, C., 15, 85

Daigo, E., 46
Daniel, S. J., 30
Darby, F., 15
Darby, J., 32
Daroedono, E., 154
Database of indicators, 137
Daukilas, S., 141
De Giusti, A., 84
de Laat, M., 32
Dede, C., 31–32
Dede, C. J., 130
Delfino, D. A. P., 30
Delgardo, M.A., 41
Demuyakor, J., 32
DePietro, A., 5
Descriptors of the Study Field, 151

Dewi, E., 30
Dewi, I. P., 30–31
Dhawan, S., 26
Diler, I., 106
Dillon, T., 32
Distance Learning / Education Guide for general education
Distance learning or organization of learning in a distance?, 136, 138
Dobinson, T., 106
Donitsa–Schmidt S., 154
Drsydale, J., 40
Dube, B., 96
Durepos, G., 107
Dutta, S., 33, 40

Egorov, G., 14–15, 25
Ehlen, C. R., 26
El-Erian, M.A., 116
Ellis, R. A., 60
Emerson, R. W., 63
Emon, E. K. H., 33
Erling, E., J., 46
Everitt, J., 41
Eynon, R., 116

Fadde, P. J., 25
Fahlevi, M., 155
Faria, A., 141
Ferguson, H. T., 5
Ferreira, N. 141
Findeisen, S., 119
Fischer, H., 59
Fleischer, M., 119
Flores M., 154
Flowers, P., 34
Foster, E. A., 59
Frankl, V. E., 147
French, S., 97
Frey, B. B., 105
Friga, P. N., 5
Frumin, K. M., 130
Fuad, N., 33

Gaebel, M., 42
Gago M., 154
Gammage, B., 119
Garrison, D. R., 120
Gaučaité R., 145
Gaus, J. M., 4
Ghazali, J. M., 154
Gibson, A., 5
Gifford, E., 45
Gilboy, M. B., 84
Ginns, P., 60
Glowatz, M., 154
Gnanam, A., 105
Godwin–Jones, R., 32
Goforth, C., 61
González Calvo, G., 155
Goodall, J., 155
Goodyear, P., 154
Google Trends., 103, 104, 114
Government of Kenya, 84, 97–99
Goyal, S., 58
Gracia, L., 45
Graham, C., 40
Grandzol, C. J., 121
Grandzol, J. R., 121
Gray, D. E., 34
Greene, F. J., 45
Greene, J. C., 107
Gregg, J., 26
Gritsenko, V., 155
Grotzer, T. A., 130
Guàrdia, L., 154
Gunn, C., 97
Gupta, I., 60
Gutman, R., 31

Haddad, C.J., 97
Haddad, M., 141
Hamidah, H., 15
Hammond, M., 25
Harada, M., 46
Hazelkorn, E., 5
Hebebci, M. T., 106
Heinerichs, S., 84
Heinz, M., 59

Heise, L., 59
Hendriyani, Y., 30–31
Herr–Stephenson, B., 31
Hiemstra, R., 145
Hiltz, S. R., 25
Hodges, C., 15, 117–118, 154
Holmes E. A., 155
Holt, D., 86
Hong, A. J., 118
Hoque, A., 60
Horrigan, J., 119
Hossain, M. A., 60
Hu, S., 5
Huang, R., 60
Huberman, A., 129
Hulett, M., 25
Hung, M., 42
Hutabarat, R., 154

Ilgaz, H., 15
Impey, C., 46
Ince, E. Y., 106
Iosifidis, C., 46
Islam, M. S., 33
Ismail, W. N. H. W., 154
Isralowitz, R., 155
Ito, M., 31
Iyer, P., 60

Jameel, R., 33
Jarvis P., 149
Jin, Y., 4
John A., 5
Johnson, S. D., 105
Jones, J. A., 30
Jones, K. M. L., 31
Juan, A., 59
Jukes, I., 31
Jung, I., 14–15, 25
Jurgen, R., 151

Kabir T., 7, 30, 32, 46
Kabir, M. M. 7, 30, 32, 46
Kabul, A., 106
Kalmukov, Y., 41

Kamarainen, A. M., 130
Kamonde, M., 85
Kamruzzaman., 33
Kang, T, 46
Kapteyn, A., 46
Karadeniz, S., 118
Kasperiūnienė, J., 141
Kassean, H., 60
Kathula, D. N. , 28
Katz, J. A., 45
Kazlauskienė A., 145–146, 148
Kebritchi, M., 46
Keith, T. Z., 61
Keller, C., 59
Kelly, K., 31
Kemp, S., 85
Kennewell, S., 86, 89
Kent, S., 106
Kerwan, A., 46
Khamenka, N., 155
Khanom, M., 60
Kharbach, A., 116
Kidd, W., 34
Kies, C., 59
Kim, H. J., 97
Kim, K. J., 118
Kitchen, J., 30
Knight, C., 155
Knowles, M. S., 145–146
Ko, S., 26, 121
Koehler, T. E., 59
Kohnstamm, T., 98
Kolo, C., 32
Konstantinov, V., 155
Koole, M., 154
KPMG, 60
Kramarae, C., 97
Kumar, S., 25, 44
Kunwar, R., 30
Kuratko, D. F., 45
Kvavadze, D., 116

Lam, S., 154
Lamagna, C., Z., 47
Lang, J. M., 15

Larkin, M., 34
Larson, M. B., 23
Latchem, C., 97
Lau, E., 44
Leask, M., 31
Lederman, D., 32
Lee, J. S., 30
Lei, H., 30
Lepore, M., 59
Lepore–Stevens, M., 59
Li, Q., 155
Li, W., 4
Li, Y., 46
Liguori, E., 30, 60
Liman Kaban, 118
Lipschuetz, A., 96
Liu, D., 60
Lloyd, S. A., 25
Lockee, B., 15, 27, 117
Lockee, B. B., 23
Lotem S., 155
Lubis, A. L., 30–31
Luckin, R., 32

Macharia, J., 85
Macleod, H., 97
Mahaffey, A. L., 59
Mahmud, A., 30
Maimunah, I., 30
Mamun, A. A., 7, 30, 32, 46
Manches. A., 32
Mansfield, C., 155
Marbán, J. M., 60, 116
Marginson, S., 5
Marinova, T., 155
Marji, D. A. S., 15
Martin, F., 25, 44, 47
Martin, L.S., 121
Martin–Barbero, S., 47
Martinez, J., 84
Martínez–Argüelles, M., 59
Masiliauskienė, E., 145
Maton, K., 31
Matsuoka, H., 46
Mazumder, D., C., L., 47

McCain, T., 31
McCarthy, S. A., 121
McCoy, T. S., 25
Mcgee, K., 119
McGee, P., 25
McIsaac, M., 105
McKelvey, M., 45
McLean, J., 149
McSporran, M., 97
Means, B., 120–121
Melnikovas A., 139
Mertens, D. M., 107
Metcalf, S. J., 130
Miao, Y., 168
Miles, M. B., 129
Miller, G. E., 26
Mills, A. J., 107
Ministry of Higher Education, 8, 69, 72, 75, 79
Mironov, C., 59
Mishra, N., 7, 60
Mitchell, A., 31
Mittal, P., 30, 40, 43
Mladenova, T., 41–42
Moebius, K., 59
Monem, M., 32
Montgomery, K. C., 31
Moore, G. C., 63
Moore, M. G., 102, 105
Moore, S., 117
Moreland, N., 45
Moyi, P., 84
Mseleku, Z., 30
Mufid, A., 155
Mulenga, E. M., 16, 116
Murillo, A., 31
Murphy, R., 9, 116
Murray, J., 34

Naciri, A., 116
Naluwemba, E. F., 60
Nath, A. K., 33
Nath, J., 33
Ndawula, S., 60
Neary, S., 41

Neck, H. M., 60
Nicola, M., 46
Nitko, A. J., 23
Norgard, C., 15
Noss, R., 32
Nurhadi, D., 15
Nyakwende, E., 85

Oblinger, D. G., 31
Oblinger, J. L., 31–32
OECD, 5, 46, 47
Ofcom., 31
Oh, C., 44
Ojcius, D. M., 60
Orellana, A., 106, 121
Osterman, K. F., 30
Own, Z., 42
Oyedotun, T., D., 46

Palloff, R. M., 121
Papa, L., 132
Papert, S., 32
Pardo–Garcia, C., 45–46
Parkinson, J., 86
Paskevicius, M., 14–15, 25
Pazzaglia, G., 84
Penfold, C., 131
Peng, X., 46
Perkowski, T., 121
Perry V.H., 155
Pete, J., 25
Pick, J. B., 119
Piggott, L., 60
Plano–Clark, V. L. P., 107
Pocevičienė R., 145, 148
Pokorni, B., 119
Pompei, F., 45
Popovici, A., 59
Potter, J., 116
Potter, K., 119
Poudel, K. K., 30
Power Transmission Expansion and Connectivity Project, 79
Pratt, K., 121
Prensky, M., 31

Price, A., 155
Print, M., 132
Prokopenko, I., 33
Purwanto, A., 155

Quezada R. L., 154
Quezada–Parker K. B., 154

Rahim, N. S. A., 154
Rahman, M. M., 33
Raiborn, M. H., 26
Ramadhani, D., 30, 31
Ramot R., 154
Rao, W. W., 4
Rapanta, C., 154
Ratten, V., 32, 33
Rea, H. R. K., 33
Redmond, P., 105
Research of Vytautas Magnus University researchers, 138
Reznik, A., 155
Richardson, A., 86
Riffee, W. R., 5
Ritzhaupt, A., 25, 44
Rofiq, Z., 30
Rohman, M., 15
Romano, L., 132
Rossen, S., 26, 121
Rotter, N. G., 25
Russo, T., 15

Sabharwal, M., 45
Sabuj, M. U., 60
Salleh, F. I. M., 154
Samors, R. J., 121
Sankaran, S., 119
Santiague, L., 96
Saridakis, G., 45
Sarkar, S., 59
Sato, S., 46
Saulle, E. , 132
Schaner, S. G., 46
Schlosser, C., 106
Schlosser, L. A., 102
Schneider, S. L., 30

Schuwer, R., 14, 15, 25
Schwab, K., 47
Seaman, J., 102–103
Sebastian, I. M., 119
Seepersaud, D. J., 102, 105
Selezneva, E., 45
Selim, H. M., 59
Selvam, S.G., 87
Sham, S., 30, 46
Sharif, P. I., 60
Sharma, S., 46
Sharpe, R., 119
Shaw, R., 34
Sheely, S., 31
Shepard, M, 32
Shohel, M. M. C., 7, 30, 32, 46
Shrestha, A. K., 30
Siagian, F., 154
Simamora, R. M., 32
Simonson, M., 85, 102, 105–106, 141
Singh V., 16
Sintema, E. J., 60, 116
Sirait, R., 154
Skugarevsky, O., 155
Slimi, Z., 96
Smaldino, S., 85, 102, 141
Smita, M. K., 33, 40
Sohrabi, C., 46
Soko, J. J., 25
Springer, M., 105
Sriwahyuni, T., 30–31
Statistica, 98
Stella, A., 105
Sterling, D. R., 23
Stone, C., 105
Strielkowski, W., 58, 60
Studies during quarantine, 139, 140, 143
Study Programme Assessment, 148
Sugandi, R. M., 15
Sumuer, E., 145
Sun, L., 59
Surani, D., 15
Suryani, P., 155
Swan, K., 121
Sykes, D., 30

Taft, S.H., 121
Takahashi, T., 31
Talbot C., 154
Tan, S., 119
Tandon, D., 60
Tandon, N., 60
Tang, Y., 59
Tanner, H., 86
Tapscott, D., 31
Tarimo, C. S., 155
Thurman A., 16
Thurmond, V. A., 105
Tiwari, S., 59
Tlili, A., 60
Tondeur, J., 85–86
Toquero, C. M., 58, 60
Tornatzky, L. G., 119
Torres, M., 25
Tracey I., 155
Trentin, G., 105
Tripp L., 31
Trust, T., 15, 117
Tu, C. H., 105
Tuson, J., 86

Uddin, E., 44
Uddin, M., 33
UN, 3, 46, 98
UNESCO, 30, 58, 116, 117, 118, 130, 131, 134
UNICEF, 33
United Nations, 32, 70, 118, 120
University Grants Commission of Bangladesh (UGC). , 32
Urmee, M. A. 7, 30, 32, 46

Valcke, M., 85
Valdes, R., 119
Valova, I., 41
Van Braak, J., 85
Van Keer, H., 85
Vanevenhoven, J., 60
Varea, V., 155
Venkatesh, V., 119
Ventä–Olkkonen, L., 46

Verawardina, U., 30–31
Vial, G., 47
Vickrey, T. L., 130
Vladimirschi, V., 14–15, 25
Vu, P., 25
Vygotsky, L. S., 85

Wadud, P., 33
Waithaka, M. W., 85
Walker, L. R., 32
Wallace, L., 86, 95
Wallace, R. M., 15
Wambach, K., 105
Wang, H., 60
Wargadinata, W., 30
Waterhouse, S. A., 86
Watermeyer, R., 155
Weeden, K. A., 4
Wessely, S., 155
What is the European Credit System (ECTS)?, 149
Whittle, C., 59
WHO., 4, 9, 58, 101
Wiebe, E., 107
Wiliam, D., 23
Willging, P. A., 105
Williams, D., 86
Williams, J., 59
Williams, A. M., 5
Williamson, B., 116
Wilson, K., 86
Windes, D., 25
Winkel, D. E., 60
Winkler, C., 30, 60
Wollina, U., 60
Woods, R. H., 24
World Bank Group, 14, 26
World Bank, 41–42, 73, 75, 85, 97
World Economic Forum, 146
Wu, C., 46, 155
Wu, J., 46, 155

Xiang, Y. T., 4
Xiao, J., 14, 15, 25
Xu, X., 46

Yan, S., 59
Yang, J., 60
Yee, A., 44
Young, A., 15
Younie, S., 31

Zaring, O., 45
Zeigler–Hill V., 155
Zeng, L. N., 4
Zeng, T., 97
Zeng, X., 46, 155
Zhang, Q. 4
Zhang, X., 119
Zhou, W., 30
Zhuang, R., 60
Zuo, W., 59
Zvacek, S. M., 85, 102

SUBJECT INDEX

Note: Page numbers followed by "*n*" indicate notes.

Academics, 5
Accessibility, 5, 71
Affiliated colleges and institutes, 32
Afghanistan, 71
   and higher education, 71–72
   ministry and readiness to combat COVID in, 72–74
   shifting scenarios, 78
   voice of stakeholders, 74–78
Alternative learning opportunities, 47
American Psychological Association (APA), 44
Amid COVID-19, 106
Assessments, 40
   relevance of, 43–47
   strategies, 40
Asynchronous online communication synchrony, 120

Bangladesh, context of HE in, 32–33
Bangladesh Open University (BOU), 32
BlackBoard, 86
Blended learning, 25
Blended online learning, 25
Blending, 25
British Educational Research Association (BERA), 36
British Psychological Society (BPS), 36

Campus life, 8, 47
Canvas, 86
Case study, 107
Catastrophe, 4

Challenges, 58
   posed by COVID-19, 10, 154
Cognition and recognition of learner's individuality, 149
Commission for University Education in Kenya, 84
Community of higher education in Afghanistan, 77
Computer-based learning, 15–16
Consensus about ODTL, 37–38
Continuity, 126–127
Continuous professional development, 40
Continuous training, 37
Convergent parallel, 34
Coronavirus, 33
Correlation analysis, 127–129
COVID-19, 7, 9–10, 58
   epidemic, 46
   impact, 59
   infection, 84
   pandemic, 14–15, 17, 30, 42, 47, 70, 72, 116, 118
Culture of trust in education, 119
Curriculum, 40
   relevance of, 43–47

Delhi National Capital Region, 60
Developing countries, 32, 60
Development of self-directed learning competencies, 148–150
Digikids, 118
Digital childhoods, 118
Digital contents and for students on online platforms, 38

Digital divide, 42
Digital inequalities, COVID-19 pandemic on, 118
Digital literacy, 118
  findings, 122–130
  literature review and theoretical background, 117–121
  methodology, 121–122
Digital materials
  mediating pathway through intention to create, 159–161
  mediating pathway through willingness to adopt, 161–162
  results of moderated mediations, 162–164
Digital natives, 118
Digital readiness, profiling needs for, 118–119
Digital skills, 119
Digital teaching, 154, 157–159, 163
Digital technologies, 46
Digital transformation of life and future of HE, 46–47
Distance education (DE), 8, 102, 150
  avenues, 9
  context, 106–107
  during COVID-19, 105–106
  data collection and analysis, 108–111
  findings, 111–113
  limitations, 113
  methodology, 107–108
  pre-COVID-19, 103–105
Distance learning in Lithuania, 136–144
Distance teaching/learning, 139–140
Doctoral students, 18

E-learning, 15–16, 59–61
  committee, 77–78
E-resources, 60
Economic disruption, 5
Economic hardships, 74
Education, 44–45
  during coronavirus, 154
  in emergencies, 50
  sector, 14
Education in a distance, 139, 141–142, 145
  in Lithuania during the pandemic, 148
Educational institutions, 58
Educational strategy, 7
Educators, 5
  perceptions and operational/ technical settings, 126
Effectiveness, 9
  of online education, 37, 43, 118, 166
Efficiency, 112–113
Eigenvalues, 63
Emergency online teaching, transition to, 124–126
Emergency remote teaching (ERT), 15–16, 117–118, 126–127, 154–155
  attitudes toward ERT and characteristics, 156–157
  mediating pathway through intention to maintain interaction during, 164–165
  results of moderated mediation related to intention to maintain interaction during, 165–166
Emergency remote teaching and learning (ERTL), 37
Emerging technologies, 31–32
Employability, preparedness of students for, 44–46
Enrollment, 70
Equality, 26
Equipping, 25
Erasmus Student Network (ESN), 43
Ethics, 26
European Credit System (ECTS), 149
Evaluation, 42

Factor analysis, 61, 65–66
Feedback, 9, 31
Financial strain, 8

Subject Index

Five-point Likert scale, 112
Fourth Industrial Revolution, 47–48
Free choice and responsibility, 148

Global pandemic, 4
Google Classroom, 33, 86

High school, 10, 156
Higher education (HE), 5, 14, 30, 58–59, 70 (*see also* Distance education (DE))
 amid COVID–19, 58
 changing landscape of, 31–32
 characteristics, 30
 context of HE in Bangladesh, 32–33
 digital transformation of life and future of, 46–47
 and employability, 44–46
 preparedness of students for future HE and employability, 44–46
Higher Education Learning Management System (HELMS), 75
Higher educational institutions (HEIs), 5, 30, 45, 47, 102
Hungarian school communities, 154
Hungarian teachers, 154

Igeneration, 118
Ikids, 118
Immediacy, 9, 105
Importance of interaction, 156
Inclusive education, 39, 42
Inclusiveness, 9, 105–107
India, 7, 58
Information and communication technology (ICT), 25, 33, 59, 85, 103
Information technology (IT), 38
Infrastructural preparedness in adopting online teaching and learning, 91–93
Instructor role online, 120

Intention to create digital materials, 159–161
Interactivity, 40
International universities, 32
Internet, 70
 at affordable cost and fund allocation for online education, 39
 connection issues, 76

Kenya Basic Education COVID-19 Emergency Response Plan, 84
Kenyan Universities, 8, 85, 91, 93
Khulna University, 32

Lanka Education and Research Network (LEARN), 14
Learner-centered instruction, 121
Learning, 4
 during COVID-19, 97
 experiences, 58
 style, 147
Learning management systems (LMSs), 14, 84, 86
Lebanon, 103
Lecturers, 19–24
Level of competency preparedness of lecturers and students, 93–95
Lithuanian educational system, 138
Lithuanian Students Union (LSU), 139–140
Lockdown, 58

M-Elimu, 86
Management Faculty, 14–15
 challenges on teaching and learning online, 20–22
 change of view on online teaching and learning, 22–23
 data collection and analysis, 17–18
 going online, 16–17
 online learning, 15–16
 perceptions on assessment, 23–24

perceptions on online teaching and learning, 18–20
Massive open online course platforms (MOOC platforms), 47
Meaningful learning, 36
Microsoft teams, 33
Minister of Education, Science and Sport (MESS), 137
Ministry of Education (MoE), 72–74
Ministry of Higher Education (MoHE), 72, 74–75
Mixed method, 9, 17, 34
Modality, 120
Modification of curriculum, 40
Moodle, 86
Moodle-based LMSs, 14
Motivating, 25
Motivation and self-motivation, 147
Multiple-choice questions (MCQs), 24

National University, 32
New normal education, 116
Novelty effect, 130

One-way ANOVA test, 109
Online assessment, 15
Online communication synchrony, 120
Online distance teaching and learning (ODTL), 30, 33, 36
   consensus about, 37–38
   system, 40
Online education, 16, 102 (*see also* Higher education (HE))
   internet at affordable cost and fund allocation for, 39
   methods, 156
   research methodology, 60–61
   results, 156–166
   results, 61–66
   revolution in Afghanistan, 77
   system, 37
   teachers' perceptions during COVID-19, 155–156
   theoretical background, 59–60
Online learning, 15–16, 102–103, 84, 118, 140
Online mode of learning, 4
Online pedagogies, 37
Online platforms, 8, 33, 38, 40, 42, 124
Online teaching, 71, 103
   aspects of, 60
Online teaching and learning, 85
   challenges on, 20–22
   change of view on, 22–23
   perceptions on, 18–20

Pacing, 120
Pandemic, 58, 72
Participation facilitation technology, 86
Pearson's test for correlation, 94
Pedagogies, relevance of, 43–47
Perceptions
   on online teaching and learning, 18–20
   toward online learning, 58–59
Phoenicia University (PU), 103
Pilot testing, 61
Planning, 24–25
Policy, 30
   and practice, 7
   preparedness for online teaching and learning, 89–90
Positive impact, 59, 77
Post-COVID, 42–43
Post-COVID-19, 116
Practice, 31, 34
Pre-COVID-19, 103–105
Preparedness, 7
Private universities, 32
Private Universities Act 1992, 32
Public HEIs, 41
Public universities, 32

Qualitative method, 110–111
Quality, 26
   in DE, 105
   of online teaching, 60
   uality and effectiveness of online education, 37, 43
Quantitative method, 108–110
Questionnaire design, 61

Questionnaire-based survey, 60–61

Reflection and reflective learning, 149–150
Reliability
  analysis, 61
  test, 61
Remote learning, 120
Remote teaching, 9, 15 (*see also* Emergency remote teaching (ERT))
Remote video conferencing, 86
Resilience
  effect of, 159
  mediating role of attitudes, 158

Science, Technology, Engineering, Arts and Mathematics students (STEAM students), 43–44
Self-directed learning, 145
Self-directed learning competencies
  development, 148–150
  in distance and online education, 145–146
  distance learning in Lithuania, 136–144
  essence and concept, 146–148
Self-efficacy
  effect of, 159
  mediating role of attitudes, 158
Self-regulated learners, 41
Shahjalal Science and Technology University, 32
Smart devices, 42, 49
Social distancing, 59
Social justice, 48
Social mobility, 5
Socio-economic status (SES), 33, 44
  diversity and lack of logistic facilities in remote areas, 39
  students, 44
Sri Lanka, 14
Standardized education plan, 67
Stress, 7, 65
Students, 18–24
  engagement, 40
  instructor ratio, 120–121
Students' participation, 126–127
Students' perspectives, 36–40
Students' preparedness, 30
  changing landscape of HE, 31–32
  context of HE in Bangladesh, 32–33
  for future HE and employability, 44–46
  implications, 48
  relevance of curriculum, pedagogies, and assessments, 43–47
  research methodology, 34–36
  teachers' and students' perspectives, 36–40
Sustainable Development Goals, 46
Synchronous online communication synchrony, 120

Teachers, 7
  collaboration, 117
  perceptions during COVID-19, 155–156
  perspectives, 36–40
  presence, 120, 130–131
  professional development programs, 131
Teaching, 4, 120
  experience, 126–127
  and learning, 85
  methods, 74–75
  new conceptualization of, 117–118
Technical capacity building, 38–39
Technological capacity building, 38–39
Technology, 9
  technology-based learning, 15–16
Telegram, 74
Tertiary students, 58, 60
Thematic analysis, 35
Themes asserted by participants, 129–130
3-way ANOVA test, 157–158
Traditional classroom teaching, 30

Traditional higher education institutions, 5
Training, 25
　to faculty members, 67
　needs for students and staffs on online teaching and learning, 37
Transformation, 6–7, 10
Trust, 119

21st Century's Higher Education, 117
2-way ANOVA test, 157

Universities, 5, 8, 71
University Grants Commission (UGC), 14, 16, 32
University of Tabish in Kabul, 77

University preparedness, 85
　findings, 89–95
　method of study, 87–89

Varimax rotation method, 63
Vice-chancellor (VC), 16

Web-based learning, 15–16
WhatsApp, 74
Willingness to borrow digital material, 161
Work–life balance, 21
World Health Organization (WHO), 4, 58
Wuhan District of China, 4

Zoom, 14, 33